Laughter
in the Living Room

Toby Miller
General Editor

Vol. 8

PETER LANG
New York • Washington, D.C./Baltimore • Bern
Frankfurt am Main • Berlin • Brussels • Vienna • Oxford

MICHAEL V. TUETH

Laughter
in the Living Room

Television Comedy
and the American
Home Audience

PETER LANG
New York • Washington, D.C./Baltimore • Bern
Frankfurt am Main • Berlin • Brussels • Vienna • Oxford

Library of Congress Cataloging-in-Publication Data

Tueth, Michael V.
Laughter in the living room: television comedy and the american home Audience
/ Michael Tueth
p. cm. — (Popular culture and everyday life; vol. 8)
Includes bibliographical references and index.
1. Television comedies—United States. I. Title.
II. Series: Popular culture & everyday life; vol. 8.
PN1992.8.C66T84   791.45'617—dc22   2004018131
ISBN 0-8204-6845-2
ISSN 1529-2428

Bibliographic information published by **Die Deutsche Bibliothek**.
Die Deutsche Bibliothek lists this publication in the "Deutsche
Nationalbibliografie"; detailed bibliographic data is available
on the Internet at http://dnb.ddb.de/.

Cover design by Lisa Barfield

The paper in this book meets the guidelines for permanence and durability
of the Committee on Production Guidelines for Book Longevity
of the Council of Library Resources.

© 2005 Peter Lang Publishing, Inc., New York
275 Seventh Avenue, 28th Floor, New York, NY 10001
www.peterlangusa.com

Printed in the United States of America

CONTENTS

ACKNOWLEDGEMENTS

I would like to express my deep gratitude to several of my colleagues for their assistance and encouragement during the writing of this book: Gwenyth Jackaway, Anahid Kassabian, Paul Levinson, Brian Rose, and especially Robin Andersen. The following students and former students also assisted in research on various topics: Jonathan D'Agostino, Philip Frezzo, Catherine Grippo, John Mann, Tim O'Leary, and Christopher Roddy. Jim Coughlin and Steve Schoenig provided invaluable technical assistance and personal counseling during my many attacks of computer-panic.

I would also like to thank the following institutions for providing a wealth of information in the form of books, journals, videotapes, microfiche, and manila folders from their archives: the Walsh Family Library and the Gerald M. Quinn Library of Fordham University, the Elmer Holmes Bobst Library at New York University, The Cooper Union Library, the New York Public Library for the Performing Arts at Lincoln Center, and the Museum of Television and Radio in New York City.

Earlier versions of three of this book's chapters have appeared elsewhere. Chapter 11 was included in *Journal of Popular Film and Television*, Volume 28, No. 3 (Fall, 2000). Chapter 12 was one of a collection of essays in *Prime Time Animation: Television Animation and American Culture* (New York and London: Routledge, 2003) edited by Carole Stabile and Mark Harrison. And Chapter 13 is included in Mary Dalton and Laura Linder's volume, *America Viewed and Skewed: Television Situation Comedies*, published in 2004 by State University of New York Press.

· 1 ·

THEY ALSO SERVE WHO
ONLY SIT AND WATCH

The venerable character actor Edmund Gwenn is credited with uttering on his deathbed, "Dying is easy; comedy is difficult." Good comedy is indeed challenging, both for the performer and for anyone
who undertakes to analyze it. Comedy on television, for instance, to be fully
understood, deserves to be studied in the context of American social, religious,
and literary traditions. Each of these elements has helped to create the distinct
atmosphere that the comic writer or performer attempts to enter.

It might seem pompous and even hubristic to require a background in soci-
ology, literature, or religion to understand what is funny about Cosmo Kramer
tumbling through his neighbor Jerry's door, or Lucy Ricardo getting bombed
on Vitameatavegamin, or Homer Simpson exercising a chokehold on his only
son. But these characters are products of their times in a medium which has
often been described as a "fun-house mirror" for the culture. Surely their concerns and dilemmas touch on the basic concerns and values of their viewers.

Comedy's fundamental nature is social, literary, and religious. It is a
uniquely social art form in its need to verify its effect with the unmistakable
response of laughter. Even though much of its patterns and techniques are
universal and timeless, it must speak in contemporary and recognizable words
and images to the society which it entertains, and the audience must certify its
success by chuckles, giggles, and guffaws. The characters and plots of television comedy come from a venerable literary tradition as well. Lucy and Ethel,
Ralph Kramden and Ed Norton, and Laverne and Shirley can trace their
roots to the scheming servants of Roman New Comedy. Homer Simpson,
Archie Bunker, and Ted Baxter are all variations of the archetypal buffoon.
Gracie Allen, Mork from Ork, Radar O'Reilly, Woody Boyd, and Phoebe

Buffay continue the tradition of the wise simpleton. They all boast a proud literary heritage, in which Miguel Cervantes can create Don Quixote or Larry Gelbart can present Hawkeye Pierce and the rest of the company of *M*A*S*H*. Comedy borrows images and tropes from more serious literature and culture as well, as the work of Philip Roth, Woody Allen, Wendy Wasserstein, Tom Stoppard, and others exemplify so well. Finally, comedy is fundamentally religious, elevating the human spirit above the burdens and fears of day-to-day existence, confronting life's demons and exorcising them, celebrating human virtues and foibles, and sometimes even managing to reconcile differences and inspire forgiveness of human vice and folly.

The social, literary, and religious character of television comedy bears the imprint of the era in which it arrived on the scene—post–World War II America. The connection between television and the mid-twentieth century was suggested recently by a bit of mock-heroic marketing presented by the television industry itself. As the ABC network began its fall season in 1997, it sponsored a series of tongue-in-cheek advertisements. Responding to the view that watching television is a brain-damaging waste of time, these billboards and magazine ads dared to proclaim television's redeeming social values. One of the ads announced: "Before TV, 2 World Wars. Since TV, 0 World Wars." While the logical reasoning and the implications of the statement may be questionable, it is an historical fact that television's entrance into American life coincided with the beginning of the era of peace and prosperity following World War II, when America's self-concept was bolstered by several developments and perceptions.

The war solidified America's role as a world power politically, as the victorious democratic alternative to Nazism, Fascism, and Japanese imperialism. The United States was the clear winner of the war, politically and economically. As Darrell Hamamoto describes the situation,

> The United States emerged from World War II as the preeminent global military and economic power. Compared to the Soviet Union, the closest political rival of the United States in the postwar era, the United States emerged from the war relatively unscathed. U.S. war dead numbered 332,000, while the Soviet Union lost approximately 22 to 24 million. Germany suffered 4.2 million dead. Furthermore, the war years were an economic boom to the United States. Vexing problems of the Great Depression—high rates of unemployment, deflation, and lackluster industrial performance—were overcome as government and industry combined to increase greatly the total wealth of the nation. The gross national product rose from $91 billion in 1939 to $212 billion in 1945.[1]

Economically, the United States had emerged as the capitalistic alternative to the Soviet brand of Marxist totalitarianism and was poised for enormous growth in a free-market economy. America's industrial capability, which had ensured its military superiority, would now be converted to the manufacture of automobiles and airplanes, houses and highways, radios and televisions, washing machines and refrigerators, and all the other conveniences and labor-saving devices within the price range of middle-American consumers. The booming job market and the opportunities for higher education provided by the G.I. Bill promised a more prosperous, leisurely lifestyle for millions of Americans. In the five years after World War II, consumer spending rose by 60 percent. By far the most significant rise was in household furnishings and consumer appliances, which increased by 240 percent.[2] One of the most popular new products was the television set, which would soon become an essential feature of this post-war Pleasantville, with television sets appearing in almost every American home by 1955.

The arrival of television also coincided with a revival of interest in family life in America, especially, as Lynn Spigel points out, among the burgeoning middle class:

> During and after the war, the marriage rate rose to record heights; of those who came of age, 96.4 percent of the female and 94.1 percent of the male populations married—and at younger ages than ever before. The baby boom, which began during the war and lasted through 1964, reversed declining birthrates of previous decades, creating a revitalization of the nuclear family as a basic social construct. The resurgence of the family unit was met with a new model for living—the prefabricated suburban tract home, so affordable that young middle-class couples, and at times lower-middle class, blue-collar workers, could purchase their piece of the American dream.[3]

As time would reveal, the television set proved particularly congenial to the lifestyle of the new American family. An identification with the family environment was imprinted on television entertainment from its earliest days and continues to guide the production and placement of television programming.

Beneath this comforting landscape was an even more reassuring bedrock of religious self-confidence. The successful outcome of World War II was understood by Americans as divinely sanctioned, the providential victory of God's Christian people over the pagan "Huns" of Hitler's Germany and the Emperor-worshippers of Japan. Soon America would also perceive itself as a nation of churchgoers in a "cold war" with atheistic communism. Prosperity seemed to be the sign of God's favor on His Chosen People, after their forty years of wandering through the desert of war and economic depression to enter the Promised Land of pasteurized milk and homogenized honey. J. Ronald Oakley's description of America in the 1950s presents some impressive statistics and details:

It is not surprising that the conservative fifties saw a major revival of religion. Year after year the statistics pointed to unprecedented increases in church membership, which grew from 86.8 million in 1950 to over 114 million in 1960. . . . Poll after poll showed that each year more and more Americans affirmed a belief in God, an afterlife, the Bible as the literal word of God, the power of prayer, and the divinity of Jesus. The radio airwaves were full of religious songs like "I Believe," "It Is No Secret What God Can Do," "The Man Upstairs," "Vaya Con Dios," and "The Big Fellow in the Sky," while Hollywood churned out *The Robe*, *The Ten Commandments*, *A Man Called Peter*, *Ben Hur*, and other movies with religious themes. The sales of Bibles reached an all time high. . . . Henry R. Luce, a close friend of Billy Graham, Bishop Sheen, and Norman Vincent Peale, saw to it that these and other religious figures got a steady stream of favorable publicity in his *Time* and *Life* magazines.[4]

While church attendance increased, religious leaders entered the mainstream. The bombast of Billy Sunday was replaced by the sensible wisdom of Dr. Norman Vincent Peale and the witty, rational arguments of Bishop Fulton Sheen. Within a few years, the words "under God" would be inserted into the Pledge of Allegiance and the Reverend Billy Graham would become the advisor and confidante of a succession of U.S. presidents. Meanwhile, the president, General Dwight D. Eisenhower, who had led America in its epic battle against evil in Europe, appeared as the divinely appointed leader of what Oakley has dubbed the "piety along the Potomac":

The president exhibited this leadership by beginning his inaugural address with a prayer, by opening each cabinet meeting with a prayer, by attending church with Mamie almost every Sunday, and by making frequent statements about the importance of faith and the close ties between Christianity and Americanism in a country battling against godless communism. The lead float in his 1953 inaugural was "God's float," exhibiting pictures of churches and other religious places and the slogans: "In God We Trust" and "Freedom of Worship" written in Gothic script.[5]

America in the 1950s saw itself as God's Country, and the new Garden of Eden was to be found in the suburbs.

This religious sensibility had a specific character, a twentieth-century version of the social and domestic life that had been practiced in America three centuries earlier: the Puritan ideal of early New England. The settlers of Plymouth Colony and Massachusetts Bay Colony, perhaps most familiar to Americans in the iconography of Thanksgiving Day, were staunch believers in a Christian theology and piety based on the teachings of the French religious reformer John Calvin (1509–1564). Calvinist Puritanism is defined well for our purposes by the historian Ralph Barton Perry as a devotion to "strictness of living and simplicity of worship, Christianity in its pristine purity, and opposed to fleshly and worldly compromises."[6] While the people who landed on Plymouth Rock in 1620 and those who founded Boston as "the city on the hill" in 1630 were few, their descendants and other Calvinist cohorts were numerous and far-reaching. Perry points out that the descendants of the original Puritan settlers spread to adjacent parts of New England, to New York, and to the Ohio River Valley. "And while they carried little baggage, they took their creed, and held to it all the more tenaciously as being their chief link with the past."[7] The Dutch who settled in New York even before the Puritans settled in Massachusetts Bay were mainly members of the Dutch Reformed Church, and the French Huguenots who settled in South Carolina and New York late in the seventeenth century were followers of John Calvin as well. The influx of Scotch-Irish immigrants to America throughout the eighteenth century brought over 150,000 Calvinist Presbyterians. Perry estimates that at the time of the American Revolution, over 40 percent of the population (1,135,000 out of 2,500,000) were "in the broad sense adherents of Calvinistic or closely allied sects." Perry concludes, "It is safe to assume, then, that the influence of Puritanism, in the broad Calvinistic sense, was a major force in the late colonial period, and that it contributed uniquely and profoundly to the making of the American mind when the American mind was in the making."[8]

Many eminent social historians have found the Puritan family to be an especially rich resource for examining the American character, especially its domestic ethos.[9] It seems especially pertinent to any study of the post–World War II culture that welcomed television into the American home.

The main elements of Puritan thought revolve around the classic Calvinist understanding of human nature as essentially depraved, as tending toward evil unless prevented by the grace of a sovereign, transcendent God. In this theology God's grace, so absolutely necessary for salvation, is freely given, not earned by any action on the part of the creature but bestowed only on those whom God so chooses. Hence, a portion of the human race, the "elect," have been predestined by God's eternal and inscrutable decision to be recipients of his saving grace, while others are doomed to eternal damnation. One's religious activity, therefore, necessarily includes a search to determine whether one is counted among the elect. The religious historian Francis J. Bremer describes what many Puritan clergy identified as "the five stages in man's progress towards God: election, vocation, justification, sanctification, and glorification."[10] The fourth stage, sanctification, is a term for the state in which someone lived after his or her justification by faith:

> One of the elect would presumably reflect his new state by his actions. He would strive harder to abide by the standards of perfection, would show true repentance

for his failings, and would lead a morally improved life. Still, he would have doubts as to the validity of his conversion, fearing lest it be a deceit of the devil to lead him into a sense of false assurance.[11]

Hence, the sanctified Puritan would understandably be quite conscientious in his or her personal conduct:

> Those who had been justified looked upon that experience as a rebirth and felt called upon to demonstrate in their new lives a reformed character marked by sober, obedient godliness. They performed diligently in all their secular roles, just as they were conscientious in the performance of their religious duties. They rejected the excesses in which so many of their fellow men indulged and imposed a rigid discipline upon themselves and their families. This did not mean that they were killjoys or prudish or in any other sense unwilling to use the fruits that God had placed in the world for them. They dressed as befitted their social class, they participated in lotteries, they drank alcoholic beverages, and they approached sex as more than a mere obligation What is often dismissed today as "puritanical" is more appropriately attributable to the Victorians.[12]

While all of this may seem somewhat arcane and otherworldly by contemporary standards, Perry, writing in 1944 almost as if he is channeling the great New England preachers three centuries earlier, translates these various doctrines and moral codes into humanistic terms that might look more familiar to the typical moral individual in post–World War II America:

> Puritanism springs from the very core of the personal conscience—the sense of duty, the sense of responsibility, the sense of guilt, and the repentant longing for forgiveness. No man, if he grows to maturity, escapes these experiences. Every man, sooner or later, feels himself rightly exiled from paradise and looks for a return. Puritanism is the elaboration of this theme, and the inculcation of its stern implications: some things are better than other things . . . and if a man is to cleave to the best he must therefore overcome the second best. . . . The best prescribes rules of action, to be scrupulously observed . . . . To live well requires the forging of a will which is stronger than any natural appetite. . . . Society, in proportion as it is human, is an association of persons in which mutual respect is mingled with solicitude and a sense of common responsibility . . . indomitable perseverance in the moral struggle.[13]

Perry also presents the logically opposite viewpoint, the denial of a moral order or hierarchy, what the Puritan mind would recognize and condemn as antinomianism:

He who would reject these ideas must be prepared to accept in some degree one or more of their opposites: a frivolous disregard of moral questions, together with aimlessness and inconstancy; a confusion or a promiscuity of values; a blurring of moral distinctions and a lack of principle . . . self-indulgence, infirmity of will, corruptibility, lack of self-discipline; a reckless irresponsibility and indifference to the true well-being of one's neighbors; a cynical admission of failure, and acquiescence in the meaninglessness of life.[14]

Duty and responsibility versus frivolous disregard of moral questions? Discovery of the best versus aimlessness and promiscuity? A strong will versus self-indulgence? Mutual respect and solicitude versus reckless irresponsibility and indifference to the true well-being of one's neighbors? It is easy to see what side most upright citizens, especially in the God's Country of 1950s America, would choose. This basic Puritan attitude, coloring all of one's personal life, imposed certain principles even on the role of entertainment in the good life of the 1950s neo-Puritan. These principles can be summarized as follows:

- eagerness to be considered among the "elect" or the respectable social groups
- avoidance of evil elements that identify one as doomed to failure and damnation
- devotion to one's home and family
- diligence in the use of one's time, both at work and at leisure

These attitudes were particularly prevalent in the post–World War II setting that introduced television into the American home.

Respectability

After World War II the nuclear family of Mom, Dad, and the kids was encouraged to abandon the evil environment of the city and create the new family in the pristine atmosphere in the suburbs. Until the mid-twentieth century the territory outside of the cities had been seen mostly as rural property or even wilderness, with its connotations of danger, isolation, and hardscrabble living. But with the extensions of electricity and other modern conveniences, the accessibility made possible by automobiles, and the arrival of supermarkets and shopping centers, the suburbs emerged as the modern gardens of the New World, combining the best of nature and civilization. The suburbs attracted upwardly mobile, future-oriented families, whose domestic life became more privatized as they found themselves more isolated from members of their extended families, who had either remained in the city or moved to other suburban locations. Relationships with their neighbors changed as well. Families who had once shared the close quarters of apartment buildings with other families or spoke to them over their backyard fences now found themselves distanced from the people next door by spacious lawns and wide driveways.

When they did interact with the other families in the subdivision, they may well have noticed the homogeneity of the group. Most of the older urban neighborhoods had developed as multigenerational ethnic enclaves, which usually kept racial groups separate. The suburbs increased the racial and generational divide, leaving minorities and older family members in the city. The community that was thus formed in these new housing developments was an even more selective environment of white inhabitants, blessed with success and looking forward to endless financial and personal satisfaction.

Suburban America was repeating the Puritan experience. The founders of Massachusetts Bay Colony, fleeing the corrupt society of English political and social life in search of a more abundant religious and economic life, had established a "city on the hill" in a pristine "new" England forged out of the wilderness of the New World. The post–World War II suburban communities, fleeing the evils of city life and desirous of moral and economic improvement for their families, were carving their own new communities out of the wilderness of undeveloped property on the urban fringe and would become modern—and more moderate—models of godly living.

Avoidance of Evil Elements of the World

Boston, Salem, and other early settlements were intended to be "communities of saints," excluding heretics and idolators and banishing or otherwise ostracizing sinners and fallen creatures with threats of death or disgrace. There is much historical evidence of such banishments, in public cases such as the pastor Roger Williams and the visionary Anne Hutchinson and the regular forced departure of any Quakers or Roman Catholics who attempted to settle in the colony. But perhaps a better sense of this dynamic can be found in the historical romances of the nineteenth-century descendant of Puritan divines Nathaniel Hawthorne. In the opening pages of his novel *The Scarlet Letter* Hawthorne depicts the typical Puritan pattern in the public scorn, the scarlet letter of shame, and the banishment to the nearby forest endured by the adulterous Hester Prynne. The clear physical boundaries between the Puritan village, inhabited by the godly "saints," and the "devilish wilderness" is depicted in another Hawthorne story, "Young Goodman Brown," in which a villager, wandering at night in the surrounding woods, happens upon a group of Satanic worshippers who bear strong resemblances to the upright inhabitants of Salem village.

Hawthorne offers a more vivid depiction of the Puritan view of the wilderness as a locus for unholy activity in another of his short stories, "The Maypole of Merry Mount." Hawthorne based his romance on accounts of the misadventures of a certain Thomas Morton, a seventeenth-century "poet and wilderness bon vivant" who established a settlement of merry-makers in the area that is now Quincy, Massachusetts, was ejected from Massachusetts Bay Colony three times for his disturbing behavior, and eventually published his own version of his experiences in 1637. While Hawthorne's imagination may elaborate considerably in the details of the particular event, the story, in its contrast between two views of recreation, merits closer examination.[15]

Hawthorne begins his tale by describing the Maytime festivities of a community of European colonists who had once been minstrels, wandering players, mummers, and "mirth-makers of every sort, such as abounded in that age, but now began to be discountenanced by the rapid growth of Puritanism" (p. 27).[16] Their festive apparel and association with forest animals suggest a pagan motif as well as the animistic practices of some Native American religions. Hawthorne suggests that the "wild throng" of maypole dancers resembled "fauns" and "nymphs" as well as "Gothic monsters." Humans and forest animals mingled together, almost indistinguishable in appearance:

> On the shoulders of a comely youth uprose the head and branching antlers of a stag; a second, human in all other points, had the grim visage of a wolf; a third, still with the trunk and limbs of a mortal man, showed the beard and horns of a venerable he-goat. And here again, almost as wondrous, stood a real bear of the dark forest, lending each of his forepaws to the grasp of a human hand, and as ready for the dance as any in that circle. His inferior nature rose half way, to meet his companions as they stooped. (p. 24)

Hawthorne reports that "all the hereditary pastimes of Old England" had been brought to the New World by this colony of revelers, with festive observances of Christmas and St. John's Eve (also known as Midsummer's Night); the annual celebration of the Lord of Misrule; harvest feasts, with bonfires; floral garlands, and the ancient Wicker Man of Celtic tradition, but, most prominent, was the maypole, a ancient lofty pine tree that the people decorated throughout the year with seasonal foliage. "Its votaries danced around it, once, at least, in every month; sometimes they call it their religion, or their altar; but always, it was the banner staff of Merry Mount" (p. 28). A central element of the celebration is the marriage of a young man and woman who are being honored that day as the Lord and Lady of the May.

Their merriment is, of course, abhorrent to the inhabitants of the nearby Puritan settlement, whom Hawthorne describes as "most dismal wretches, who said their prayers before daylight, and then wrought in the forest or the cornfield till evening made it prayer time again" (p. 28). A company of armed men from the village, led by no less a personage than Governor Endicott himself, interrupts the festivities. He confronts the priest who is leading the festivities, calling him "a priest of Baal" and proclaiming:

> Thou art the man who couldst not abide the rule even of thine own corrupted church, and hast come hither to preach iniquity, and to give example of it in thy life. But now shall it be seen that the Lord hath sanctified this wilderness for his peculiar people. Woe unto them that would defile it! (p. 30)

Endicott proceeds to cut down the maypole, "this flower-decked abomination, the altar of thy worship," commands that the "heathen crew" of revelers be taken into custody and punished with whippings, branding, and cropping of ears, and, finally, orders that the bear be shot in the head. "I suspect witchcraft in the beast," says Endicott. Finally, he orders that the young bride and groom be clothed in more severe clothing and brought to the village: "There be qualities in the youth, which may make him valiant to fight, and sober to toil, and pious to pray; and in the maiden, that may fit her to become a mother in our Israel, bringing up babes in better nurture than her own hath been" (p. 33).

Hawthorne's romance is a powerful description of the Puritan attitudes toward the dangers of "mirth and jollity" as pagan and devilish, as frivolous and sensualist, as animalistic and antinomian. If the Puritan community is to continue to foster characters that are "sober to toil and pious to pray" and more skilled at "bringing up babes in better nurture," its inhabitants must forcefully oppose the pagan pleasures of the maypole.

Such steadfast efforts to remove all immoral or otherwise dangerous influences from the colony stem from the intense sense of solidarity felt by the Puritan settlers, which included a concern to preserve themselves from any "contagion" of evil. Perry explicates the logic of such a view:

> The puritan's social interest was also actuated by a sense of solidarity—by the belief, namely, that the good of each is bound up with the good of all. . . . Among the social conditions of piety the simplest and most evident is contagion. Whatever be the deep psychological explanation in terms of imitation or suggestion, it is an unquestionable fact that the members of the same social group are in such close physical and mental proximity that that good and evil propagate themselves from next to next. The evil condition of one corrupts those about him; no

matter how careful a man may be of his own condition, he is exposed and susceptible to evil originating elsewhere. His solicitude for himself will, therefore, include a solicitude for his immediate human environment. This effect of contagion is operative on every level. . . . Since unrighteousness was conceived not merely as a private but as a public evil, concerted measures were taken to prevent or to eradicate it, and to create a uniformity of righteousness in the community at large.[17]

The fear of moral contagion was mirrored in the similar exclusionary practices in the new suburban communities of postwar America. As Perry, writing in 1944, comments,

Belief and unbelief, like diseases, are contagious. . . . The fact that ideas and sentiments are spread by contact is undeniable. Modern enlightenment has confirmed, and not discredited, the puritan's sense of the dependence of his private creed on the creed prevailing in his immediate neighborhood.[18]

Similar fears of moral or social contagion inspired the exclusionary practices in the development and marketing of the new suburban communities of postwar America. This attitude was bolstered by the pattern of racist discrimination that had pervaded American society since the era of black slavery and had continued in the Jim Crow laws and other segregationist patterns in American life. Associating the minorities of the inner city with crime and moral degradation, especially in family relations, the suburban developments, with the help of the policies of the Federal Housing Administration and the Home Owners Loan Corporation, excluded black families or other minorities from buying homes while encouraging white families to leave the cities and populate the new domestic colonies on the metropolitan edges.[19] Thus the Puritan pattern of excluding sinners from the new Jerusalem was repeated in the restrictive covenants, red-lining, and other discriminatory policies of the suburbs.

Devotion to the Family

By virtue of their very newness, the suburban communities could not immediately provide the social cohesiveness of the old urban neighborhoods and extended families left behind in the cities. The members of the nuclear families in the fresh new subdivisions, therefore, needed to look inward to one another for an emotional bond that would survive through the upward mobility that suburban life promised. Television was promoted as a valuable aid in creating this new dream of "togetherness." According to Spigel:

Television, it was said, would bring the family ever closer. . . . In its capacity as unifying agent, television fit well with the more general postwar hopes for a return to family values. It was seen as a kind of household cement that promised to reassemble the splintered lives of families who had been separated during the war.[20]

The television set was to be nothing less than the new family hearth, encouraging family cohesiveness and, as Cecilia Tichi has illustrated, promoting patriotism and other traditional American values.[21] Tichi documents the reference to the Revolutionary War era in the design and titles of various models of television sets and the connection to the colonial revival era in American architecture, furniture, and the literature of the Fireside Poets of the mid-nineteenth century. The interweaving of domesticity, militarism, and patriotism all evoked the world of the earlier New England of the original Puritan colonists.

The importance of good order in the family was a great concern to the religious and civic leaders of the early Puritan communities in America. John Demos quotes the great Puritan divine, Cotton Mather's, description of the family as "the very *First Society* that by the Direction of Providence of GOD is produced among the Children of Men."[22] The fathers were referred to as "the family governors," who would supervise their families' behavior. "Having taken such care to bring everyone under the authority of a family ruler, the state did its utmost to support such rulers in the proper exercise of their authority."[23] For example, "it punished tavern keepers and anyone else who entertained children or servants without the consent of their parents or masters."[24]

With the primarily locus for entertainment and leisure situated in the home, the family could enjoy their leisure time together under the watchful eye of parents. Much was made of this point in the marketing of television sets in the family-friendly environment after World War II. Lynn Spigel documents the portrayal of television sets as the center of family life in magazine advertisements:

Typically, the magazines presented the television set as the new family hearth through which love and affection might be rekindled. . . . Indeed, the magazines included television as a staple home fixture before most Americans could even receive a television signal, much less consider purchasing the expensive item. . . . In the span of roughly four years, television itself became *the* central figure in images of the American home; it became the cultural symbol par excellence of family life.[25]

Indeed, the television set was portrayed as a sort of unifying agent fostering a return to family values:

In 1950, *Better Homes and Gardens* literally merged television with the family room, telling readers to design a new double-purpose area, a "family-television room." But one needn't build a new room in order to bring the family together around the television set; kitchens, living rooms, and dining rooms would do just as well. What was needed was a particular attitude, a sense of closeness that permeated the room.[26]

More than any other mass medium, television began to be understood as "coming into the home." It was often depicted by its critics as somehow "invading" the domestic environment, a Trojan Horse to be viewed with suspicion. While newspapers and magazines arrived on a daily basis and radio and phonograph records were found in every home, television's powerful combination of sounds and images, often provided by live presenters, had a way of dominating the room and demanding to be noticed far more aggressively than the magazine lying on the coffee table or the record playing in the background. Hence, parents were often reminded of their responsibility to control what arrived via television into their homes. The defenders of television responded by reminding the parents that they were now in a better position to control their children's entertainment since children had more opportunity for entertainment right in their homes. Instead of wondering what their son or daughter was doing or seeing at the movie theater or what music they were hearing at the school dances or on the radio in the bedrooms, parents could oversee such activity in the safe quarters of the living room. Another Puritan dream was coming true.

Diligence in the Use of One's Time, at Work and at Leisure

Television's closest link to the Puritan tradition can be found in its efficiency and economy. In Calvinist theology, leading the good life included discovering and pursuing the work which was one's divine calling in life. One is chosen by God to aid in the creation of the Kingdom of God on earth by the use of one's divinely given talents and opportunities to their best advantage, and a great psychological tension was created by the constant anxiety about one's diligence in such use. This moral concern is well illustrated in the famous sonnet of John Milton, the seventeenth-century Puritan poet–political thinker. The poem is often identified by its title, "On His Blindness." At the age of forty-three, having achieved considerable success as a writer of political and religious tracts and greatly admired for his poetry, Milton became totally blind and found himself severely hampered in the pursuit of his calling as a scholar and writer. In the opening lines of his sonnet, the poet ponders:

> When I consider how my light is spent
> Ere half my days, in this dark world and wide,
> And that one talent, which is death to hide
> Lodged with me useless. . . .

The poet fears that God, the great taskmaster, will call him to account for not performing his divinely appointed duties, which require the gift of sight. He finally resolves his doubts by recalling that the omnipotent Diety can find many ways to use his creatures to achieve the Divine Plan. Rather than give specific orders, God asks only that a good man do the divine bidding, whatever that may be:

> . . . who best
> Bear his mild yoke, they serve him best.

Milton reflects that even the angels are asked only to do God's will:

> Thousands at his bidding speed
> And post o'er land and ocean without rest.

But some of the angels only stand by in expectation of God's command:

> They also serve who only stand and wait.

Like some of the angels, therefore, Milton has been given a way to serve God by standing by and waiting for the next sign of the divine will for him. Thus even the enforced idleness of his blindness is seen by Milton as "work" for the Kingdom of God, an expression of dedication to one's divine calling in this life.

For the Puritans the greatest sin was wasting time. The wrath of the early New England preachers was not directed, as many have characterized it, toward sexual misbehavior or drunken carousing but to the misuse of one's time. Insofar as frivolity or overindulgence occupied time that was better spent performing one's duties, such activities were condemned. Hence the Puritan colonists were particularly inimical to the theatrical performances and other festivities associated with holidays. Just as the Puritan rulers of England in the interregnum period had outlawed the theaters throughout the country in 1642, so the Puritan colonists continued to pass laws against theatrical productions. The theater historian Hugh F. Rankin cites several condemnations by leaders in New England and other colonies throughout the seventeenth and early eighteenth centuries, culminating in the proclamation of the Massachusetts legislature in 1750 prohibiting theatrical performances because they "not only occasion great and unnecessary expenses, and discourage industry and frugality, but likewise tend generally to increase Immorality, impiety, and contempt of religion."[27] Notice the concern for industry and frugality. Leisure time was to be used only to refresh one's body and spirit for a return to work in one's divine calling and should avoid lavish expenditure of time and money.

Citing the same concerns for public morality and private frugality, the Puritan leaders of the interregnum period in England had also outlawed the celebration of Christmas, the major holiday in England at the time. In legislation enacted in 1644 and 1645, Parliament declared Christmas a working day and announced that anyone found celebrating Christmas with any of the traditional feasting, dancing, singing, masques, or games associated with the season was subject to arrest. The Puritan leaders of Massachusetts outdid their British counterparts by outlawing the celebration of Christmas with legislation that remained on the books until the middle of the nineteenth century.

The same distrust of leisure prevailed, oddly enough, in the formation of a new domestic ideal for the suburbs and the place of television in the well-behaved family. Tichi devotes considerable attention to the careful connection television marketing made between the new technology and a proper view of leisure. She points out in one illustration of a 1950s family gathered around their living room television set watching *Kukla, Fran, and Ollie* that a clock sits atop the television cabinet. Tichi ponders the possible symbolism of the clock in the family's viewing environment:

> The whole family is well groomed and respectable, and prosperous in middle-class terms. Atop their TV cabinet, we see, they have put a clock, perhaps to remind them of the hour when the program changes, but more likely of the children's bedtimes and the adults' too, since father and mother must not allow television to distract them from scheduled commitments. The clock tells us the family will not be led astray by their new TV set, just as clothes tell us that they could, if they choose, go out of the home at any moment, to pay an evening call or to dine. Television will not tempt them into slovenly domestic ways.[28]

Tichi also examines the contents of an article in a special issue of *Life* magazine entitled "The Good Life" (December 1958). The article, entitled "Leisure Could Mean a Better Civilization," remarked:

> There is nothing new about mankind's abhorrence of too much leisure. No matter how much we talk about the necessity of leisure in an age in which machines are taking over more and more mental as well as physical work, our relatively recent Puritan past screams in protest. Since the first settlers at Jamestown starved, the need for work was firmly stamped upon the minds of the early colonizers. . . .

> Work gained an aura of religious respectability. . . . We still have a profound feel-
> ing that work is good, and that the enjoyment of leisure for more than a short
> time is vaguely immoral.[29]

Even with its inaccurate identification of the Puritans with the Jamestown colonists, the *Life* article clearly expresses the viewpoint of 1950s America that
too much leisure is a sign of moral depravity. In light of such an attitude Tichi
proceeds to show how television viewing was presented as an energetic activity, not a sedentary occupation. One 1949 advertisement for Dumont television sets shows couples in evening attire gathered in a living room as if they
were sitting in a private box at the theater and watching a cultural event on
television. Tichi observes:

> Television in the living room was thus offered to the housewife as an excursion
> out of the household and into an expensive private box for an experience of high
> culture. With television, the housewife was not an isolated suburban drudge but
> a theatre-goer, participant in urban social forms of high-culture night life.[30]

Two other illustrations provided by Tichi show the lengths to which television marketing would go to deny that television viewing was a sedentary, pas-
sive experience. A magazine advertisement for Panasonic televisions announces that the picture is "so lifelike you'll feel you're part of the picture"
while the visual image shows a television viewer startled to see a football
kicked out of the screen and into his den, sailing over his beer and pretzels:

> In the next moment, he will become a player. And that is the point of such adver-
> tising texts, that at heart the seated TV watcher is really a teammate-activist only
> temporarily on the sidelines but ready at any moment to join the action. He may
> appear to be sedentary but underneath is kinetic in mind and body. . . . The fig-
> ure of the armchair activist functions as an anodyne against anxieties about
> American work and leisure.[31]

Tichi concludes her survey of such marketing techniques by declaring:
"The corporation ads for TV receivers, the trade association messages, the reports on work and leisure authorized by representations of cultural and social
institutions all reach consensus on one point, namely, that leisure in antitheti-
cal to the ideology of the United States."[32] Television, in this view, will be entertaining and culturally enriching, but it will not lead to the evils of the leisurely life.

They need not have bothered to make such a case. Television fits very
neatly into the American embarrassment about overindulgence in leisure, insofar as television viewing is a relatively efficient and modest investment of

time and money in entertainment. The couples in that 1949 advertisement have found a way to enjoy the theater and still remain neo-Puritans. Instead of paying for tickets to the sporting event, playhouse, concert hall, or movie theater, one can enjoy all of these events for free. Viewers do not have to spend hours getting the tickets, driving to the event, meeting others for a pre-theater dinner, or hosting a tailgate party in the stadium parking lot. They can simply walk into their living rooms and turn on their television sets. One need only consider the hours that a rock music fan spends in line with a sleeping bag in the overnight vigil for the precious (and often expensive) tickets, the logistics of meeting up with one's concert companions, the acquisition of whatever is to be consumed during the concert, the inevitable hour or two spent waiting for the delayed appearance of the concert stars, and, finally, the traffic crawl out of the venue's parking lot to appreciate the relative efficiency of the hour or two spent watching the rock star performing at a scheduled time on television. Given the options, a godly Puritan would much prefer television for its efficiency and economy.

How does television comedy fit into this picture of American life, permeated with Puritan ideals and fears? The most fundamental fact is that television is situated within the hallowed precincts of the home. As this study will show, all the creators of comic programming have been forced to negotiate this basic reality. Throughout recorded history, comic performance has thrived in a multitude of environments: the amateur games and tropes of folk culture; the popular art of traveling troupes, pantomimes, and circuses; the lavish presentations in the courts of royalty; the sophisticated venues of theaters and playhouses; and finally, in the twentieth century, in the mass medium of film. All of these shared one characteristic: they occurred outside the home. Only with the advent of radio did the comedian cross the sacred threshold into the family environment.

The second inescapable truth is that television is a commercial environment, providing mostly free entertainment and information through the kindness of sponsors. In their abiding desire that the televised material offers a suitable environment for the promotion of their product, the sponsors can prove as suspicious of "unsuitable" material as any Puritans were of the festivities at Merry Mount. This commercial imperative coincides neatly with Puritan morality, as Max Weber established clearly in his classic study of the interrelationship of capitalism and the Protestant work ethic.[33] Hence, most of the comedy on American television illustrates and reinforces the values and attitudes of the middle-class family and capitalist society.

However, it is also the function of comedy to challenge the prevailing mores in the form of the foolish and the carnivalesque, in the mockery of social standards, and in the exploration of alternatives to the status quo. In his treatment of film comedy Gerald Mast states that "the most thoughtful film comedies are iconoclastic. . . . The greatest comedies throw a custard pie (sometimes literally) in the face of social forms and assumptions." He claims that such outrageous defiance serves a social purpose:

> Perhaps comic iconoclasm provided the audience with a useful emotional release, an opportunity to indulge their own antisocial urges without damaging the social fabric; perhaps the iconoclast was free to speak against social and moral values because he used the entertaining comic form—a traditional privilege of comedians since Aristophanes.[34]

This tendency of comedy toward iconoclasm and rebellion has found expression in many types of comic literature and performance. Much of the shock takes the form of the "dirty joke." The Greek satyr plays and Roman comedy are infamous for their licentiousness and frank sexual humor. The literature of Boccacio, Chaucer, and Rabelais are replete with bawdy jokes and puns. Gypsy Rose Lee, Sophie Tucker, Redd Foxx, Moms Mabsley, and other comedians of the Golden Age of burlesque and night clubs had their repertoire of naughty material. Another strain of iconoclastic humor takes the form of zany physical comedy bordering on the violent. The Keystone Kops, the Marx Brothers, the Three Stooges, Buster Keaton, and the teams of Laurel and Hardy, Abbot and Costello, and Martin and Lewis have entertained millions of moviegoers for almost a century. Surely such popular material has a place on the small screen. Or does it? The history of television comedy shows that this wilder comedy of sexual and slapstick humor has appeared far less frequently in the living rooms of America than it has elsewhere. Only recently has such transgressive humor found a place on the television schedule.

Television comedy: a welcome guest into the home or an intruder? Free entertainment or a disguise for advertisers? A moral guide or an iconoclast? In its first fifty years, comedy on the small screen has negotiated its way through all of these roles and been alternately praised and blamed for all of the above. From the neo-Puritan 1950s to the postmodern twenty-first century, television comedy lives on and continues to do more than entertain us. It has moved in with us.

·2·
___

A NIGHT ON THE
TOWN—AT HOME?

The history of the comedy-variety shows in prime time most vividly illustrates the accommodation of television comedy to the domestic ethos. What began with Milton Berle's, Sid Caesar's, and Jackie Gleason's legendary achievements in bringing something akin to the The Ziegfeld Follies or Las Vegas into everyone's home eventually gave way to the milder character comedy of Jack Benny, the simpler folksy humor of Red Skelton, and the informality of Arthur Godfrey. The pioneer Milton Berle enjoyed phenomenal success in television's earliest years, but his popularity dwindled as television grew and a host of other comedians copied his show, which ended its run after eight seasons (1948–1956). Sid Caesar's two comedy-variety shows, *Your Show of Shows* (1950–1954) and *Caesar's Hour* (1954–1957), which television critics admired at the time and have revered ever since, did not, for various reasons, achieve the same level of popularity as Berle's. Jackie Gleason, experimenting with several different formats and supporting casts, including one season of his classic situation comedy, *The Honeymooners*, maintained an intermittent television presence from 1952 to 1970.

With varying degrees of success these three comedians hosted the type of program that network programmers presumed would be most welcome into the homes of America, a "night on the town" in the comfort of their living rooms. Television offered viewers free and convenient access to the sort of musical and comedy revues that were previously available only in Broadway theaters or nightclubs. In the comfort of home, viewers could enjoy live performances by some of the biggest stars from the worlds of Broadway, grand opera, popular music, and, to a more limited extent, Hollywood. Such variety programs seemed destined for widespread popularity in the new entertainment medium, but time would prove otherwise.

While historians tend to group their shows under the label "vaudeo" because of the numerous "acts" by various musical and comic performers and the lavish production values on each show, Berle, Caesar, and Gleason had distinct approaches, and each presented his own comic persona. Milton Berle pioneered the form by offering the closest equivalent to a vaudeville master of ceremonies who presented his own monologue, introduced the other acts, and participated in some of the comedy sketches and musical productions. Sid Caesar did not serve as the host of his shows, preferring to appear only in the sketches with the regular ensemble or in scripted monologue routines in which he portrayed a particular character, not himself. Jackie Gleason was a flamboyant host, orchestra leader, and general ringleader of his shows, joking with the chorus girls and guest stars and starring in most of the sketches and his own wide variety of character monologues. Although each of these larger-than-life talents would meet with some success in occasional forays into theater or film, their greatest triumphs came by way of the small screen, and all three of them today enjoy distinguished places in the pantheon of television comedy.

In terms of steady popularity and longevity, however, these three titans of early television comedy are surpassed by three comedians who chose less flashy formats. Jack Benny, who brought his very popular radio show almost intact to television, sustained a presence in prime time from 1950 to 1965. Red Skelton also transferred his radio show to television for a continuous, albeit rocky, run of twenty years (1951–1971). The mildest of the three comedy-variety hosts was Arthur Godfrey, another popular radio comedian who, when he moved to television, made his mark by becoming the only personality in TV history to have two top-rated programs running simultaneously in prime time for an extended period. His comedy-variety show, *Arthur Godfrey and His Friends*, aired as an hour-long show from 1949 to 1957 on Wednesday nights and for the 1958–59 season in a half-hour format, while *Arthur Godfrey's Talent Scouts* appeared on Monday nights from 1948 to 1958. Both of Godfrey's programs showed up regularly among the top-rated series almost every year of their run. The popularity of Arthur Godfrey should not be overlooked in any study of comedy-variety shows.

Milton Berle's place in television history is secure. Early in his career in the medium he was dubbed "Mr. Television," and the title stuck. He was the host of the very first NBC telecast of their new variety show, *The Texaco Star Theater*, on the night of June 8, 1948. During that summer a group of comedians rotated as the host each week, but by September Berle was made the permanent host.[1] The show was a phenomenal success, making Berle the first television superstar. At one point in its first season the show's 97.4 share of the audience meant that almost every television set that was turned on at that time of the evening was tuned to Milton Berle. Restaurants, theaters, and nightclubs adjusted their schedules so that patrons would not miss the program on Tuesday nights. Some restaurants even closed on that night of the week. Movie exhibitors and Broadway producers claimed that Berle had made Tuesday night "poisonous at the box office."[2] On November 2, 1948, NBC delayed broadcasting election returns of the Dewey-Truman presidential race until Berle's program was over.[3] Berle's picture appeared on the cover of both *Time* and *Newsweek* on May 16, 1949. Philip Hamburger, reviewing the show quite unfavorably in *The New Yorker,* described the audience mania in an age before most viewers had television sets in their homes:

> All over town during the Berle program, in taverns equipped with what the industry refers to as "the magic kaleidoscopic eye of TV," people are reported to be standing four deep at the bar, laughing, nudging one another, and neglecting their warm beers. A traffic problem of sorts has been created in front of television stores, where crowds gather to watch Berle as people once clustered at the doorways of radio stores, a generation ago, when Amos 'n' Andy were getting underway.[4]

For several years Milton Berle dominated the medium. In his second year on the air, while *The Texaco Star Theater* was honored with the Emmy Award for Best Kinescope Show, Berle also received the Emmy for Most Outstanding Kinescope Personality in 1949. The show's change of titles over its eight-year run nicely illustrates the tightening of the spotlight's focus on the star of the show. What began in 1948 as *The Texaco Star Theater* became *The Buick-Berle Show* in 1953 and then simply *The Milton Berle Show* from 1954 to 1956.

Television made Milton Berle a star, but his comedy career had begun long before he exploded onto the TV screens of America, and he was hardly an unknown in the entertainment industry. For almost forty years he had been working quite successfully in every entertainment medium. Born in 1908, he began his career as a child actor at the age of five, appearing in memorable silent films such as *The Perils of Pauline* and *Tillie's Punctured Romance* and performing in vaudeville children's acts. When he was twelve he made his Broadway début in the hit show *Floradora*. A year later he played New York's Palace Theater; a few years later, at the age of twenty, he became the youngest master of ceremonies in the Palace Theater's history. He went on to a highly lucrative career as a nightclub entertainer, a popular master of ceremonies on the vaudeville circuit with top billing, and eventually a headliner in lavish Broadway reviews such as *Earl Carroll's Vanities* in the 1930s and *The Ziegfeld Follies* as late as 1943, as well as starring in many other Broadway productions.

Berle developed an act characterized by a fast-paced monologue and a flippant, wiseguy personality. As a master of ceremonies, "he opened with a clever monologue, introduced the acts, and often obtruded in their performances to get laughs. His rapid-fire delivery of successive one-liners and compressed jokes . . . typified the urban vaudeville stand-up comic."[5] He appeared in numerous Hollywood films in the 1930s and 1940s, but he never starred in any of them. In the late thirties he moved to radio, starring in the *Texaco Star Theater* from 1939 to 1948, which, along with many other popular radio programs, made its move to the television medium in the late 1940s. Having displayed his talent on the vaudeville and Broadway stage, Hollywood films, and network radio, Berle was eager to try the new medium of television because he judged it to be well suited to his particular talents. The future "Mr. Television" was certainly right about that.

His rise to fame coincided with the rapid increase in production and sales of television sets to bars and other public gathering spots and homes across the cities of the East Coast. Television sales grew at impressive rates, and Berle's popularity has always been credited with creating the huge demand for sets. No longer content with seeing "Uncle Miltie" at the neighborhood tavern, Americans wanted television in their homes. There were approximately half a million TV sets in America when Berle went on the air in 1948. In 1949 that number doubled, and by 1950 six million sets had been sold. During Berle's reign on the air, the percentage of American households with television sets increased from 9 percent in 1950 to more than 70 percent in 1956.[6]

Gerard Jones's study of television comedy takes care to qualify the reports of Berle's success, noting that, especially at its peak in the early years of the show, its popularity was a matter of geographic region and social class:

> In 1949, only twenty-four cities got network broadcasts, most of them in the Northeast. Of the million TV sets in use, 42 percent were in New York City. The FCC contributed to the situation when, in the fall of 1948, it became nervous over the boom in TV sales and clamped a freeze on new station licenses . . . the freeze dragged on for nearly four years. Well over half of Berle's viewers were thus in East Coast cities. A lot of them watched in working-class bars; even in 1950 only 9 percent of American homes had television. Berle was a sensation with the people who had always favored his kind of comedy: working- and lower-middle-class New Yorkers, gathered in bars and friends' houses, enjoying a party atmosphere. As TV became a home appliance nationwide, his ratings fell quickly and far.[7]

The format of the show took full advantage of the burgeoning medium, translating the comedy of vaudeville and nightclub acts onto the small screen and grainy black-and-white images of primitive television. It originated live from Studio 6B in the RCA building at Rockefeller Center. Berle worked on many of the details of the show each week. He edited the writers' lines, selected the musical arrangements, directed the dancers and musicians, chose the scenery and costumes, and checked the camera angles.[8] The May 16, 1949, *Newsweek* article claimed that "Berle runs the rehearsals of his show—cast, band, and guests— with an iron hand, and indeed of so rough a grade of iron that there are some performers who will not repeat their visits on the program" and goes on to conjecture whether this pressure is caused more by Berle's personality or by the "frantic demands of a wild and unexplored new medium."

The pressures to produce a weekly live show were enormous; it was particularly challenging to come up with new comedy material each week. In the days of touring the vaudeville circuit, a comic had years to perfect his act, and he could repeat the same routines for different audiences in various cities. "Now Berle was faced with staging a live weekly program for thirty-nine consecutive weeks and creating new jokes and skits for every show."[9] Production of the show was expensive. Each show featured elaborate musical routines with a chorus of showgirls in lavish costumes, flashy sets, and a live orchestra. Every week boasted a roster of popular guests from the worlds of Hollywood film, popular music, and the nightclub circuit who would participate in banter with Berle, the zany but congenial host, and engage in sketches with Berle and his resident comic ensemble.

Berle's own comedy tended toward the burlesque, with his outlandish costumes—a caveman, Cleopatra, a bride, Superman, Carmen Miranda—and corny, even naughty one-liners. Steven D. Stark quotes one reviewer who described Berle as the king of "the yak, the blacked-out teeth, the idiot's wig, the lisp, the swagger, the falling pants."[10] David Marc describes Berle and other stars of the early comedy-variety shows as an "electronic *toomler* . . . a kind of combination social director/trickster figure who flourished in the Catskills from the 1920s . . . kidding the guests, introducing the sketches, and providing continuity between program and commercial."[11] While Berle's monologues often included some topical satire, most of the jokes would consist of comments about the audience and mild self-deprecatory remarks. The comedy usually depended on Berle's willingness to be the fall guy. Most of the show's humor, in the monologues as well as the sketches, was visual, making use of outlandish costumes, pratfalls, and other slapstick material.

Berle added one feature to his stand-up persona, however, one night in 1949, which serves to illustrate that even this loudmouth master of ceremonies needed to become more aware of the family viewers who had now replaced the nightclub customers and theater-goers of his previous experience. To fill some air time that remained at the end of the live show, Berle addressed himself to the children in his audience. He had reportedly received numerous messages from parents complaining that their children insisted on staying up past their bedtime to watch his show. So he spoke to the boys and girls at home: "I want to say something to any of you kiddies who should be in bed getting a good night's rest before school tomorrow. Listen to your Uncle Miltie and kiss Mommy and Daddy goodnight and go straight upstairs like good little boys and girls." From then on, until the day he died, Berle would be referred to as "Uncle Miltie."[12] The vaudeville beast had been domesticated.

Berle's comic roots, nevertheless, remained East Coast urban. As Arthur Frank Wertheim has observed, "Berle's rapid delivery, frenetic activity on stage, and even the swift progress of the show matched the fast pace of city life. . . . He personified a flippant city slicker."[13] Hence, as the reach of television programming expanded across the country, NBC realized that Berle's brand of citified comedy did not seem to appeal to viewers in other regions. For example, an Arbitron survey published in *Variety* in May 1954 reported that in Charlotte, North Carolina, Berle's ratings were only 1.9, compared to a figure of 56.3 for his competition, a western dramatic series called *Death Valley Days*.

The format of Berle's show changed significantly about halfway through its run. For the 1952–1953 season the producers hired the talented writer Goodman Ace and a new writing team to create the programs. They did away with much of the slapstick and created a "less boisterous" Berle. Instead of coming onstage in drag or another outrageous costume, Berle was dressed in a tuxedo. Each program was organized "around a comic situation in which Berle was seen behind the scenes having some difficulty while preparing for his TV broadcast."[14] The show relied less on guest stars and more on the regular comic ensemble. In some sense, the show was developing into more of a self-reflexive situation comedy about producing a variety show.

In the fall of 1955, in what would become Berle's final season, the format changed again, doing away with the resident ensemble and alternating the format of the show among the variety-show patterns, satirical episodes, and book musicals. One week, for example, the show was an hour-long political satire, with music, written by the sophisticated Broadway playwright and novelist Gore Vidal. Berle also began sharing his Tuesday night time slot, alternating with other variety shows starring Martha Raye, Steve Allen, or Bob Hope.

The show's phenomenal audience share was bound to decline with the onset of serious competition from the growth of the other networks and their more extensive roster of programs (many of them simply attempts to copy Berle), and the show finally ended its run in June 1956. Berle returned two years later, however, in a new half-hour variety series for NBC called *Milton Berle Starring in the Kraft Music Hall*, but the new show lasted only one season. An attempt at a comeback on the ABC network in the 1966–1967 season fared even worse with viewers.

In 1951 Berle had signed a contract with NBC guaranteeing him $200,000 a year whether he worked or not, and in 1956 the contract was renegotiated to allow him to appear on other networks. This enabled Berle to continue to work in films and appear in television specials. Over the next forty years Berle was honored with nearly every show business tribute and award, but after the early years of his television superstardom, Berle never found a permanent place in television comedy. Nothing, however, can take away from his accomplishments as the "king of comedy" in television's early days.

Berle's eight-year season was quite respectable, and yet historians of television comedy seem determined to see the program as some sort of failure. Wertheim, for example, describes Berle as "one of television's first victims, and, perhaps, one of its most poignant ones."[15] Several reasons are suggested for the demise of the show. The main consensus seems to be that Berle's urban vaudeville comedy reflected the energy and excitement of the new medium, especially for viewers in the major cities of the Northeast. By 1952, however, when the installation of the coaxial cable across the country had made possible the simultaneous nationwide viewing of network programming and the FCC ended its "freeze" and allowed many more local television stations beyond the East Coast to go into operation, television viewing became a much more national experience. It gradually became clear that Berle's wiseguy abrasiveness and outrageous shtick did not play as well in the farm communities, small towns, and, most importantly, the suburbs of Middle America. David Marc argues that the racier humor and revealing costumes of nightclubs, vaudeville, and burlesque were deemed unsuitable for the American home.[16]

Others critics maintain that the very format of the variety show could not be sustained, in terms of its expense, pressure on its writers, and audience appeal, all of this in the face of the rise of situation comedy, which was less expensive to produce, required fewer writers, and appealed to the broader television audience. It seems that the networks had misjudged the taste of the public for variety shows, since so many other attempts had even less success. Viewers were not interested in the electronic "night on the town," provided by the television equivalent of Broadway theater, vaudeville, and nightclub entertainment.[17]

Another star of television variety shows would encounter the same pattern of viewer response to his more sophisticated approach to comedy variety that offered a Broadway experience to viewers across the country. Unlike Milton Berle, who had already enjoyed a lucrative thirty-year career in show business before his television début, Sid Caesar was relatively unknown when he first showed up on the small screen. His road to television stardom began when he was performing as a musician in the Coast Guard during World War II. While playing in the service show *Tars and Spars*, Caesar was overheard improvising comedy routines among the band members, and the show's producer, Max Liebman, switched him over from music to comedy. Caesar went on to perform his "war" routine in the stage and movie versions of the review, and after the war he appeared regularly in theatrical reviews in Florida and the Catskills and in the Broadway review *Make Mine Manhattan*, also produced by Liebman. In 1949, when Liebman developed his first variety show on television, *The Admiral Broadway Revue*, he naturally cast Caesar as part of the regular ensemble and teamed him with the brilliant comedian Imogene Coca.

The show premiered on January 28, 1949. Simultaneously broadcast on both the NBC and DuMont networks, it adopted the format of a Broadway revue with top-name guest stars and lavish production numbers. Liebman described it as an attempt to bring Broadway comedy to television:

> At the time that television began to capture my attention, I realized that most of the programs being presented really originated in vaudeville and nightclubs or were an extension of radio. My emphasis was influenced, more or less, by the legitimate theater. There was a level of maturity and, if you will, an element of sophistication that was compatible with what I had done all my life before that. I wanted to bring this into the medium, without denigrating anything else . . . the legitimate theater; the element of sophistication.[18]

From 1934 to 1940 Liebman had been producing weekly original revues for the fifteen hundred guests at Tamiment, the adult summer camp in the Poconos, offering opportunities for many budding writers and performers, such as Danny Kaye. He brought the best of his material to Broadway in 1939 in a revue entitled *The Straw Hat Revue*, a showcase for Kaye, Coca, the singer Alfred Drake (destined for Broadway stardom as the original Curly in *Oklahoma* and other hit musicals of the 1940s and 1950s), and a young Jerome Robbins dancing in the chorus. Liebman was convinced that there was an audience eager to see such material on television, and so *The Admiral Broadway Revue* offered a more sophisticated bill of fare, with comedy sketches that "dared to satirize modern painting, psychiatry, movie epics, advertising, and other themes not commonly treated on television."[19]

Liebman's instincts were correct. The show was a huge success, perhaps too successful. The sponsor, Admiral, a major manufacturer of television sets, found that the public's demand for its sets outpaced its manufacturing capacity and had to withdraw its sponsorship. *The Admiral Broadway Revue* ended its run in early June, after only seventeen weeks of phenomenal popularity.

But Liebman soon came up with a replacement. On February 25, 1950, the comedy-variety program *Your Show of Shows* made its début on the NBC network. The "Broadway" motif was evident in the opening theme song of the program, which promised the appearance of "stars over Broadway" and invited the viewers to "join Broadway on parade." *Your Show of Shows* adopted its predecessor's format—monologues, skits, and parodies of movies and plays—with some changes. The new show depended less on guest stars, showcasing instead the talents of the remarkable resident ensemble of Caesar, Coca, Carl Reiner, and Howard Morris. It was hosted by a different guest star every week, usually a well-known film or theater personality, who would introduce each number and perform in some of the sketches. The first few shows were hosted, for example, by Burgess Meredith, Rex Harrison, and Melvyn Douglas, all from the worlds of theater and film, not from vaudeville or nightclubs. The program also benefited from developments in the use of the television camera:

> No longer resembling a filmed intimate stage revue, the program made greater use of camera movement to catch Sid Caesar's bellows or rage or suffering and Imogene Coca's infectious grin or lascivious wink. Where the Admiral show had occasionally seemed detached and precious, the sketches on "Your Show of Shows" brought the viewer in close to the action—Caesar and Coca, alone or together, in pantomime or sketches.[20]

The show's success depended a great deal on its brilliant team of writers, who have been described as a virtual who's who of post–World War II American comedy, Mel Tolkin, Lucille Kallen, Larry Gelbart, Mel Brooks, Neil Simon, and many others who went on to their own successful careers in television, musical theater, and film. Caesar always attended the writing sessions to suggest ideas and offer criticism, and Coca frequently participated as well. The weekly writing schedule for the show has become infamous, demanding ninety minutes of material that would be written from Monday to Wednesday, rehearsed and rewritten from Thursday to Saturday, and presented live on Saturday night from 9:00 to 10:30 p.m. from the NBC studios in New York. The frenzy of coming up with knock-'em-dead material week after week is hilariously recorded for posterity in the ex-writer Neil Simon's 1993 Broadway comedy *Laughter on the 23rd Floor*.

Mark Williams offers a succinct description of the show's content:

> Both raucous and urbane, it combined revue and sketch comedy with a rather sophisticated sense of satire and parody. . . . Caesar, notorious for his deviations from the script, was skilled at mime, dialects, monologues, foreign-language double-talk, and general comic acting. . . . Not a rapid fire jokester like Berle or Fred Allen, Caesar was often compared in the press to the likes of Chaplin,

Fields, or Raimu. The 90-minute show usually featured a guest host (who played a minor role), at least two production numbers, sketches between Caesar and Coca, the showcase parody of a popular film (e.g., "Aggravation Boulevard," "From Here to Obscurity"), further sketches (as many as ten per show), Caesar in monologue or pantomime, and the entire company in a production number.[21]

While Caesar resembled Berle in his daily involvement with the writing and production of the show, his on-screen presence was quite different. First, Caesar was not the master of ceremonies of the show and seldom spoke directly to the viewers as Berle did every week at the show's conclusion. Caesar did not have any distinct persona to match Berle's combination of wiseguy and buffoon. Caesar was not a stand-up comedian, preferring to appear in the mask of a character, even in his monologues. He developed several recurring characters, most famously a Germanic professor, the storyteller Somerset Winterset, and the beatnik jazz musician Progress Hornsby. Caesar and Coca developed the recurring characters of the battling married couple, Charlie and Doris Hickenlooper. Most of the sketches made good use of the rich comic ensemble of the show.

Sid Caesar's whole approach to comic performance differed significantly from the gags and slapstick of Milton Berle. Liebman once described Caesar's comic style:

> Caesar tells no jokes and elicits terrific crescendos of mirth. Characterization, not gags, is the main ingredient of his techniques. He is blessed with a kind of magic truth, the uncanny ability to project the core and humanity of the character he is playing. Beneath the surface humor there is a wry commentary on the conventions and hypocrisies of life. . . . Sid could never be a stand-up, one-line comedian. In fact, he didn't like one-line jokes in the sketches because he felt that if the joke was a good one, anybody could do it. One-liners would take him away from whatever it was that drove him into his completely personal approach to comedy. He wanted to do things only the way he could.[22]

Another critical analysis pointed to the contrast between Caesar and Berle, observing, "Mr. Caesar needs no insult routines, stale gags, shabby sketches to garner his laughs. In his comedy approach he has found the greatest source of humor to be people themselves."[23]

Although he engaged in sketches and production numbers on the show, Caesar was probably at his best in his solo performances. Ted Sennett describes Caesar alone on camera:

> With his physical being intensely involved in a specific situation, he was at his most riveting, his most remarkable. . . . With a face that could express various degrees of happiness, fear, loathing, dismay, surprise, desperation. . . . Caesar

was like a man possessed, reaching for the inner being of the perennially anxious, hopeful, exasperated character he was playing.[24]

Your Show of Shows ran for four seasons, totaling 160 live telecasts. It was honored with the Emmy Award for Best Variety Show in 1951 and 1952, and Caesar and Coca received the Emmy for Best Actor and Best Actress in 1951. Only in its fourth season (1953–1954) did the show drop below the top 20 shows in the Nielsen ratings, along with other signs of its waning popularity. Its schedule was changed so that it appeared three out of four weeks, alternating with another variety show, *The All-Star Revue*. The song-and-dance portions of the program became more prominent, and, as various critics observed, the comedy did not seem to approach the level of earlier seasons. The observations of Jack Gould in *The New York Times* describe a show that seemed to have run out of steam:

> Perhaps it is the horrendous number of commercials that prevent any continuity or sustained warmth in the show but somehow it has gone cut and dried and impersonal. "Your Show of Shows" bears the imprint of a production that has had a long run. It needs some first night sparkle and excitement. . . . Mr. Caesar and Miss Coca have not lost their technique or artistry. Their performances individually may be just as good as they were four years ago. The difference is that millions of persons now know "Your Show of Shows" backward and forward. Within its framework there is hardly anything that Mr. Caesar and Miss Coca can do that seems fresh and bright.[25]

Your Show of Shows was not picked up for the 1954–1955 season. Perhaps NBC was disappointed with the show's ratings or the critical reviews, but the more likely explanation for the discontinuation of *Your Show of* Shows is offered in Max Wilk's assessment that "whatever the reasons, management thinking went like so: if Liebman, Caesar and Coca had been triumphant as a trio, then by splitting the three, triple success would be guaranteed."[26] Caesar's own comments at the time, published in *The New York Telegram*, offered a polite interpretation of that strategy:

> The truth is that Max, Coca, and myself have to split up because there just isn't time for the three of us to express ourselves on one show any longer. . . . During the past five years, we've done everything that's possible to do within the confines of one show. It's time we were given a chance to express ourselves differently. I know Coca is capable of doing more, and so is Max.[27]

The last episode of *Your Show of Shows* aired on June 5, 1954. The following season saw the implementation of the "triple success" strategy, with mixed success. Coca showed up in *Your Show of Shows*'s previous time slot as the star of her own half-hour show, which experimented with both the situation-comedy and comedy-variety formats and got cancelled after only one season. Liebman moved on to produce a series of Saturday and Sunday "spectaculars," called *Max Liebman Presents*, which continued to provide more sophisticated entertainment with televised versions of past Broadway successes *(Lady in the Dark, Babes in Toyland)*, some original musicals *(Heidi)*, and musical revues as showcases for major musical stars of the era (Judy Holliday, Frank Sinatra, Jimmy Durante, and others). But Liebman gradually withdrew from television as network production moved to filmed and taped programs in Hollywood.[28]

Caesar, however, fared much better. He returned as the star of *Caesar's Hour*, a shorter version of *Your Show of Shows*, employing the same team of brilliant writers and many of the same supporting players, but with a wider variety of formats. One week's entry might be the standard comedy-variety show, another week might be categorized as a musical revue, and another week might be closer to a full hour of situation comedy about a suburban husband and wife and their neighbors. Occasionally, the show would offer some combination of all of the above. The suburbanite sketch, entitled "The Commuters," proved popular with the viewers, whose preference for situation comedies like *I Love Lucy* was already sending an ominous message to the comedy-variety shows. The hour-long presentations of "The Commuters" was testing the waves of the future for these talented writers and performers who could very well move into a situation-comedy format on a full-time basis. Although the show won an Emmy Award for Best Series in the 1956 season and several of the supporting actors won Emmys as well during the show's run, *Caesar's Hour* did not do as well in the ratings as its predecessor and was cancelled after three seasons.

The third major star of comedy-variety shows that offered "a night on the town" was Jackie Gleason. *The Jackie Gleason Show* appeared in two incarnations on the CBS network. Its first run extended from 1952 to 1955 and was replaced for the 1955–1956 season with thirty-nine half-hour episodes of the now-legendary situation comedy *The Honeymooners*. While *The Honeymooners* managed to live on in reruns for many years and, now available in DVD format, has achieved classic status, its ratings for its one season did not match those of Gleason's variety show. So Gleason returned to the variety format, only to find that his ratings were even lower than the previous season of *The Honeymooners*, and the show was cancelled in 1957. After Gleason's unsuccessful attempts to appear in other formats, *The Jackie Gleason Show* returned with its lavish variety-show format and enjoyed a longer run, from 1962 to 1970.

Born in Brooklyn in 1916, Jackie Gleason had led a hardscrabble life in and around New York City. His alcoholic father had abandoned the family. Gleason dropped out of school at an early age and tried his hand as a pool hustler, a boxer, a carnival barker, and had finally settled into a moderately successful career as a stand-up comic and a master of ceremonies in nightclubs. He got his first break into television in 1949 as the star of the television version of a popular radio series, *The Life of Riley*, about a Brooklyn-born factory worker who had moved out to California for a job in an aircraft plant. Gleason was a substitute for the original star of the radio series, William Bendix, who was too tied up with movie commitments to take the role.

The show was mainly a domestic comedy set in a working-class home, with the hard-hat father usually creating rather than solving problems for his long-suffering wife and bumptious children. Unfortunately, Gleason's portrayal of Chester A. Riley was too broad for the character who had become so familiar to the program's fans, and the series was cancelled after only one season. The series would be revived three years later when Bendix became available and would enjoy a five-year run and impressive ratings. But by then Jackie Gleason had found a far better path to stardom as the host of a lavish variety show that offered wider scope for his larger-than life physical comedy and character portrayals.

When it first appeared on the air, *The Jackie Gleason Show* in many ways resembled Milton Berle's program. Gleason, the ebullient, jovial master of ceremonies, dressed in a tuxedo, often holding a cigarette in one hand and a drink in the other, would open the show with a monologue, ending with his boisterous phrase, "And awaa-aay we go!" and the evening's entertainment would proceed. Virginia Wright Wexman has examined Gleason's television persona as a noteworthy exception to the general pattern of the "aesthetic of realism" surrounding television performers. Critics are prone to observe that, unlike the larger-than life images cultivated by movie actors, "TV characters strike us as being just like the actors who play them, who, in turn, seem like the audiences who watch them and fantasize about them."[29] Viewers have become accustomed to think of Mary Tyler Moore, Bob Newhart, or Ray Romano, for example, as "regular people." Gleason's persona, however, was more glamorous both on- and off-screen:

> Though not a romantic idol in terms of physical appearance, Gleason's money and fame allowed him to cultivate a lifestyle based on popular fantasies about successful and desirable males. Such fantasies were acted out through well-publicized anecdotes about the star's personal life and in his widely distributed record album "For Lovers Only." These themes were further developed in the presentational

mode of his appearances as master of ceremonies . . . where beautiful women called "Glea Girls" announced his entrance and served him liquor in a coffee cup as he confided to the audience, "How sweet it is." Gleason was later to marry a showgirl, thereby providing such images with a further dimension of documentary verisimilitude.[30]

The show boasted a full orchestra (sometimes conducted by Gleason, who had composed the theme music for the show), a bevy of showgirls who appeared throughout the show, musical production numbers, musical and comic guest stars, and Gleason, "the Great One" himself, playing a variety of characters he had perfected over the years: Joe the Bartender, The Poor Soul, Reggie Van Gleason III, the Loudmouth, and other characters who played off Gleason's facial dexterity, booming voice, or occasional dip into pathos. Jackie Gleason's monologue was not composed of the quick one-liners of Milton Berle, but he surpassed Berle in his ability to create a full comic character. "The Honeymooners," which originated as extended sketches in the variety show, showcased Gleason's talent for character comedy best as he became Ralph Kramden, the Brooklyn bus driver living from paycheck to paycheck, always falling for a get-rich-quick scheme with his pal, Ed Norton, and battling with his loving but sardonic wife, Alice.

As it began its second run, from 1962 to 1970, Gleason's show bore the more grandiose title of *The Jackie Gleason Show: The American Scene Magazine.* Gleason returned to his old master-of-ceremonies persona, along with the orchestra, the showgirls, and all of Gleason's characters. The comedy featured more topical satire than had been present in the previous show, more appearances by famous guest stars, and numerous experiments with various hour-long formats. There were entire episodes done as musical comedies. In 1964 the entire production moved from New York to the studios of Gleason's showplace in Miami Beach, Florida, for the rest of its run. In 1966 Gleason brought back Art Carney to play Ed Norton as he resumed production of "The Honeymooners" sketch as a main element of the program. Throughout the last four seasons of the show's run, over half of the episodes were full-hour presentations of "The Honeymooners," sometimes done as musical comedies with songs and production numbers.[31]

Of all the variety-show comics, Gleason was the most persistent. Over the years, with rich inventiveness, he seems to have tested every possibility for the variety-show format in prime-time television, even attempting some sort of convergence of the variety show and the situation comedy. Like Sid Caesar a decade earlier, Gleason's talent for character comedy and the chemistry of a great comic ensemble insured a deep vein of comic material for the sketches, while the glamour and bluster of his master-of-ceremonies role resembled the more sophisticated, less flamboyant persona Milton Berle adopted in his last few seasons. Meanwhile, the toss-up between situation comedy and comedy variety must have been fascinating for Gleason and his writers and producers.[32] Was there any place in the living room for someone who was larger than life?

·3·

———

SURVIVAL OF THE NICEST

T he rise and fall of the great comedy-variety shows of television's early years seem to indicate that the new medium was not the place for lavish spectacle or outlandish comedy. There have been a number of variety shows over the ensuing years that can be characterized as vaudeville-style shows with big-name guest stars and elaborate production numbers, but the most successful ones have been hosted by musical stars—Dean Martin (1965–1974) and Sonny and Cher (1971–1977), for example. Only one major comic talent, Carol Burnett, succeeded in hosting a long-running variety show with the sort of sets, costumes, musical numbers, guests, and other high production values associated with the golden age of Berle, Caesar, and others. By combining the star's genuine likeability, her comic versatility, and her musical talent with the sort of sketch-comedy ensemble reminiscent of *Your Show of Shows*, Burnett's show enjoyed a twelve-year run from 1967 to 1979.

The careers of Milton Berle, Sid Caesar and Jackie Gleason show how difficult it was to re-invent the Ziegfeld Follies or Las Vegas for the home audience. Viewers preferred to chuckle over the adventures of Lucy Ricardo and her many successors in the more familiar surroundings of the home rather than split their sides over the zany antics of Uncle Miltie, the sophisticated routines of Sid Caesar, or the raucous behavior of Jackie Gleason. But the comedy-variety format did not disappear with the departure of the big-time boffo comics. There were more modest successes in the ensuing years, and a few genuine stars who achieved great success with less flashy formats.

Flip Wilson hosted a popular comedy-variety show for four seasons (1970–1974), and George Gobel offered a minimalist-variety show which, for most of its six-year run (1954–1960), appeared in a half-hour format filled with Gobel's monologue, a sketch or two, and a musical number. Garry Moore, who was more of a genial host-humorist than a full-fledged comedian, hosted a similarly low-key variety show that garnered good enough ratings to achieve a run of six years (1958–1964). Comedy-variety even ventured into country humor for a brief spell. *Hee Haw*, a music-and-comedy show hosted by the country-guitarist Roy Clark, lasted only two years (1969–1971) on CBS, but went on to enjoy an amazing tenure in first-run syndication from 1971 to 1992. These few successful ventures in the comedy-variety genre over the years pale in comparison to the flood of situation comedies that were filling up the prime-time schedule every season.

Certain comedians, however, figured it out and achieved true television stardom in the comedy-variety mode by taking it down a notch. While studies of the comedy-variety format tend to emphasize the spectacular "night on the town" variety shows of Berle, Caesar, and Gleason, three other popular comedians—Jack Benny, Red Skelton, and Arthur Godfrey—found their own niche with less lavish formats that centered on the likeability of the show's star and the willingness of the viewers to "invite him into our home" week after week. In all three of these cases, the longevity of their uninterrupted runs on television exceeded that of Berle, Caesar, and Gleason. Their success suggests that a more informal approach to comedy-variety fit the television screen better, pleasing viewers and advertisers alike.

Jack Benny was the most famous radio personality of his day to make the move to television. Like so many comedians of his era, Benny had begun in vaudeville. In fact, his early career closely resembles that of Milton Berle. In 1912, at the age of 18, Benny began touring as one-half of a novelty-music act with occasional comic touches. After serving in World War I, during which he appeared in some military shows, Benny returned to vaudeville with a solo act consisting mainly of ragtime music and comic effects with the violin. By the mid-1920s Benny was playing the Palace Theater, appearing in Broadway revues, and starring as a master of ceremonies in vaudeville shows. His style as master of ceremonies, a significant departure from the wiseguy jokesters such as Berle and others, would eventually serve Benny well in the monologue segments of his television shows:

> He stood on the stage expressing unhurried ease and exuding great confidence. He almost seemed to feel that nothing mattered very much. As he spoke, in a slow and bored fashion, he would fix his tie or straighten his breast-pocket handkerchief or pick invisible bits of dust off his suit. He didn't seem at all to care that there was an audience out there.[1]

In the early 1930s, as vaudeville was dying, Benny signed a contract with MGM and managed to appear in several unimpressive films. (One exception was his starring role in Ernst Lubitsch's 1942 screwball anti-Nazi comedy, *To*

Be or Not to Be.) Finally, in 1932, on the advice of his close friend George Burns, Benny found his way into radio, and, in the process, he created a new formula for comedy, of which Benny himself would become the consummate practitioner. Realizing early on that "radio was an insatiable monster that swallowed scripts and demanded new ones incessantly,"[2] Benny and his main writer Harry Conn abandoned the typical vaudeville pattern of bizarre situations and exaggerated characters and strings of gags, puns, and punch lines, which up until then was the standard fare for Ed Wynn and other popular radio comics, and developed comedy based on more recognizable character traits and relatively realistic situations and dialogue:

> Now, instead of reciting lines to the listener at home as if he were speaking from a stage, Benny developed a framework of situations and a set of characters on which amusing complications and funny pay-off lines could be hung. . . . Conn developed fairly real and human characters and situations and had the humor arising out of the characters and situations; his dialogue sounded conversational instead of artificial. He eschewed puns and other forms of low comedy. Soon many of the situations were written around Benny's home life, and this meant even less exaggeration and even more credible situations.[3]

Maurice Zolotow has called this new formula "the great revolution in radio comedy," and he quotes the observations of Benny's great radio-humorist rival Fred Allen, who said:

> [Jack Benny] was the first to realize that the listener is not a theatre with a thousand other people but is in a small circle at home. The Benny show is like a one man's family in slapstick. When they tune into the Benny show, it's like tuning into somebody else's home."[4]

And audiences at home tuned in. *The Jack Benny Show* (under various titles depending on the identity of the sponsor, Canada Dry, Chevrolet, Jell-O, or others) became a major Sunday night fixture first on the NBC network and then on CBS. It slowly and steadily found its audience until by 1937 it was first in the ratings and continued to stay among the top-rated shows until its twenty-three-year run on radio ended in 1955.

Even while starring weekly on the radio, Benny started to explore television with an experimental scheduling strategy. His half-hour show on the CBS television network began airing in 1950 as an occasional "special." From 1953 to 1960 it ran every other week. It became a weekly show from 1960 to 1965, and finally returned to a series of occasional specials from 1965 until Benny's death in 1974. Another series of occasional hour-long shows, *The Jack Benny*

Hour, began airing in 1959 and continued even while Benny's half-hour show was appearing on a weekly basis.

The format of the show and the personality of Jack Benny, so well honed over two decades on radio, remained basically the same in the move to television. This in itself was a gamble; most of the other beloved radio comedies—*Amos 'n' Andy*, *Fibber McGee and Molly*, and *The Edgar Bergen-Charlie McCarthy Show*, for example—did not succeed in their transitions to the small screen. However, the formula that Harry Conn and the other writers had developed for Benny's comedy offered something different from the other radio hits. Benny's radio show had communicated the illusion that the listeners were allowed "to eavesdrop on the lives of actual persons" since Jack and most of the cast of characters appeared under their actual names and remained consistently in character.[5] Tinky Weisblat describes the basic pattern:

> Benny played a fictional version of himself, Jack Benny the television star, and the program often revolved around preparation for the next week's show—involving interaction between Benny and a regular stable of characters that included the program's announcer, Don Wilson, and its resident crooner, Dennis Day. Until her retirement in 1958, Benny's wife, Mary Livingstone, portrayed what her husband terms in his memoirs as "a kind of heckler-secretary, a wise-cracking friend of the family and the television program." . . . Jack Benny's ever-present butler/valet/nanny, Rochester (portrayed by Eddie Anderson) . . . viewed Benny with slightly condescending affection—and frequently got the better of his employer in arguments that were obviously battles between peers. He was, in fact, the closest thing the Benny character had to either a spouse or a best friend.[6]

Other members of the ensemble included Frank Nelson as a preening department store salesman, bank teller, travel agent, or some other functionary who could easily intimidate Benny, and the multitalented Mel Blanc, the "master of a thousand voices" (including Bugs Bunny) who appeared frequently as Professor LeBlanc, Benny's long-suffering violin teacher, and as various ethnic characters. Blanc also provided various sound effects, especially the engine of Benny's ancient Maxwell automobile.[7]

Benny employed a relatively small and permanent group of writers, whose tasks seem simpler than those required for the writing of all the sketches and satirical pieces needed for Sid Caesar's sixty-minute or ninety-minute programs or the hour of gags and skits required by Milton Berle each week. The writers needed only to rework variations of the well-defined Jack Benny persona, with the addition of some visual material not possible on the radio, which continued to provide a consistent source of comedy:

Jack's stinginess, vanity about his supposed age of 39, basement vault where he kept all his money, ancient Maxwell automobile, and feigned ineptness at playing the violin were all part of the act—and were, if anything, bolstered by their visibility on the TV show. Added to Jack's famous pregnant pause and exasperated "Well!" were a rather mincing walk, an affected hand to the cheek, and a pained look of disbelief when confronted by life's little tragedies.[8]

The persona worked both in Benny's monologue, which usually opened the show, and in the sketches that followed, which generally amounted to a behind-the-scenes situation comedy that portrayed Benny as prey to his own foibles, low self-esteem, and image of himself as an outsider constantly vulnerable to the condescension of friends and strangers. Weisblat remarks on his minimizing of his Jewish identity and his sexuality, managing "to transcend those categories, rather than deny them. Beneath his quickly lifted arrogant façade lurked an American Everyperson."[9]

In real life Benny was, in many ways, the opposite of his comic persona. His general disposition was low-key and introspective, with no desire for public attention or to be the life of any party and not given to witty conversation or any expressions of personal vanity. He drove a Cadillac, not a Maxwell; he paid his writers and cast members some of the highest salaries in the business, was a heavy tipper, lavish giver of gifts, and a generous philanthropist who gave numerous benefit performances every year, revealing—contrary to all the jokes—that he was actually a very accomplished violinist.[10] The contrast between Benny's actual personality and the Jack Benny persona, of course, only added to the joke.

The Jack Benny Show also regularly featured guest stars. Most well-known Hollywood actors had avoided television in its early days; in fact, many had been forbidden by their studios to appear on the new medium. Benny, a beloved figure in Hollywood, lured many of these stars to test the television waters with guest appearances in a most congenial environment. His guest list included such established Hollywood deities as Humphrey Bogart, Barbara Stanwyck, Jimmy Stewart, Claudette Colbert, Gary Cooper, William Holden, Betty Grable, Kirk Douglas, and Gregory Peck, as well as up-and-coming stars of the era like Marilyn Monroe, Tony Curtis, Natalie Wood, and Rock Hudson. A large and impressive assortment of other comedians also appeared as guests. Over the years George Burns and Gracie Allen, Fred Allen, Milton Berle, Phil Silvers, Carol Burnett, Dick Van Dyke, Lucille Ball, Bob Hope, Groucho Marx, Jackie Gleason, Johnny Carson, George Gobel, Red Skelton, and the Smothers Brothers all visited the show. The show also provided some rare television appearances by personages such as the violinist Isaac Stern, the baseball manager Leo Durocher, the evangelist Billy Graham, and President

Harry Truman.[11] For some of his musical guests Benny changed the show's format; he would serve as the comic master of ceremonies for a variety show featuring sketches and musical performances by stars such as Ginger Rogers, Frankie Avalon, Robert Goulet, Andy Williams, Jack Jones, and others.

Benny's popularity and prestige can be clearly seen in the ratings and awards. *The Jack Benny Show* appeared in the top 20 in the Nielsen ratings almost every year of its fifteen-year run. Benny was honored with an Emmy Award for Best Continuing Performance in 1957 and for Best Actor in a Comedy Series for the 1958–1959 season, and the show was awarded an Emmy for Best Comedy Series in the 1958–1959 and 1960–1961 seasons. It won the Emmy for Best Writing of a Single Program of a Comedy Series in the 1959–1960 season. Meanwhile, the alternate series, *The Jack Benny Hour Specials*, received an Emmy for Outstanding Directorial Achievement in Comedy in the 1959–1960 awards. It seems that everybody, inside and outside of Hollywood, loved Jack Benny. While Berle and the other stars of television comedy variety saw their shows cancelled for one reason or another, Jack Benny is the only one whose show ended its run only because of the death of its star.

Red Skelton, another transfer from radio to television, achieved the longest uninterrupted run of a weekly prime-time comedy-variety show in television history. *The Red Skelton Show* premiered in September 1951 and aired its last episode in August 1971. During his two decades on television Skelton developed an extremely loyal following among his viewers; his show ranked among the top 20 in the Nielsen ratings sixteen times and among the top 10 shows of the season nine times. The show would have enjoyed an even longer run had it not been for the CBS network executives' decisions to reshape their programming to appeal to a younger, urban professional demographic.

Like so many others of his era, Skelton began his comedy career in vaudeville. His comedy was primarily visual, consisting "mainly of pantomimes, pratfalls, funny voices, crossed eyes, and numerous sight gags."[12] When he began his weekly show on the radio in 1941, he had to abandon the purely physical gags and concentrate on some of the characters he had been developing in his vaudeville act. Tim Brooks and Earle Marsh describe them succinctly:

> Among the best known were The Mean Widdle Kid, who left chaos wherever he went (his favorite expression: "I dood it!"); Clem Kadiddlehopper, the befuddled rustic; Sheriff Deadeye, the scourge of the West; boxer Cauliflower McPugg; Willie Lump-Lump, the drunk; San Fernando Red, the con man; and Bolivar Shagnasty.[13]

When Skelton moved to television he was able to add another character, Freddie the Freeloader, a hobo who never spoke and was a regular feature of the show, appearing in "The Silent Spot," a mime sketch performed with no words but usually with a soft musical accompaniment. With such a variety of characters who became so familiar to his viewers over the years, Skelton could move from broad slapstick to warm sentiment, endearing himself to his viewers as a comic willing to take a pie in the face or bring a tear to the eye.

He developed an affectionate relationship with his millions of faithful viewers. Skelton often laughed at his own jokes, further identifying himself with his viewers as someone who enjoyed his own jokes as much as he presumed they did. At the end of every show Skelton would address the viewers and thank them for allowing him into the privacy of their homes, and then he would close with his trademark line, "Good night and God bless."

Critical opinion of Red Skelton varies widely, from those admirers who compare him to Chaplin for his ability to evoke sympathy for his tramp-like characters, or to Buster Keaton for his remarkable physical pratfalls, or to Marcel Marceau for his skill at delicate pantomime. Other critics fault him for his unsophisticated baggy-pants humor, tendency to go for the quick laugh, reliance on his old shtick, blatant sentimentality, and that tendency to laugh at his own jokes, which many of them found annoying and unprofessional. He developed something of a sad clown persona similar to the famous Ringling Brothers circus clown of the era, Emmett Kelly. The image was fostered by the exhibit of Skelton's oil paintings in the mid-sixties, which consisted of his many pictures of clowns, most of them sad. It was also reinforced for anyone who knew much about his private life. Skelton's father died from the effects of alcohol two months before Red was born, leaving a wife and four sons in poverty. Skelton's early career in show business provided an unusually harsh apprenticeship: working with a traveling miracle-elixir salesman, entertaining the audiences at dance marathons, and providing the laughs in burlesque houses. His first marriage ended in divorce. His only son died of leukemia at the age of nine. Red's second wife, also alcoholic, committed suicide. And Skelton himself went through a long period of alcoholic binges that threatened his career, marriage, and life. If anyone was entitled to play the sad clown, it was Red Skelton.

When Skelton came to television he had already been one of the highest-paid performers in vaudeville, had appeared in dozens of Hollywood films, many of them very successful, and he was starring in one of the top-rated radio shows in the country. Many of his colleagues had moved from radio to television. Some of them—Bob Hope, Jack Benny, and Jackie Gleason—would find great success in the new medium. Others—Jimmy Durante, Fred Allen, and Eddie Cantor—would not do so well. Skelton, therefore, was very careful when he began his show on NBC.

One element crucial to the show's success, according to Skelton, was the importance of doing the show on film, not live. He felt that there were too many opportunities for mistakes and accidents in his kind of physical comedy that a theater audience could tolerate, but they would not fit the requirements and expectations for the neatly packaged entertainment that came into people's homes. The network, however, worried that filmed programs were generally not produced in front of a live audience and Skelton needed a live audience for his style of spontaneous comedy. The network won this battle, and the show went on as a live production. However, the producers did not seem to realize that the audience situation in the television studio was quite different from a vaudeville theater. The large cameras, lighting equipment, boom microphones, and other technical paraphernalia on the television stage blocked the audience from viewing Skelton's performance directly. They had to be content with watching the show on several monitors placed overhead.

A second element of the show's success came about as a matter of fortunate timing. The month that Skelton's first show went on the air, the coaxial cable had just gone into operation, greatly increasing the reach of the show beyond the urban population of the Northeast who had made Milton Berle such a hit. Skelton, the veteran of traveling elixir shows and small-town theater tours, knew how to appeal to viewers in the small towns and rural communities of the Midwest, South, and West. Even many of the suburban viewers seemed to find his friendly disposition and his bumptious brand of humor more to their liking than the New York–based comedy of Milton Berle and Sid Caesar.

The twenty-year run of the show was not achieved easily, however, with different attempts at live and filmed production, a change of network, and several personal difficulties hampering Skelton's performance. For more than half of its run *The Red Skelton Show* was a half-hour production, but in 1962 it was expanded to an hour, renamed *The Red Skelton Hour*, and experienced its peak in ratings popularity until it was cancelled in 1970. The format of the show consisted of Skelton's opening monologue, some musical presentations, and a few comedy sketches featuring his various characters. He did not work with a permanent ensemble, only a rotating list of some of the best supporting players in the business: Mel Blanc, Hans Conried, Verna Felton, and others. The only other regular cast member was his bandleader, and close friend, David Rose. Unlike the Hollywood insider Jack Benny, Red Skelton did not, as a rule, invite other major comedians or many other big-name performers on his show. He seems to have felt intimidated by the presence of any talent that could steal the spotlight.

Skelton captured viewers' hearts by making it obvious that he would go to any extreme to entertain them. Arthur Marx tells of one very successful bit done at the end of his monologue on his first show that became a recurring gag throughout the years:

While Red was standing in front of the curtain taking a bow and smugly acknowledging audience applause, two hands reached out from under the curtain, grabbed him by the ankles, and whisked him out of view under the curtain. This surprise conclusion to Red's monologue threw the audience into hysteria. . . . Flat out frontwards is perhaps the most dangerous way to take a fall, however, and though it never failed to get a huge laugh, Red later wound up having to go to the hospital to correct internal injuries sustained from being thrown forward and dragged under the curtain week after week.[14]

Another moment in his premiere show as described by Marx captures a second element essential to Skelton's appeal to the folks at home. As he had been doing for ten years on his radio show, just before signing off, Skelton spoke to the audience:

Ladies and gentleman, I want to thank you for putting up with my nonsense. I sincerely hope I haven't said or done anything to offend anyone. If I have, I didn't mean it. I hope you have had as much fun as I have had. It is a lot of fun to try to make people laugh. Regardless of what your heartaches might be, while laughing for a few seconds, you have forgotten about it. Thanks for coming, and good night.[15]

The show was an immediate success with critics and viewers. However, the bane of the comedy-variety format appeared once again—how to come up with new material every week. The problem was complicated in this case by Skelton's personal aversion to learning new material. He had difficulty memorizing the lines and found that relying on cue cards was difficult for the sort of farcical knockabout comedy that he did best. The emotional strain was too much for him. So NBC relented, and, as the second season began, Skelton was allowed to film the show. While this greatly lowered the stress level, it allowed for only the crew and a few invited friends to attend the filming, and, as NBC had predicted, Skelton lost the spontaneous interaction with a large, appreciative audience. His ratings dropped considerably, and soon the show went back to live production. The combination of the show's drop in popularity, stress of live production, and Skelton's problems with his marriage and drinking led to even more difficulties, and, at the end of the second season, NBC dropped the show from its schedule.

But CBS picked up the show, and the next season (1953–1954) found Skelton back on television. His ratings remained very low. CBS, however, had signed a three-year contract and was stuck with the show. As it turned out, three years was the magic number for Skelton, because in the third season, the show took off again, thanks to the comic insight of a new writer hired for the 1955–1956 season, Sherwood Schwarz, who would eventually make his mark in television history as the creator of *Gilligan's Island* and *The Brady Bunch*. In Schwarz's opinion the constant parade of Skelton's various characters on each show evoked very little emotional involvement from the viewers. If the viewers, however, could feel more connection with a particular character, it would take much less of a joke to amuse them. Hence, the format of the show was changed into more of a story involving only one of the characters. This had the added benefit of leaving the viewers wondering who would show up on a particular week as the main character. The strategy worked. The show's ratings started climbing up to the top, as viewers identified with the many lovable losers Skelton portrayed as well as the eager-to-please persona he presented at the end of the show. (It was when he moved to CBS, by the way, that Skelton had begun his characteristic practice of ending every program with "Good night and God bless.") Steve Allen remarked that the viewers "actually seemed to be rooting for Red as he came smiling onto their TV screens week after week."[16]

In 1962 the show was expanded to one hour and made into more of an extravaganza similar to Jackie Gleason's show. It continued to be a major ratings winner, and even the critics agreed that the hour-long format gave Skelton a more expansive environment for his type of visual slapstick. Skelton developed a large and loyal viewership in his show's final years, but he apparently could not command the same attention from his industry peers. In the 1951–1952 season, its first year on the air, the show had won an Emmy for Best Comedy Show and Skelton was honored with the Emmy for Best Comedian. Its only other Emmy came in 1961, for its writers. Over twenty years that was relatively little industry recognition.

Despite its high ratings (it was the #1 show in the 1966–1967 season), the show was cancelled in 1970 because of the programming philosophy of the new president of CBS, Robert Wood, who wanted the network to appeal to a younger, more urban, and more affluent audience. The hour-long show was also, like its variety-show predecessors in television's early days, proving to be an expensive proposition for the network. So Red Skelton was out, along with popular, but rural, comedies such as *The Beverly Hillbillies* and *Green Acres*, to be replaced by a new brand of comedy that Wood accurately predicted would appeal to a hip, young audience of the 1970s, *The Mary Tyler Moore Show*, *M*A*S*H*, *All in the Family*, and other megahits destined for the Comedy Hall of Fame.

Skelton attempted one more reincarnation. He went back to NBC, which developed another half-hour show for 1970–1971, but it only lasted one season. Skelton was understandably bitter about his show's removal at the height of its popularity, and at the end of a performance in Las Vegas in 1972, in the course of one of his traditional sentimental sign-offs to his audience, he let his feelings be known:

It was a warm and sentimental speech up to a point; then just when he was about ready to walk into the wings for possibly the last time of his career, he had an unexplained attack of paranoia. Suddenly turning bitter and maudlin, Red blamed his premature retirement on the shabby treatment accorded him by TV executives who had been unappreciative of his contribution to the industry. Red concluded with, "My heart has been broken" and walked off the stage, seemingly a beaten and broken man, a shadow of his former self.[17]

Late in his career Skelton was invited by President Richard Nixon to entertain at the White House for an audience that included the vice president, cabinet members, and members of Congress. In his introduction Nixon said of Skelton, "The American people like him because he has heart."[18] Nixon's observation was accurate and insightful. Of all the variety-show comedians, Red Skelton survived the longest on television not because he was a comic genius revered by his peers, as Sid Caesar or Jack Benny were, but because he had "heart" and presented the sort of amiable personality that viewers felt comfortable inviting into their homes.

A figure who seems to have been forgotten in histories of comedy-variety shows was a genuine superstar who, in his day, enjoyed a tremendous following on both radio and television, Arthur Godfrey. His disappearance from the usual surveys of television comedians is especially ironic, since, as his biographer Arthur J. Singer reminds his readers in the beginning of his biography, Godfrey was a major public personality in his day:

Arthur Godfrey was once the most recognized man in America. His voice was listened to by more people each day during the 1940s and 1950s than anybody in history up to that time. In his heyday, he was on the air for ninety minutes each weekday morning on the CBS Radio Network and for sixty minutes each weekday morning on the CBS Television Network. Each Monday evening, he hosted a top-rated series on radio and televison. And to top it off, each Wednesday evening he had a top-ten hour-long variety show.[19]

Another assessment of Godfrey's popularity comes to a similar conclusion:

Arthur Godfrey, despite common sense declarations that he had "no talent," must be counted as one of television's greatest stars. Prior to 1959 there was no bigger TV draw than this freckled-face, ukulele-playing host. There was something about Godfrey's wide grin, his infectious chuckle, his unruly shock of red hair that made millions tune in not just once, but again and again.[20]

Godfrey was one of the many radio stars who were lured to television. His morning radio show, *Arthur Godfrey Time,* had begun airing on the CBS network in 1945 and remained on the air until 1972. From 1951 to 1965 it was also simulcast on morning television. His prime-time presence was even more impressive when compared to the other comedians who hosted their own variety shows. From 1949 to 1958 Godfrey appeared on CBS's prime-time schedule twice a week. The comedy-variety show *Arthur Godfrey and His Friends* aired from 1949 to 1959 on Wednesday nights, while *Arthur Godfrey's Talent Scouts* appeared on Monday nights from 1948 to 1958. Both programs showed up regularly among the top-rated series almost every year of their run. In the 1951–1952 season, in fact, *Arthur Godfrey's Talent Scouts* was the #1 show, ahead of Milton Berle, Sid Caesar, Red Skelton, and Jack Benny, not to mention *I Love Lucy* (in its first season), while Godfrey's variety show enjoyed the #6 spot in the ratings. In the following season, as *I Love Lucy* rose to the #1 spot that it would enjoy almost continuously for the rest of its run, the two Godfrey shows were in the #2 and #3 spots in the Nielsen listings. These two weekly shows served as a cornerstone of the CBS-TV network's programming strategies during the 1950s.

CBS designed Godfrey's prime-time variety show along the same lines as his morning show. It was live and unscripted, with Godfrey as a casual host sitting at a desk, speaking informally to the television audience, interviewing guests, ridiculing his sponsors, and interacting with "The Little Godfreys," an ensemble of musical performers, mostly young and clean-cut, some of whom went on the successful recording careers on their own—the McGuire Sisters, Pat Boone, and (after Godfrey fired him on the air) Julius LaRosa. As an unscripted show, it was unpredictable. NBC attempted to compete by launching its own variety show during the same Wednesday night time slot. The program, *Four Star Revue*, featured a rotating roster of top-flight comedians—Ed Wynn, Danny Thomas, Jack Carson, and Jimmy Durante. But it lasted only three seasons. Major stars and lavish production values were no match for the spontaneity and likeability of Arthur Godfrey.

As Singer also points out, Godfrey is not easily categorized; he was primarily a host and a raconteur, not an entertainer in the mold of Berle, Caesar, Benny, or Skelton. But he could be called a humorist, and, along with his other accomplishments as a host, interviewer, and recording artist, Godfrey was generally jovial and mischievous. Steve Allen, who often served as a replacement for Godfrey, has recalled that he had often been told that he was funnier than Godfrey. Allen's reaction was:

> It is not difficult to be funnier than Godfrey, as he is not essentially a comedian. . . . People laugh at what Godfrey says because they like him, not chiefly because what he says is amusing. His material is often, as a matter of fact, lamentably weak, if not in poor taste, but it is an indication of the tremendous power of his personality that he triumphs over the material. . . . He has such a vital per-

sonal magnetism that it is difficult not to be pleased by any halfway acceptable idea he presents.[21]

While Fred Allen once called him "the Huckleberry Finn" of radio, Arthur Godfrey might better be compared with Will Rogers for his folksy humor, populist political views, overt patriotism, and way with a novelty song. (Godfrey's recording of "Too Fat Polka" sold over one million copies in 1947.) Like Rogers, Godfrey became famous primarily as a beloved personality who was welcomed into the homes of America and whose personal life was interwoven into his public persona. Steve Allen's analysis of Godfrey's appeal focused on his voice, which "just sounds so damn natural," with no provincial accent and a certain fatherly tone, conveying an image of the common man, a middle-of-the-road personality with mediocre singing ability, intelligence, or any other talent.

Godfrey's comic talents were best displayed in his delivery of the commercial messages on his program. In the economic boom of postwar America, with new goods and services flooding into the marketplace and into the homes of suburban America, Godfrey's unparalleled blend of entertainment and advertising was a network executive's dream come true. Both the comedy and commercial pitches were based on his self-presentation. Godfrey never advertised a product that he did not personally use or approve. He seldom stayed with the advertising copy he was given, preferring to speak spontaneously (although, as Steve Allen points out, Godfrey employed a sizeable staff of writers). He would talk for as long as he felt it necessary to convince his viewers of his message, frequently running over his allotted time for the commercial. The more he liked the product, the more he would kid the sponsors, shocking viewers and sponsors with his irreverence but making the product memorable. As Douglas Gomery describes the approach:

> Godfrey made it sound like he was confiding to you and to you alone, and early television viewers listened to Godfrey's rich, warm, resonant descriptions and went out and purchased what he endorsed. . . . Despite all his irreverent kidding, advertisers loved him. Here was no snake-oil salesman hawking an unnecessary item, merchandise not worth its price. Here was a friend recommending the product.[22]

Arthur Singer recounts several typical comic moments during what were supposed to be standard commercial pitches. One of Godfrey's major sponsors was Lipton Soup. He would regularly offer such commentary as the following:

> Lipton chicken noodle soup? . . . There's plenty of noodles in it. Chicken? I didn't see any, but maybe one walked around the pan or somethin'. Somehow

they got the flavor in there. . . . But I'll call it "Noodle with a chicken flavor" if I were you. 'Cause you're never gonna get very far on the chicken that's in there.[23]

Singer also describes Godfrey's irreverent treatment of Lipton Tea. As he actually brewed a pot of tea, he would offer this sort of commentary:

It's a very simple matter to make one if you have the tea bags and the hot water nearby. I think I'll try one. [pause] I always try to get the tag out of it if I can. . . . Doesn't add much to the taste. [pause] Notice the finger. When handling tea you must always keep one finger in the air. I don't know why. [pause] I pour the boiling water on it . . . and let it sit there and stew . . . and it's amazing what comes out of there! Amazing! You see how droopy I am now. [laughter] Just wait till I have a shot of that tea—That Lipton Tea.[24]

Another sponsor was Pepsi Cola. On one occasion Godfrey played the phonograph record with their familiar jingle, which mentioned that the consumer got "twice as much for a nickel." When the commercial finished, Godfrey said, "You know, everywhere I go, it's seven cents." Then he took the phonograph record and smashed it, and said, "I've been drinking Pepsi downstairs for the past week, and it costs *seven* cents. . . . It's a great *drink*, it's worth *more* than seven cents, but it *ain't* a nickel." [25]

Godfrey's comedy even got a bit crude and racy for its time. Singer tells of a commercial for Nabisco crackers that occurred on the first telecast of the morning show *Arthur Godfrey Time:*

Arthur goes into a plug for Nabisco. He takes a bowl of crackers and begins crunching them up with his fingers. "Listen to these crackers. . . . Hear how crispy they are! And to go with these dainty little crackers today, we have an eighty-pound turkey!" The sponsor, he explains, wanted to present the turkey to Arthur and the cast in advance of Thanksgiving Day. The crew places the turkey in front of Godfrey, who notices that they have garnished the bird with parsley. Godfrey grabs a bunch of the parsley, saying, "I know exactly what to do with it!" and he stuffs it into the backside of the turkey. The audience roars, while Godfrey comments, "I think you'll agree that's the proper place for par-sa-ley."[26]

Godfrey's ad-lib humor often lapsed into bad taste. Steve Allen reported that scarcely a week went by that CBS did not receive letters of complaints about Godfrey's vulgarities or off-color remarks. Local stations who broadcast Godfrey by delayed transcription would occasionally edit the offensive material before airing it. Godfrey was usually surprised to find that "a coarse reference to a bull's activities on his Maryland farm or a chance remark about a woman's girdle" had shocked some of his audience. But the barnyard humor would be offset by his "frequent and frank references to God and religion," including his regular close of each show with the remark that he would be back the following day "be the good Lord willin'."[27]

In the 1954–1955 season ABC finally launched a successful assault on Godfrey with *Disneyland*, the network's first hit series, which regularly defeated *Arthur Godfrey and His Friends* in its time slot, causing it to drop from 6th place to 22nd place in the Nielsen ratings that season. By 1956 the television landscape was changing considerably. There were now three major networks, most of the production was being done on the West Coast, and much less programming was being telecast live. Adult westerns and situation comedies, all filmed in Hollywood, would soon dominate the ratings; *Gunsmoke*, for example, premiered in the fall of 1955 and would go on to #1 in the Nielsen ratings for four seasons, from 1957 to 1961. Godfrey's type of television—live, unscripted, with Godfrey doing his own commercials, almost all of it coming from New York—was fading out of prime time. But CBS held on to Godfrey, changing the name of the variety show to *The Arthur Godfrey Show* and running the show for one more season, until June 1957. It was revived in a half-hour format for the 1958–1959 season and finally cancelled in April 1959.

An overview of the careers of these six major stars of early television comedy serves to exemplify three "modes" of television personality defined by David Marc:

> The television personality develops in one or more of three general modes: the representational, in which he dons the mask of a frankly fictional character; the presentational, in which, as "himself," he addresses the audience within the context of the theatrical space; and the documentary, in which his "real life"—his exploits, his opinions on matters of public concern, his Lifestyle—becomes the subject of other television programs or presentations in other media.[28]

For example, Marc analyzes Jackie Gleason's development of all three modes of his television personality, showing a certain consistency in the characters he portrayed, his master-of-ceremonies persona, and his real life:

> Gleason, of all the clown-auteurs of the fifties, put the least distance between himself and his "act.". . . Ostentatiously displaying his expensive tastes in booze, broads, and life itself, the Cincinnatus of the Brooklyn tenements wallowed in the admiration of the masses. . . . In both life and art he projected the persona of the Depression-bred blue-collar ethnic who demanded the right to live like a king. Like a Damon Runyon mobster, he held daily court at Toots Shor's Times Square restaurant for the New York press. His car? An immense Cadillac, complete with bar and chauffeur—a personal gift to The Great One from Frank Sinatra himself.[29]

Gleason was not the only star to exploit all three of Marc's "modes." When the six stars of television comedy-variety—Milton Berle, Sid Caesar, Jackie Gleason, Jack Benny, Red Skelton, and Arthur Godfrey—are studied under Marc's rubric, there is almost an exact corollary between the length of the comedian's television career and his willingness to go beyond mere representational performance to engage in a presentational approach to the viewers and, in several cases, to appear in the documentary mode of entertainment. Sid Caesar, perhaps the most critically admired comedian of the group, had the shortest tenure in prime time, with his two variety shows lasting a total of seven years and the second show never receiving blockbuster ratings. Caesar limited himself almost exclusively to the representational mode, performing in the sketches and monologues, seldom addressing the television audience as a master of ceremonies, and sharing nothing about his personal life with the viewers. The attempt of the shows' producers to evoke the tone of a Broadway presentation rather than vaudeville discouraged the use of Caesar as a host or as a television "personality." Milton Berle likewise shone in what Marc would call representational comedy in his outrageous costumes and slapstick comic performance, but Berle also engaged in presentational direct address to his audience as "Uncle Miltie," the congenial host who opened and closed every show and offered a gag-laden monologue each week. Berle developed a distinct personality as the put-upon, incompetent star of the show, and the irreverent attitudes of his ensemble and guests were often at his expense. His show, which enjoyed phenomenally high ratings in its early years, lasted for eight seasons. Jackie Gleason, by employing all three modes of presentation, as Marc demonstrates, managed to star as a prime-time comedy-variety host for thirteen seasons.

The pattern applies even more strongly to the entertainers who seemed more accessible in terms of their performance and personal lives. Jack Benny was particularly skilled at combining the presentational and representational modes of performance. Adapting a format that had proved so successful on the radio, *The Jack Benny Show* allowed the comedian to begin the show as the host with an opening monologue and conversations with his guest stars, à la Milton Berle, and then transition into something akin to a backstage situation comedy, in which Jack played himself along with the ensemble cast, most of whom also played themselves, with most of the comedy focusing on Jack Benny's famous comic flaws of vanity about his age, inability to play the violin, reluctance to part with any money, and his vocal and facial mannerisms. Benny's comedy was heavily weighted toward the presentational. With rare exceptions—notably his film roles in *Charley's Aunt* (1941) and *To Be or Not To Be* (1942)—Benny always played "Jack Benny." Meanwhile, it was generally agreed that this popular and instantly recognizable comic persona did not mirror Benny's real life.

His friendship with George Burns and others in the Hollywood community, philanthropic activity, happy marriage to Mary Livingston, and other details of Benny's personal life were well known. The much-beloved comedian's willingness to combine the three modes formed the basis for a fifteen-year run of his comedy-variety show on prime-time television (1950–1965) with frequent appearances in "specials" until his death in 1974.

At the same time, while Red Skelton's array of characters offered him the opportunity for a variety of representational performances in monologues, sketches, and pantomime, he developed his own method of grounding his comic performance in a presentational mode. Like most of the other variety-show comedians, Skelton served as a likeable, eager-to-please host of the show, ending every episode with a sincere "God bless." He also tended to break character in the midst of performance, breaking into laughter at his own routines, thus endearing himself to his fans as almost a member of his own audience and reminding them that behind the character he was portraying was Red Skelton, the loveable, sentimental clown under the makeup. This use of a presentational mode resulted in a steady television presence with two years on NBC, another eighteen season on CBS, and, after CBS's cancellation, a few months back on NBC, making *The Red Skelton Show* the longest-running prime-time comedy show in television history.

But the master of familiarity was Arthur Godfrey. In terms of representational comedy he never engaged in comic sketches, but he offered a certain type of comic performance in his singing and ukulele playing of many novelty songs. Godfrey was more entertaining when he moved into the presentational mode, speaking directly to his viewers as a jolly, mischievously comic host, inspiring a huge outpouring of affection and trust from his millions of viewers. However, Arthur Godfrey surpassed all of his fellow variety-show hosts, even the high-living Jackie Gleason, in the presentation of himself in the documentary mode, with his own revelations of his personal opinions and feelings as well as the attention paid to his personal life by the media. Godfrey shared, on a daily basis, detailed accounts of his personal life, both pleasant and unpleasant. His love of flying, his life on his farm in Virginia, the beauty of Miami Beach and Hawaii, firing of his staff, disagreements with his critics, medical crises, enthusiasm for American military prowess, and honest endorsement of every product he advertised—these were the raw material of his daily radio and television programs. When Godfrey underwent hip surgery in 1953 he shared every detail of the operation with his fans; it is estimated that he received forty thousand cards and letters a week during his months of recuperation. His first night back on live television on July 17 received an audience share of 91.4.[30] Later that year when Godfrey fired the popular young singer Julius LaRosa during a live broadcast, the incident made headlines for weeks.

Godfrey's temper often got him unwanted publicity, as it did when he had his pilot's license suspended by the Federal Aviation Administration in 1954 for defying the instructions of air traffic controllers.[31] The public's fascination with Arthur Godfrey demonstrated, as Singer observes, that "the growing medium of television—still somewhat of a novelty for most Americans—had shown, for the very first time, its ability to generate its own news and dominate the American mind, superseding for a time concerns about or interest in government, business, sports . . . or even daily life.[32]

The subsequent decades have offered even more evidence that American viewers prefer likeable personalities rather than oversized talents as hosts of any sort of comedy-variety show on television. Dean Martin's (1965–1974) laid-back "rat pack" personality did not include any gift at comic impersonation, rapid-fire one-liners, witty monologues, sketch comedy, or heavy-duty slapstick. With his legendary casualness in rehearsal and performance, Martin never claimed or attempted to be the next Milton Berle or Jack Benny. Sonny and Cher (1971–1977) exchanged insults and engaged in some sketch comedy, but no one even thought of comparing their performance with the brilliant teamwork of Sid Caesar and Imogene Coca. George Gobel's (1954–1960) semi-rural comic style gave new meaning to the term "low-key." In his monologues he constructed his Lonesome George persona of a henpecked husband who was also prone to intimidation and humiliation in his other personal relationships and who was also moderately talented at playing the most humble of musical instruments, the harmonica. Gobel's "punch lines," such as "I'll be a dirty bird," were so easily imitated that they became household expressions during his tenure on television. Whether they exuded a Las Vegas high lifestyle or a hippie flair or a rural eccentricity, these hosts capitalized on their presentation as everyone's amusing friend, not a television superstar like the early comedy-variety legends.

Even the two comedy-variety hosts who displayed a far wider ranger of talent, Flip Wilson (1970–1974) and Carol Burnett (1967–1979), attracted their large viewership by their strong and direct rapport with the viewers at home. Donald Bogle's description of the mood of Wilson's show emphasizes its more intimate approach:

> Producer Bob Henry . . . insisted that the show be shot in the round before a live studio audience, which created the perfect type of intimacy for Wilson's particular style. . . . Banished were the familiar chorus lines, production numbers, and windy introductions that were so much a part of variety shows at the time. Simplicity became crucial to Wilson's effects.[33]

Carol Burnett, even though her show benefited from high production values in general, rooted every show in her relationship with her studio audience.

Her poignant Chaplinesque charwoman character tugged at the viewer's heartstrings, and a caricature of the beloved figure would eventually be incorporated in the show's logo during the teasers and credits. Burnett's famous Tarzan call resembled the sort of amateur-night bit that a favorite relative might be called on to perform at family gatherings. Most effective was Burnett's weekly question-and-answer sessions, in which she would turn up the house lights and engage in spontaneous interaction with the audience in the theater seats. Even the carefully written and rehearsed sketches would be enhanced by the cast's ad-libs and breaking of character that would be retained in the taped versions of the show, demonstrating the camaraderie of the ensemble and letting the viewers in on the fun.[34]

The comedy-variety shows of television's early years promised to provide Middle America with opportunities to enjoy virtual front row seats at a Broadway show or a front table at a Las Vegas revue. But, as the years went by, the networks found that the viewers preferred to pass up those free tickets to the nightclubs and theaters and, instead, just stay at home and invite the more likeable comedians to drop in for a nice, neighborly visit.

·4·

. . . AS LONG AS WE BOTH
SHALL LAUGH

As television reached out across America, it soon became clear that the viewers preferred the milder format of situation comedy rather than the raucous revelry of the comedy-variety show. It also became clear that the favorite situation was the familiar region of the home. However, three of these early comedies, which are now considered classics, focused primarily on the relationship between the husband and the wife, with three distinct origins, approaches, and audience reception. These "marriage comedies" comprise a specific phase in television situation comedy that has never been revived. They might best be examined in chronological order.

The George Burns and Gracie Allen Show (1950–1958) starred the real-life husband-and wife comedy team playing themselves in a suburban home environment. *I Love Lucy* (1951–1957) featured another real-life husband and wife, Lucille Ball and Desi Arnaz, as a fictional couple, Lucy and Ricky Ricardo, living in a middle-class apartment in Manhattan (at least for the first few seasons of the show) with Arnaz's character closely resembling his real-life situation as a Cuban American bandleader. *The Honeymooners*, which appeared in the standard half-hour situation-comedy format for only the 1955–1956 season but reappeared regularly as part of Jackie Gleason's comedy-variety show from 1966 to 1970, portrayed the life of a bus driver and his wife living in a noticeably run-down apartment in Brooklyn. Each of the series offered a distinct presentation of married life.

The George Burns and Gracie Allen Show, which made its début on October 12, 1950, maintained a modest but healthy popularity with viewers, leaving the air eight years later only because Gracie wanted to retire from show business. It has long remained a favorite among television fans and historians because of its experimental approach to the possibilities of the medium. Like many other early television shows, it was a carry-over from their very popular and long-running radio program (1932–1950). In its early days the program was broadcast live from the CBS studios in New York City, but at the beginning of its third season, production moved to Hollywood, where the show was filmed for weekly showings. The show's basic structure was a visual translation of the domestic sitcom formula that had been developed so successfully on radio by Burns and Allen and many other similar series, such as *Fibber McGee and Molly* and *My Favorite Husband.* The husband and wife were a respectable, financially comfortable couple leading relatively leisurely lives without any children living at home. Their home was the sort of suburban dwelling well appointed with all the modern conveniences that viewers were being encouraged to purchase. The wife, Gracie, stayed at home but managed to involve herself in the standard comic plots of mistaken identity, schemes, surprises, and misunderstandings. The husband, George, wore a suit and tie around the house and never spent much time away at whatever work he did as a professional comedian. They lived next door to some slightly goofy neighbors, who felt free to drop in on George and Gracie without knocking or to engage in conversations with them through their own kitchen windows, on the front porch, or across the fence, in a world of suburban contentment.

The framework for this typical domestic sitcom, however, was quite sophisticated, with what David Grote has described as "a complex series of overlapping layers within each episode, which has rarely been matched even in the most complex feature films or avant-garde novels."[1] At the beginning of every episode the show's title was written across a stage curtain that was framed by a proscenium arch reminiscent of Burns and Allen's vaudeville days. The curtain would then rise to reveal the show's domestic set. Grote describes a typical episode:

> Gracie needed some money, as wives in fifties comedies often did, and George did not particularly want to give it to her. As the show began, they both appeared on their front porch and did a routine directly to the camera audience. Then they went into the living room and began a "normal" sit-com scene. Next, we cut to George sitting upstairs in his office watching Gracie's plot on his own TV, which he turns off to turn to tell us his plan to thwart her. Then we cut to Gracie, who is now watching George on her TV, and she explains her plan to us. When everything is solved, the curtain falls and George and Gracie appear to do their final routine in front of the curtain for the studio audience. Thus, at one point we have a film audience watching a "live" audience watch a real man and wife on a stage playing an imaginary man and wife at home, where he watched her watch him on their television sets. And even more important, all these layers had to be understood by the home viewing audience before the plot of the episode could make any sense.[2]

Other semi-absurdist, self-reflexive elements were included in the show. The program's announcer, Harry Von Zell, would show up as a neighbor in the situation-comedy plot. Sometimes his appearance in their home or on their front porch would segue into a commercial for the program's sponsors. George and Gracie would often be shown in the commercial actually using the product, such as Carnation Milk, in their kitchen. George's monologues, addressed directly to the television viewers, would often make self-referential comments. "Here's a good one: Gracie and I have a fight. It's amazing that we could come up with such innovative ideas with only five full-time writers."[3] In another episode George solves a problem by calling Gracie on his telephone from his den and the viewers see Gracie on George's TV screen. After he hangs up the telephone, George turns to the camera audience again:

"I'm glad that's over with," announces George, "but now there's no story and we've still got some time left on the show. Maybe there's something else on." He turns the channel to a cowboys-and-Indian movie; the cavalry is chasing thousands of screaming warriors on horseback. We watch this with George for about five or so seconds. Cut to commercial. The episode ends with Gracie stepping across the proscenium and joining George in a reprise of a Burns and Allen vaudeville routine.[4]

At the heart of the situation-comedy plots, however, was the persona of Gracie Allen. From their earliest days in vaudeville, the team of Burns and Allen had developed their comic routines around the naïveté and contorted logic of Gracie's view of life. Her reactions to every situation were consistent with her character: well-meaning but ill-informed, eager to please George and everyone else, gullible and sympathetic in any encounter. For instance, in one episode Gracie has written a story for *Look* magazine about her life with George. To make the story more appealing she had invented an elaborate anecdote about George's beating up a famous gangster, Fuzzy Thompson (a guest appearance by the great television character actor and producer Sheldon Leonard). The gangster comes to the home to wreak revenge on George. Gracie welcomes him into her kitchen, treats him like a naughty child when she discovers his gun, and so confuses the mobster with her peculiar logic and innocent responses that he forgets about revenge in his eagerness to escape her insanity. The befuddled mob boss comments at one point, "Whaddya know! I come here to blow somebody's brains out, and I find out that somebody already did it!"

Each episode usually included a conversation between George and Gracie, one of the main carryovers from their vaudeville stand-up routines, which would usually include the typical Gracie non sequiturs, confusion of names and other information, and misuse of pronouns in the style of Abbott and Costello's "who's on first?" routine. The combination of Gracie's confusion and George's patient endurance in these dialogues created a reassuring portrayal of marital fidelity for better or for worse, in confusion and in resignation. In the security of the American home and suburban neighborhood, Gracie's innocent madness could be objectified and interpreted by the mordant wit of her understanding husband.

The success of this program is also a tribute to the ingenuity of its creators, who managed to transfer the performance of one of the greatest stand-up comedy acts of the vaudeville era to the new environment of the television screen by distilling George and Gracie's conversations and George Burns's monologues to segments of two or three minutes within the familiar sitcom format. They also confined the potentially anarchic behavior of Gracie Allen, whose absurdity matched the zaniness of the Marx Brothers, especially Harpo, whose childlike innocence she also mirrored, within the characterization of the goofy housewife that Lucille Ball would soon shape to comic perfection.

Another message was being communicated to George and Gracie's loyal followers. A mature couple such as George and Gracie, who had been vaudeville stars since the early 1920s and familiar voices on the living room radio for almost twenty years since the 1930s, now became a visual presence in the home, appearing as the very model of the perfectly stylish, if slightly older couple (she was at least in her mid-forties; he was in his mid-fifties) fitting right into suburban life in the 1950s. Their home was tastefully decorated in middle-class style; they made use of all the modern home appliances and automobiles. George wore well-tailored suits and ties and smoked the best cigars; Gracie's clothes were as fashionable as anything soon to be worn by Lucille Ball, Donna Reed, Harriet Nelson, or even the career girls such as Ann Sothern in *Private Secretary*. Vaudeville may have died, and radio may have been fading away, but these two beloved comedians of those eras fit right into the new televised world of post–World War II America.

The second sitcom to gain significant popularity went on to become a phenomenon. *I Love Lucy* premiered in October 1951, finished its first season as #3 in the ratings, and then reigned as the most popular show every year for almost its entire run. In the 1955–1956 season *I Love Lucy* was pushed down to #2 by the temporary sensation of the quiz show *The $64,000 Question*, helping to make CBS the #1 television network. On April 7, 1952, thanks to the completion of the coaxial cable, *I Love Lucy* was the first television show ever to reach ten million households all at once.[5] While still at the top of the ratings, *I Love Lucy* ended its run in June 1957, but that did not stop CBS from continuing to air the comedy. As early as April, 1955, CBS had already begun offering reruns on other nights of the week even while *I Love Lucy* was airing in its first-run phase. For example, in the 1955–1956 season the first-run episode would run in its usual 9:00 Monday night time slot while a rerun was aired on Saturday night at 6:30 p.m. When the original run of the show ended in 1957, CBS continued to program reruns of the show in its prime-time schedule until 1959.

This gold mine of programming was made possible because of the creative instincts, business savvy, and persistence of Lucille Ball. While some television historians tend to describe Ball's film career as relatively unsuccessful, it should be acknowledged that from her arrival at MGM in 1933 until her venture into television in 1951, Lucille Ball appeared in more than fifty-five films with virtually all the major musical-comedy stars at MGM, with some excellent performances in *Stage Door* (1937), *Big Street* (1942), *Best Foot Forward* (1943), and starring roles in *DuBarry Was a Lady* (1943), *Miss Grant Takes Richmond* (1949), and *Fancy Pants* (1950). In other words, by 1951 Lucille Ball was a wealthy, well-respected Hollywood actress who knew everybody in the business and had no reason to think that her career in films would not continue apace. But in 1947 Ball took the route of several other successful Hollywood stars, like Bing Crosby, Bob Hope, Ronald Colman, and others, and starred in a highly successful radio comedy called *My Favorite Husband,* in which she created her persona of a wacky housewife. When Lucy agreed to move the program from radio to television, she changed the direction of television comedy production forever.

As Gerard Jones recounts the story, the birth of *I Love Lucy* is replete with the irony of hindsight. This television classic almost did not happen. Lucille Ball knew what she wanted and had to fight the experts for every feature that eventually made the program into the television phenomenon it became. At first, everything seemed simple enough. CBS wanted her to move her radio show to television as other hit shows had done or would do with varying success. But Ball had one major insight: television was not radio. Nor was it the motion pictures. Most Hollywood studio executives saw television only as the threat to the film industry that it appeared to be, as Americans began to stay away from the movie theaters and gather around their television sets. Many Hollywood studios actually forbade their major stars from appearing on television. Many of the more glamorous stars were more than happy to keep their images away from the harsh studio lights and the grainy transmission of television. Unlike her colleagues, however, Ball was fascinated with the new medium, and, fortunately, she was not a big enough star for MGM to forbid her venture into television.

However, when Ball agreed to work on a television comedy series, she insisted that her co-star should be her real-life husband, a moderately well-known Cuban American bandleader, Desi Arnaz. Network executives balked at the idea of the Latino husband. To convince them, Ball and Arnaz spent a summer traveling to various movie palaces presenting a stage version of their comedy, about a Latin bandleader and his movie-star wife. When the network was unimpressed even by this successful tour, Mr. and Mrs. Arnaz, who had already created their own production company, Desilu Productions, invented a new relationship among television producers, sponsors, and network executives. At the time the common practice in radio and television production was that the advertising agency for a company—Texaco or Philip Morris, for example—would act as the producers and creators of a show, financing the production and reaping the benefits in increased sales and public recognition. Instead, Desilu Productions put up the money for *I Love Lucy*, and, instead of getting big salaries, Lucy and Desi gained complete control of the product. They tweaked their stage-show concept a bit into the story of Ricky and Lucy Ricardo, a middle-class entertainer and his stay-at-home housewife, living in a New York City apartment.

Then Lucy dropped the big bomb. She said that she wanted to produce the program from Hollywood instead of New York City, where, at the time, all television programming was being produced and broadcast live. She had two personal reasons for this decision. First, Lucy was pregnant and, fearful of a repeat of the miscarriage she had endured once before, she wanted to be near her doctors. Second, Lucy felt that working together every day and coming home to their family dwelling in Beverly Hills every night would help to rein in her attractive husband, whose life as a bandleader on the road had led to womanizing and other misbehavior. The stunned executives responded that there were no facilities for producing live television in Hollywood. Ball's response was simple and revolutionary: film the program in a Hollywood studio and send it to New York for airing from their studios. The filming of *I Love Lucy* started a trend.

The filming of the program was done with three cameras simultaneously, supervised by the Academy Award–winning cinematographer Karl Freund. The technique allowed for the rapid use of reaction shots, close-ups, and the middle and wide shots so crucial for the slapstick comedy of Lucy and Ethel in the chocolate factory, Lucy in the Italian winepress, and other legendary scenarios.

Lucy and Desi also insisted on filming in front of a live audience. Despite their success, this particular practice would not be adopted by their many imitators. It would not be done again until the early 1970s, when a new wave of situation comedies such as *All in the Family* would begin each episode with a voice-over announcing that the show "was filmed in front of a live studio audience."

The unexpected result was that once the shows were finished and "in the can" and the show proved so phenomenally successful, the network executives, as well as Desilu themselves, realized what they had. The episodes could be safely finished and shown to network executives and sponsors well before deadline. These programs could be shown repeatedly and sold into syndication forever. Within two or three years almost all television comedy production moved to Hollywood and began to be filmed for original runs and repeats on networks and syndication to local affiliates.

The phenomenal popularity of *I Love Lucy* during its original run can be seen as a matter of perfect timing, both artistically and sociologically. Jones describes several features of the show's comic brilliance as a synthesis of television comedy up to that time:

> In terms of the number and force of its gags it was the first sitcom to rival the comedy-variety shows. Ball's timing and shticks were always at least equal to Berle's and Skelton's. Yet this comedy was presented within a sitcom structure, with constant and likable characters, which the variety shows lacked. In some respects *I Love Lucy* was a complete synthesis of TV comedy up to that time: It had the music and burlesque of Berle, the plot strength and slickness of *Amos 'n' Andy*, the behind-the-scenes charm of *Burns and Allen*, the naturalism of *The Goldbergs*. Even technically it was a synthesis, blending the rapidity and intensity of live TV with the editing and sleekness and shifts of angle associated with Hollywood movies. *Lucy* seemed to have achieved what all prior programs had only been groping toward.[6]

However, as Jones and others have pointed out, *I Love Lucy* can also be examined as a barometer of gender relations in the early 1950s. As Jones has analyzed it:

> *I Love Lucy* came along at the moment when Americans were finally putting the depression and the war behind them and trying to shift back into "normalcy," which for women meant domesticity . . . and the housewife was again a feminine ideal. . . . The big catch, of course, which every woman knew but few had the nerve to say, was that housewifery got boring.[7]

In such a problematic situation for many women, the Lucy Ricardo character arrived in American living rooms as "the embodiment of female energy with no valid outlet":

> She is the mid-century American woman with no job, no power, no reinforcement for her aspirations, no kids, not even much housework (this being the age of the laborsaving device), yet with a mind and spirit excited by the possibilities of the twentieth century. She is a comic demon called forth from the boredom and frustration of an entire generation of housewives. She is what happens when a woman is allowed to go to college, tantalized by career possibilities, asked to give her all to war-work, and then told to retreat to the kitchen because that's what good girls are supposed to do.[8]

Jones argues that the show "simultaneously legitimized yearnings of women for fuller lives and assured them that they would be better off keeping their dreams in their heads."[9] He quotes Lucille Ball's description of the marital situation in the show as one in which "the man would be the master of the house. She would be a scatterbrain, but wily enough to get her own way in a comedic sort of fashion.[10] The usual comic plot revolved around Lucy's schemes to get into show business, get a job outside the home, meet someone famous, or make some extra money to supplement her household allowance. Another recurrent source of comedy was Lucy's wifely jealousy, shown in her constant suspicions about the attractive showgirls Ricky encountered at his club (an ironic reflection of a genuine source of tension in the actual Arnaz household). A third motif was Lucy's frequent complaints that Ricky did not appreciate her enough, did not find her attractive enough, or took her care of the household for granted. All of these situations, as Jones points out, would be resolved by the end of the half-hour episode, usually by Lucy's learning a lesson and by Ricky's expressions of appreciation and affection for his zany wife.

Jones is also correct in observing how these issues reflected the situation of the American housewife in mid-twentieth-century America. As Betty Friedan would point out soon enough, the middle-class suburban housewife, with a high school and in more and more cases a college education, who may have learned even more from her recent experience in the wartime labor force outside the home, may well have felt trapped in her role of wife and mother. The flood of laborsaving devices were providing women with a degree of leisure time their foremothers had not enjoyed. Betty Friedan's exposé of "the problem that had no name" would articulate the discontent of many women with their restricted roles in an American society that was bursting with opportunities for their male counterparts. *I Love Lucy* can be profitably studied as a comic commentary on the situation of the American housewife in the early 1950s. Lucy Ricardo's situation was a comic version of the "strange stirring, a sense of dissatisfaction, a yearning that women suffered in the middle of the twentieth century in the United States" that Friedan would explore in her landmark report.[11] Lucille Ball's professional achievements, as well as that of so many women in television comedy after her, also provide their own sort of answer to Friedan's closing question, "Who knows what women can be when they are finally free to become themselves?"[12]

The squelching of Lucy Ricardo's desires for adventure and fulfillment suggest a larger pattern, a new formula for comedy, which, according to Grote, separates the television sitcom from the entire tradition of comic theater in Western culture. To understand this development one needs to see some ways in which *I Love Lucy* both imitates and departs from classical comedy.

On first glance one may find that both the situation and the character of Lucy Ricardo bear a resemblance to classical comic heroes. Lucy-as-schemer is rooted in some of the earliest Roman comedies of Plautus featuring scheming slaves and the wily servants of Molière and Restoration comedy. (Larry Gelbart did all students of comic history a big favor when he offered a legitimate modern version of Roman comedy in his 1962 farce *A Funny Thing Happened on the Way to the Forum*, with the larger-than life Zero Mostel as the wily slave Pseudolus.) It is sociologically telling that the plots traditionally concocted by slaves and servants in times past were so believable when enacted by a modern housewife such as Lucy Ricardo and her accomplice, a similarly entrapped Ethel Mertz. Wifely jealousy was also a pattern in these classical comedies, but in those cases the wives were usually domineering, and their worries about their husband's activities stemmed from their general desire for control of their household, with the husband usually portrayed as the innocent victim, too terrified of his wife to engage in any extramarital dalliance. Lucy's fears, however, stemmed from her genuine feeling of helplessness and isolation, as she remained in their apartment while Ricky went out every day (and many nights) to his work in the glamorous and highly sexualized environment of nightclubs. The comic conflict in classical theater was usually resolved in favor of more freedom for the servant, more trust between the spouses, and various other compromises in the new order established at the end of the play. Not so for Lucy, however.

The fundamental difference between Lucy and her predecessors is illustrated perfectly by her lack of progress toward any real change in her wifely situation. Northrop Frye describes comedy as the "mythos of spring," a "movement from one kind of social order to another," from the old, old, life-stifling regime to a new arrangement "which causes a new society to crystallize around the hero . . . frequently signalized by some kind of party or festive ritual."[13] The young lovers in *A Midsummer Night's Dream* who refuse to marry according to the Duke of Athen's wishes; the daughter in Molière's *The Miser* who rebels against her father's choice of an elderly but wealthy man for her husband; and so many other young lovers in classic comedy are granted their true desires by the end of the play, which celebrates their young and passionate love in the new order in the archetypal victory of spring over winter.

However, according to Grote, for the first time in the history of comedy, in television situation comedies, there is no new order at the end of the episode. In fact, nothing really changes:

> Individual episodes may begin with a threat to the equilibrium of the situation, but by the end of the episode equilibrium is restored. . . . The basic plot of the

television situation comedy is a circle rather than a line. In the traditional comic plot, some characters, usually a boy and a girl, start at point A and want to get somewhere else, usually in bed together, at point B. No matter how many twists and turns, no matter what the confusions, at the end of the play the characters have moved from A to B. In the usual situation comedy, however . . . the principal characters meet situations and deal with them and then go on, except that they never go on to anything.[14]

Grote even uses *I Love Lucy* to illustrate the pattern:

In several different episodes, Ricky plans something special or unusual in his nightclub act. Lucy, as always, wants to break into show business and tries to horn in, over Ricky's opposition. Somehow, she sneaks into the act, wrecks it, and makes a fool of herself. However, Ricky forgives her, and everyone is restored to happiness at the fadeout. . . . Everything goes back as it was at the beginning of the episode. Lucy never learns to stay out of the nightclub shows, and Ricky never relents and makes her a part of them. In a few weeks, she will do the same thing again, with exactly the same results.[15]

The reason why viewers—including her fellow housewives—tuned in to watch Lucy Ricardo rebel against her domestic confinement and enter into adventures was not a desire to see Lucy win these battles. They wanted to see how the life force, her female energy, drives her to hilarious extremes. Over fifty years of television, viewers have continued to enjoy Lucy's frantic confusion as she stuffs chocolates in her mouth while the candy conveyor belt at which she is working speeds up; her helplessness as she is pinned against the kitchen wall by a hugely oversized loaf of bread that protrudes from her oven; her desperation as she slowly gets coated in ice in the walk-in freezer in which she has locked herself. They have delighted in seeing her embarrass herself by becoming intoxicated with the alcohol-laden Vitameatavegamin, by her inappropriate behavior in the presence of Hollywood heartthrobs such as William Holden and John Wayne, by her failed attempts to disguise herself to spy on Ricky whom she suspects of cheating on her. They welcome her frequent appearances in various outlandish costumes, from the country bumpkin with the missing teeth to the cigarette holder–wielding Manhattan sophisticate. Viewers also seemed to be rooting for Lucy as she tested the boundaries of wifely behavior. Steven D. Stark suggests:

I Love Lucy was both of and ahead of its time; one only has to look at the satisfied, conformist mothers on *Father Knows Best* and *Leave It to Beaver* a few years later to see that Lucy—by contrast—was in unending revolt against the conventions of her age. Moreover, by defying her "place," she symbolically rebelled against all middle-class norms. Though these crises were portrayed humorously, they were often not laughable subjects. . . . It is one of the best-known secrets of television that it always presents its most radical ideas in the form of comedy, the better to beguile the masses while preaching to them.[16]

In all of this Lucy exhibits the life force that lies at the heart of the Bergsonian comic hero and, true to the comic formula, always survives even the riskiest of adventures. Yet, in Grote's analysis, she survives only to return to her original situation: "At the end of the episode, the original order is restored, as if the middle never existed at all, almost as if all occurrences were a dream."[17]

But what a great dream!

One distinctive, and perhaps disturbing, feature of the *I Love Lucy* dream, however, was the unusual amount of argument and quarrelling between the married couple, with its comic roots in the *commédia dell'arte* and the Punch and Judy tradition. Jones finds the intensity of their battles quite unusual for domestic comedy and comments on "the vitality and intensity of the conflict" between Ricky and Lucy:

Ricky is no bland, smugly knowing sitcom husband but a mercurial mass of cockiness, anger, self-delight, and stubborn authority, all made grotesquely funny by Arnaz's accent and awkward delivery. . . . And Lucy is a force unto herself, a housewife who has put herself under her husband's command because she assumes that's the thing to do but who rebels against him constantly with every erg of her misdirected energy and every leap of her distorted imagination.[18]

This pattern of domestic argument would soon disappear from television comedy, giving way to what Jones has called the "corporate" resolutions—the pattern of discussion, surrender of disruptive urges, consensus for everyone's good—of the *Father Knows Best* mold of family comedies that would come later in the decade. But, especially in the years before the birth of Little Ricky and the general mellowing of the show's tone, life in the Ricardo household was frequently a domestic battleground that reflected the "nervous, feisty energy of Americans at the beginning of the '50s."[19] Only one other comedy of the era would engage in similar domestic battles, and the attempt would not prove quite so successful.

The Honeymooners, starring Jackie Gleason, lasted only one full season in the half-hour format of the typical situation comedy. It had appeared as a popular segment of the comedy-variety program, *The Jackie Gleason Show*, beginning in 1952. In 1955 Gleason temporarily abandoned the variety-show format and produced thirty-nine half-hour segments of *The Honeymooners*. The result in terms of viewership must have been disappointing. While the variety show had been #8 in the ratings in the 1953–1954 season and #2 in the ratings (right behind *I Love Lucy*) in 1954–1955, *The Honeymooners* managed only to make it to #19. It may have been a fatal mistake for Gleason overall. When he returned to the variety-show format the following season, using several different approaches for the next fifteen years, Gleason's programs experienced a bumpy ride in the ratings, appearing only a few times among the top 20 shows of any season.

Gerard Jones has described *The Honeymooners* as "one jubilant, defiant explosion of noise and pain and marital rage"[20] The show was simply a development of one of Gleason's many skits; in this case he played Ralph Kramden, an overweight and irascible bus driver living in a dingy Brooklyn apartment with his feisty wife, Alice. His best buddy was his upstairs neighbor Ed Norton, a sewer worker who was married to a former striptease dancer named Trixie. As Jones points out, the development of the *The Honeymooners*, in its original form as a five-minute comedy sketch, dared to explore some darker aspects of American life:

> A couple of years earlier Gleason had played a similar figure on the first TV incarnation of *The Life of Riley* but was constrained by the tameness and sentimentality of sitcoms. Now, controlling his own material for his own variety show, he could rip off the gauzy veneer and let all the venom of a frustrated blue-collar Brooklyn marriage pour out. . . . Ralph evolved into a classic American type, a perennial loser who persisted insanely in seeing himself as a man of the world, a master of his destiny, an opportunist eternally on the brink of making it big. . . . Toss in Alice, the homemaker who seemed utterly helpless against the perpetual degradation of her shabby apartment, and we may have the bleakest picture ever of working-class life in American entertainment.[21]

The action of the show was usually confined to a single set, the kitchen of their small apartment. Virginia Wright Wexman's analysis of *The Honeymooners* sees the combination of Ralph's physical bulk and the limited apartment space as symbolic:

> Ralph's very name suggests a person who must be "crammed in" to his surroundings. The Kramden apartment . . . is conspicuously cramped, and Ralph, especially when he is angry (which is much of the time) can hardly be contained by it. As he stalks around the kitchen, his gestures constantly threaten the space of others in the room as he throws his arms wide, jabs his finger in the air, or thrusts his head aggressively forward. On one occasion, when Ralph belligerently tells his wife that "There isn't enough room in here for both of us," she pointedly replies, "There isn't enough room in here for you and *anybody*."[22]

The visual presentation of the show matched the comic situation in its sparseness. The single camera barely moved, making very limited use of the type of close-ups or reaction shots that *I Love Lucy* constantly employed. The Kramdens' kitchen was minimally furnished with an old table and well-used chairs, a stove, a sink, and a non-electric icebox. They owned none of the modern labor-saving devices that Burns and Allen enjoyed. While Alice, played by the attractive Audrey Meadows, was always neatly, if modestly, dressed and groomed, Ralph was usually close to bursting out of his bus driver's uniform. Wexman, in fact, describes Ralph's appearance as "grotesque," especially when contrasted with Gleason's self-presentation as the tuxedo-clad host enjoying the attention of the chorus girls on his variety show:

> As the star moves from the role of gracious host to that of harried bus driver, his body image changes from classical to grotesque. In particular, the smooth, finished appearance of Gleason the host is transformed in his portrayal of Ralph Kramden into ungainly clownishness. Though in his role as host Gleason's sizable stomach is concealed by well-cut clothing, his corpulence is exaggerated by Ralph's bus driver's uniform, and it repeatedly makes Ralph the butt of the other characters' "fat" jokes. As host, Gleason's utterances are mellow and measured, but as Ralph his laugh often ends in loud, uncontrolled coughing. Ralph's eyes habitually bug out. He is frequently characterized as having "a big mouth," a description which contains literal as well as figurative truth, in view of the fact that his mouth is often agape as he roars in rage and pain.[23]

The plot of each episode, as described by Jones, resembles those of *I Love Lucy*, with gender changes:

> Ralph has a scheme: become a prizefighter; marry off Alice's meddling aunt to the local butcher; form a songwriting team with Norton; hypnotize Alice so he can go to a convention of the Raccoon Lodge. The scheme backfires horribly; Alice gives Ralph his comeuppance; he rages at her, his volume and ferocity increasing as his own idiocy becomes more painfully apparent. Finally he accepts his own humiliation and feels grateful that, for some reason, Alice goes on loving him. "Baby," he says, "you're the greatest!" The honeymoon continues.[24]

And, of course, nothing changes.

The Honeymooners in its classic half-hour format appeared as a regularly scheduled situation comedy for only one season (1955–1956). The Kramdens reappeared, however, during the last four years (1966–1970) of Gleason's resurrected variety show. Over half the telecasts of those seasons consisted of full-hour "The Honeymooners" episodes. Sometimes the episodes would take the form of musical comedies with songs and production numbers, set in different locations around New York City or around the world, with or without guest stars, but always featuring the Kramdens and the Nortons.[25] Gleason and his writers, well aware that this pair of comic couples had won the hearts of their viewers, wisely kept experimenting with various modes for presenting them other than the typical domestic situation-comedy format, which had failed to find a large audience.

At a time when viewers were delighted to see the Ricardos arguing with each other and were accustomed to watching Lucy's schemes come to naught, why were they not similarly enthusiastic about this similar version of married life? Did they find the setting of the Kramdens' economic situation too dreary in comparison to the Ricardos' pleasantly furnished, full-appliance apartment on Manhattan's Upper East Side? Grote sees *The Honeymooners* as a violation of the rules for situation comedies and the commercials surrounding them:

> It there is a single characteristic that unifies almost all of the sit-com heroes, it is prosperity. Many have been comfortably middle-class, often living in modern suburban homes . . . There is a process used in the making of commercials that seems to be reflected in the placement of comedy series. A standard pattern in the commercial is to determine the social status of the potential customer, then to illustrate the use of the product in the home of someone just a step or so higher on the socioeconomic ladder. . . . In the same way, the homes of sit-com characters seem to be always just a bit better than they could afford in the real world, given the salaries and backgrounds they are supposed to have. Jim Anderson of *Father Knows Best*, an insurance salesman, lives in almost exactly the same home as Doctor Stone of *The Donna Reed Show*.[26]

It was made perfectly clear to the viewers, however, that the Kramdens were a couple "who were just scraping by and who would be in bad trouble if Ralph ever missed a paycheck, a feeling you never get from even the poorest sit-com principals since then."[27] According to Jones, Audrey Meadows reported that "every season hundreds of viewers mailed her pretty aprons and hairbrushes and curtain rods so that she and her environs wouldn't have to look so damned dowdy." He suggests that the Kramdens served to remind post-Depression Americans of some of their deeper fears:

> America was on its way to becoming a land of universal prosperity after all, and soon everyone who wanted to be—or deserved to be—would be a member of the contented middle class. . . . [But the Kramdens] reminded people that even the new America had its losers, that maybe everyone was more a loser than anyone wanted to admit, that maybe the ultimate happiness of our secular, suburban paradise was just as unattainable as Ralph Kramden's dreams of wealth.[28]

This puncturing of the American Dream balloon seems to have been unsatisfactory for both the viewers and sponsors.

Perhaps the Kramden household was a bit too angry for viewers. In an age of "togetherness," husbands and wives were being encouraged to treat each other with more respect and settle differences with compromise. Even *I Love Lucy* eventually adopted a more modern approach to marital conflicts. In the first couple of seasons Ricky often threatened Lucy with physical punishment, and, in fact, in some episodes he actually took her over his knee and spanked her. But as Jones has pointed out, after the birth of Little Ricky in January 1953, the husband-and-wife relationship mellowed significantly:

> Ricky became much more solicitous of his wife now that she was the mother of his baby. He gave in to more of her whims and seemed far less eager to "teach" her a lesson." For her part, Lucy became less rebellious, her schemes less frequent and bizarre.[29]

Ralph Kramden, however, kept bellowing and fuming. In almost every episode he would threaten to strike Alice, uttering his classic expressions, "One of these days, Alice, *one of these days* . . . POW! Right in the kisser!" or, shaking his fist in her face, "To the moon, Alice, to the moon!" To his credit, Ralph was never seen carrying through on such threats, but he left little doubt that he was capable of such behavior. His temper was a regular feature of every episode.

It is significant in this context that *The Honeymooners'* relatively poor showing in the ratings was partially due to its competition on NBC, a variety show hosted by the extremely mild-mannered pop singer Perry Como, whose relaxed, intimate but unthreatening presence contrasted sharply with the ferocious Ralph Kramden. Como's musical-variety show lasted for fifteen consecutive years on television from 1948 to 1963, varying its format from a fifteen-minute show airing three nights a week on CBS to a full-scale hour-long show during its last eight years on the NBC network. His family-friendly music hour, featuring Como's many hit recordings as well as the frequent presentation of religious songs to close the show, just barely beat out *The Honeymooners* in the 1955–1956 season in Como's first year as host of an hour-long program, and it continued to do well enough in the ratings—sometimes quite well—to run for another seven years. Given the choice between an oversized, bellowing loser and a maturely handsome, laid-back crooner, viewers made their preference clear.

Viewers may also have been uncomfortable with the pattern of Alice's reaction to Ralph and her frequent use of sarcastic put-downs about his weight, stupidity, and powerlessness. She was able to halt his tirades by simply saying, "Now you listen to me, Ralph," and then proceed to belittle him or trim his outsized attitudes and schemes. This sort of marital discord may have been a bit too close to the deeper realities of married life for 1950s viewers. As Wex-man has pointed out:

> The show's depiction of such gender conflict was connected to uncertainties re-garding gender roles in the culture as a whole during the 1950s. On the surface the relations between men and women appeared untroubled, and images of har-monious interactions within the nuclear family were frequently promoted. However . . . this surface masked deeper currents of unrest. . . . Taken together these developments reflected growing instabilities within the established system of patriarchal power, which was largely founded on a principle of male domi-nance in the realms of sexuality and family life.[30]

While they were content to see the hotheaded husband put his zany wife in her place in the Ricardo household, viewers may well have been nervous watching a wife so successfully deflate her husband's authority. There may have been a bitter aftertaste to the exchanges in which the husband's mastery was so effectively tamed. Was there some harsh truth being explored when Ralph shouts at Alice, "Look here, Alice, around here I'm the king . . . and you're nothin'," to which Alice responds, "Big deal! King over nothing"?

Finally, as the show's creators intuited, the basic material may have been ill suited for the situation-comedy formula in general. Jones explains:

> When "The Honeymooners" was a sketch within a variety show, it sat one step further from reality. Set up by Gleason's monologue as emcee, buffered by kits-chy numbers with the June Taylor dancers, the sketches had the quality of non-sense, of grotesque fantasy. . . . But a *sitcom*—with no reality other than the play itself, with no grinning host to gloat, "How sweet it is!" and reassure us at the end that it was all a joke—was another thing entirely. Suddenly the Kramdens existed on the same plane of reality as the Andersons, the Nelsons, and the Wil-liamses. As such, they were disturbing.[31]

These three examples of married couples in early television comedy point to the persistent presence of the Puritan ideal of domestic life, which was en-joying such a resurgence in American society in the 1950s. The Ricardos and the Burnses, with all their faults, approached that ideal much more closely than did the Kramdens.

Husbandly Authority

The wife could be dim-witted or zany, but she should be properly submissive to her husband, and, in the Ricardos' and Burnses' homes, the husband would resolve all comic confusion and restore order to the home.

Housewifery

The wife tended to the affairs of the home and, in Lucy's case, even the needs of a baby. She was often shown doing housework. For Lucy Ricardo and Gracie Allen that meant using the latest appliances to clean the living room and prepare meals, while for Alice Kramden it meant darning socks, washing clothes, and taking daily trips to the corner grocery store.

Virtuous Living

George Burns could amuse himself by watching his wife's antics on his own television set in his personal den, or Ricky Ricardo could revert to his native Spanish to express his husbandly frustration, but there should be clear limits to their displays of anger and threats, which were not observed by Ralph Kramden. Sexuality, for all its central importance to a married couple, is not to be mentioned. One need only recall that, throughout the well-publicized period of waiting for the arrival of Little Ricky, his parents and others were never allowed to mention the word "pregnant" and the Ricardos were allowed to share a bed only because of the viewer's presumed awareness that Lucille Ball and Desi Arnaz were married in real life. While Lucy often suspected Ricky of romantic activity with other women, her suspicions always proved to be unfounded. Lucy never considered straying, and the issue of marital infidelity never even arose in the other two shows.

Financial Success

Although the couple may not always be able to afford the fur coat or expensive new dress for which the wife pines, the couple should live in comfortable surroundings, relatively free of financial worries, as befits the blessings of the good life. The husband should be steadily and successfully employed, even if his success has been earned in the world of show business, so disapproved of in the Puritan worldview.

Despite the enormous popularity of *I Love Lucy*, television comedy soon moved away from the dynamics of married couples to the richer comic possibilities of full-fledged families with children, which had already struck a nerve with viewers. Two popular shows in the early days of television, *The Goldbergs* (1949–1954) and *Mama* (1949–1956), had featured lovable teenagers. *The Adventures of Ozzie and Harriet, Father Knows Best, The Danny Thomas Show, The Donna Reed Show, My Three Sons,* and other tales of the nuclear family, mainly in suburban homes, would soon be the norm for situation comedy in the 1950s and 1960s. Most of the comic problems would revolve around the children, and the husband and wife would be depicted not so much as spouses but as parents, the voices of reason and sources of nurturing affection.

It is revealing to note that the legitimate theater—from Noel Coward and Philip Barry to Neil Simon, A. R. Gurney, and other contemporary playwrights—has thrived on comedies that focus on the relationships of husbands and wives. Many classic Hollywood films have explored marriage in the screwball "remarriage" comedies of the 1930s, in Nick and Nora Charles of *The Thin Man* series and some of the Hepburn-Tracy romps of the 1940s, and in many of the best of Woody Allen's films. Yet network television has never quite returned to the simple relationship of husband and wife as the focus of the comic situation.

One possible exception to this pattern was the popular and award-winning series *Mad About You* (1992–1999), which concentrated on the relationship of a newly married couple in Manhattan without even one child, at least until their fifth season. In place of children, however, many of the comic complications in *Mad About You* involved the couple's parents, siblings, and other relatives as regularly recurring characters, some of them played by veteran comic stars such as Carol Burnett, Carroll O'Connor, and Mel Brooks. (How many relatives of the Ricardos, Kramdens, or George and Gracie did viewers ever meet?) In 2002, on cable television, Larry David, the creator of *Seinfeld*, premiered an HBO comedy starring himself *as* himself, Larry David, living with his wife (played by an actress—this is not Burns and Allen) and no children in Los Angeles. Otherwise, one searches in vain for any successful domestic comedy series focusing exclusively on a married couple without involving their children or a workplace situation.

One explanation for the lack of husband-and-wife comedies on television might be tied to the development of the situation-comedy genre over the years. Steven D. Stark's analysis of *I Love Lucy* addresses the issue in terms of the type of comedy these early shows employed. Stark observes that "in a medium notorious for shamelessly copying any formula that works, television rarely returned to Lucy's slapstick-rebellious form of situation comedy."[32] He attributes this anomaly first—and quite rightly—to the uniqueness of Lucille Ball's comic talent. But he also points to the preference for softer story lines in the family sitcoms that would follow in the 1950s. And, third, Stark observes that there was a certain blurring of reality and fiction in *I Love Lucy*. "It was hard to tell where Lucy and Ricky stopped and Lucy and Desi started—they even had babies at the same time."[33] The same could be said for George Burns and Gracie Allen's blending of their personal married life and their presentation of it on television. After these two marital comedies went off the air, only one other actual married couple, Ozzie and Harriet Nelson, succeeded in presenting a facsimile of their marriage in a television comedy. Their married life, however, included two growing sons, Rick and David, and during its fourteen-year run *The Adventures of Ozzie and Harriet* turned more and more of its attention to the boys and their adventures.

Perhaps marriage is, oddly enough, too sensitive a subject for comedy in the home. Studies have shown that marriage still retains a sacred character in the American consciousness. Most people—86 percent in a 2003 poll—still are married in a religious ceremony. As one expert expressed it, "Marriage is the one institution that touches on everything that Americans really care deeply about. . . . People who would never step inside a church for religious reasons will get married in one. That's what churches are for many people these days."[34] Could it be that marriage—in its comic form—is a lovely idea, but you really should not bring it into the home?

· 5 ·

OZZIE & HARRIET AND
ROCK & ROLL

America in the 1950s, as Lynn Spigel has described it, "invested an enormous amount of cultural capital in the ability to form a family and live out a set of highly structured gender and generational roles."[1] It should not be surprising, then, that a show such as *The Adventures of Ozzie and Harriet* would have become popular at the time. The Nelson family offered the perfect image of the American family, living in what David Halberstam has called "a wonderfully antiseptic world of idealized homes in an idealized, unflawed America."[2] Many other versions of the ideal family became popular on television at the same time; *Father Knows Best*, *My Three Sons*, *The Danny Thomas Show*, *Leave It to Beaver*, and *The Donna Reed Show* were the most successful examples. *The Adventures of Ozzie and Harriet*, however, deserves special attention because its fourteen-year run of original programming not only outlasted all the other suburban family comedies but for many years—until *The Simpsons* surpassed it in 2003—held the record as the longest-running prime-time comedy in television history. The show maintained a steady presence on television from 1952 to 1966. The secret of its longevity lies in the decision of its creator, Ozzie Nelson, to feature his son Ricky as a suburban model of the rock-and-roll teenager. While Ricky went on to a stunningly successful recording career as a "teen idol"—the term was first coined to describe him—his father used his success to sustain the popularity of a televised portrayal of family life that was coming to an end in the real world, if indeed it ever existed.

Mary Beth Haralovich describes the genre of the 1950s domestic comedy as "drawing on codes of verisimilitude to present portraits of everyday life in the white middle-class suburbs."[3] Nina C. Leibman goes so far as to deny the title "comedy" to shows such as *Ozzie and Harriet* and *My Three Sons*, preferring to deal with them as "domestic melodramas."[4] Spigel contends that "these programs worked to 'naturalize' family life, to make it appear as if this living arrangement were in fact the only one possible."[5] Halberstam's description of the sitcom pattern offers a quick summary of the "only possible" living arrangement offered on these shows:

> Everyone belonged to the political and economic center, and no one doubted that American values worked and that anyone with even an iota of common sense would want to admire them. In that sense the family sitcoms reflected—and reinforced—much of the social conformity of the period. There was no divorce. There was no serious sickness, particularly mental illness. Families liked each other, and they tolerated each other's idiosyncracies. . . . The dads were, above all else, steady and steadfact. They symbolized a secure world. . . . Moms in the sitcoms . . . were at once more comforting and the perfect mistresses of their household premises, although the farther they ventured from their houses the less competent they seemed. . . . No family difference was so irreconcilable that it could not be cleared up and straightened out in the allotted twenty-two minutes.[6]

There seemed to be a contract between the producers and viewers to sustain this image of the family during prime time. Even in the 1950s American housewives and others who watched the daytime dramas were seeing far darker images of marriage and the family, including the divorce, mental illness, and irreconcilable differences that Halberstam has seen as off-limits for prime-time comedy. People surely knew that Ozzie and Harriet's family life was not "the only one possible," even on television. Yet everyone seemed content to endorse its hegemony during the sacred hours of prime time.

Even in the context of television's attempts to "naturalize" its image of family life, *The Adventures of Ozzie and Harriet* had a unique level of verisimilitude. Halberstam describes the process as one of "fashioning a mythical family out of a real one."[7] Unlike every other example of the genre, this program starred an actual family, Ozzie and Harriet Nelson and their sons, David and Ricky. The show's set was closely modeled after their actual home in suburban Los Angeles. Ricky and David grew up over the show's fourteen years, and when they got married, their real-life wives joined the cast.

Ozzie Nelson not only starred in the show; he also wrote, produced, and directed every episode and was "an authoritarian, almost dictatorial presence on the set," quite the opposite of the laid-back, casual, occasionally bumbling paterfamilias he portrayed on the show.[8] He was, however, authentically middle-class wholesome. Born in Teaneck, New Jersey, in 1906, Nelson gained some attention as a star quarterback for Rutgers University. After college he became a bandleader, and by the age of twenty-five he already enjoyed national prominence. He became the bandleader on the Red Skelton radio program and eventually married the band's vocalist, Harriet Hilliard. Once they were married, Skelton would feature them on the radio, joking with them about their life as newlyweds. One summer, as a replacement for Skelton, they starred in their own radio show and were promoted as "America's favorite young couple." Their show lasted on the radio from 1944 to 1954.

In 1952, during the run of the radio show, they moved to television. Ozzie Nelson gave the show a sharp, clear, almost antiseptic look, with top-notch production talent. In one of his first production decisions, Nelson hired William Mellor, a top Hollywood cinematographer, to supervise the filming of the program in the crisply defined black-and-white style that had won him an Academy Award the year before for *A Place in the Sun*. Harriet was always fashionably dressed for a housewife, while Ozzie was more casual, often in shirt and tie, but usually wearing a cardigan sweater, looking a bit younger than his actual age of forty-six. The decor of the Nelson home struck just the right chord of comfort and middle-class refinement. Harriet no longer had the assistance of a maid that she had enjoyed on the radio show, but she never seemed to be overwhelmed with housework, spending much of her time with her bridge club or at the country club. Although references were made to Ozzie's former career as a bandleader, no clue was given as to his present occupation. He spent a lot of time around the house, commenting on and giving advice to Harriet and the boys.

This template of the ideal suburban household, the nuclear family of Mom, Dad, and the kids, living in relative affluence and trying to maintain traditional family values, was being offered to a population of viewers who, whether they knew it or not, were facing major changes in gender and generational roles. It has even been suggested that *The Adventures of Ozzie and Harriet* should not be analyzed as a situation comedy with the standard formula of ludicrous characters and situations, but rather it should be seen as a tentative forerunner of the prime-time teen dramas of the 1990s, which explored much more self-consciously a variety of ethical dilemmas and personal values in the diverse family settings of *Beverly Hills 90210*, *Party of Five*, or *Dawson's Creek*. The roles of middle-class men and women were undergoing severe readjustment in the 1950s. *The Adventures of Ozzie and Harriet* presented a new, and apparently attractive, view of family life in the mid-twentieth century, especially a new definition of the role of husband and father.

The first adjustment that many married couples had to make was finding themselves in new locations, as the forces of government and industry were strongly encouraging the move of white middle-class families to the burgeoning suburbs. Gerard Jones writes:

By 1953 one out of five Americans lived in the suburbs, and the number kept growing. The burbs were growing at fifteen times the rate of the rest of the country. . . . Clearly the powers that were supported the exurban flight. Federal Housing Administration and Veterans Administration housing loans, the last great program of the New Deal, accounted for nearly half of all new home mortgages during the first decade of suburban expansion. The vast majority of that money was concentrated on brand-new houses; government money withdrew from the cities. . . . Corporate America knew what it wanted, too. The new suburbanites were prime consumers, prime targets of the manufacturing and advertising worlds. . . . No one, it seemed, dragged old furniture and appliances from the city apartment to the new "ranch house." Besides, there were so many astounding laborsaving devices rolling off the assembly lines. Everything was bought new and at remarkably low prices: refrigerators, deep freezes, barbecues, washer-dryers, butterfly chairs, massive cars, and, of course, televisions.[9]

Jones shows how this move to the suburbs gave a new significance to the nuclear family structure:

Suburbia separated people from their neighbors, sealing them in the comfort of their dens and family rooms. It pulled people from familiar neighborhoods and ethnic conclaves. Along with fertility and prosperity, the new life brought unprecedented mobility. Corporate positions could mean frequent transfers. For those who were simply seeking a new promised land the abundance of jobs made it easy to pull up stakes. Extended families were left behind in the cities or rural areas, often a continent away. Spouse and children were often the suburbanite's only close, long-term social group.[10]

In the context of such major changes in family life, television portrayals began to change as well. In retrospect, Ozzie Nelson's creation of the New Dad of postwar America, the suburban husband and father as democratic authority figure, is quite remarkable. The husbands and fathers of early radio and television comedy were usually simple bumblers, such as the working-class Chester Riley on *The Life of Riley* or Fibber McGee of *Fibber McGee and Molly*, a major hit on radio that, significantly, did not replicate its enormous radio popularity when it moved to the television screen. Apparently viewers were willing to imagine these buffoons on the radio, but viewers did not want to see such humiliating behavior on television. They preferred to see more authoritative characters heading the households. In comedy, however, authoritarian figures easily turn into tyrants or bullies, so their behavior in these domestic comedies had to be tempered by genuine husbandly affection. In episode after episode of *I Love Lucy*, Ricky Ricardo was shown reestablishing his control over his irresponsible wife, sometimes in the form of a spanking, but always because he "loved Lucy." Ralph Kramden on *The Honeymooners* alternated between threatening his wife, Alice, with physical assault and glumly surrendering to her commonsense approach to managing their marriage. But he usually ended each episode by gazing into her eyes and proclaiming, "You're the greatest." Loud arguments were the usual method of discussion for the Ricardos and the Kramdens. *The George Burns and Gracie Allen Show* was, as in so many other ways, something of an exception to the rule. George, self-assured and eternally patient, lived in resigned acceptance of Gracie's eccentricities and generally agreeing with the neighbors and others who considered her somewhat mad.

Ozzie Nelson maintained but redefined the image of male authority over the household. In Ozzie viewers saw a husband who commanded respect but remained remarkably free of any desire to dominate the family, preferring instead a type of partnership with his wife, a mature, attractive woman who had enjoyed her own years of professional work outside the home and had settled into domesticity. Ozzie and Harriet faced every crisis and settled every dispute by quiet, intelligent, and even whimsically humorous discussions, and any misunderstanding was settled quickly before it got out of hand. Ozzie's approach to child rearing was similarly mild. As Gerard Jones defines it:

> As a father, he was just "ol' Dad." . . . He was the picture of an America that didn't have to be tough and serious anymore. . . . He was the antithesis of Ricky Ricardo and a couple of evolutionary steps beyond him; all the conflicts of the postwar world were comfortably behind him.[11]

Such domestic tranquillity, however, had its price:

> No one would say out loud, of course, that the endless quiet twilights of suburbia were a bit of an anticlimax to the tumult of the '40s, but many a man must have shaken his head over the contrast between his past as War Hero and his present as Domesticated Dad. With sly self-parody Ozzie helped American men chuckle at their retreat from heroic maleness.[12]

Much critical attention has been given to the character of Harriet Nelson and the other mothers and wives on these suburban sitcoms. They certainly represented a change from the "wacky" housewives and secretaries portrayed by Lucille Ball, Joan Davis, Ann Sothern, Gracie Allen, and others in the early 1950s. In many ways, of course, the suburban version of wifely contentment was just as unrealistic. It can be argued, however, that at least the external features of Harriet's life and the lives of other suburban housewives replicated the actual situation of middle-class suburban wives and mothers of the 1950s, who were generally homemakers without outside employment, with lives revolving around the home and family. Diana Meehan, in her treatment of the sitcom figure she calls "The Goodwife," observes the images of these housewives as at least competent and efficient household managers, in contrast to the scatter-brained Lucy Ricardo and others. (Meehan, however, also cites statistics indicating that, contrary to the television stereotype, many married women could be found in the workplace, with married women comprising half the female workforce in 1950 and the ratio increasing over the decade. The percentage of these working women who could be considered members of the suburban middle class, however, was not given in these studies.)[13]

The depiction of the typical suburban husband and father, as embodied in Ozzie Nelson, was not as factual. Ozzie seemed to have an unrealistically large supply of time to spend freely around the home and to deal with his wife and children in a leisurely fashion. This was not, in fact, an accurate reflection of the American father at any time in the twentieth century. With the rise of urbanization and industrialization after World War I, most husbands and fathers of almost every socioeconomic level spent long hours away from the home, often six days a week, at work in factories, offices, and stores, and by the time they got home they were often too weary to give much attention to domestic matters. The post–World War II movement of families to the suburbs often translated ironically into even more hours away from home for the commuter father. Ozzie Nelson's constant presence around the home and steady involvement in the activities and interests of his wife and sons presented a dream image of the perfect head of the household of the 1950s. As Halberstam describes it:

> In a way, Ozzie and the other sitcom dads seemed to have it both ways compared to the new breed of real-life suburban dads, who had to go off every day very early to commute to work and often returned late at night, when the children were ready for bed. By contrast, Ozzie seemed to work such flexible hours that he was home all the time. He never seemed to be at work, and yet he was successful.[14]

In its view of the husband and father, as in all other aspects of family relations, *The Adventures of Ozzie and Harriet* took a decidedly optimistic view. Postwar American families were beginning to experience a sharp rise in divorce rates, illegitimacy, and sexual experimentation and the first stirrings of feminism among middle-class women. There was already great concern for the problems of the young, generally phrased in the vague term "juvenile delinquency." Meanwhile, America in the 1950s was dealing with the challenges of court-ordered racial desegregation and accompanying problems of urban poverty and unrest. None of these issues made it into the conversation around the Nelson dinner table. It may be too harsh a criticism to say, as Rick Mitz has written, that Ozzie and Harriet "took family life—a hotspot of American insecurity—and trivialized it to the point of innocuousness."[15] Did such a portrayal border on denial? Or is it more accurate to see this as the building of barricades against the first waves of social change that would turn into a social revolution within the next decade?

A good example of Ozzie Nelson's approach to the changing social order is his treatment of adolescence, certainly an issue that was becoming a "hotspot" in American life in the late 1950s. One of the reasons Ozzie chose to address the topic was the happy coincidence of Ricky Nelson's stardom. As the series had evolved over the years, the basis for the comic "adventures" of the show tended to arise more often from the activities of David and Ricky rather than the parents in the show's title. This too represented a major departure from the sitcom formula of early television. The most popular family comedies of the early 1950s tended to exclude child characters; Ralph and Alice Kramden were childless, George Burns and Gracie Allen's son was grown and out of the house, and Lucy and Ricky Ricardo had a baby who only had the chance to turn four years old before the series ended its run. But even in the radio version of *The Adventures of Ozzie and Harriet*, the boys were part of the regular story line. On television the clean-cut good looks of the Nelson boys garnered them even more of a following, especially from the growing number of teenagers in the baby-boomer audience. The younger brother, Ricky, who was already entering his teen years when the show moved to television, was portrayed as a basically nice kid who was irrepressible, noisy, and occasionally impudent. But soon he would become an icon of cool suburban adolescence.

It happened in 1957. Rock and roll had entered the mainstream of popular music, especially with the arrival of Elvis Presley. Elvis began recording songs with Sun Records in 1954, got a recording contract with RCA in 1955, and exploded onto the popular music scene in 1956. While his record sales would make him a major star on the radio and on the phonograph, the real Elvis experience was a visual one as well, and it would be television that would demonstrate what an antithesis he presented to the bland American popular culture of the Eisenhower era. Elvis's television début could not have been more symbolic. In late January 1956 Elvis entered the homes of America in the staid, big-band context of the Dorsey Brothers' *Stage Show*, where he stunned the white-bread audience with his raw and surly combination of blues and rock, "Heartbreak Hotel," and was booked for five more consecutive appearances. Later that year Elvis shocked the even larger audience that watched *The Milton Berle Show* with his rockabilly hit "Hound Dog." By September, when Elvis appeared on the highly rated *The Ed Sullivan Show*, Sullivan earned an 82.6 share of the viewing audience, an estimated 54 million people.[16] Elvis's smoldering good looks, the combination of growl and moan in his voice, his rebellious sneer, and especially his blatantly erotic pelvic and thigh movements thrilled the teenagers and terrified their parents. His music was sending a message as well, with the pounding beat of his guitar and his backup group and the suggestive lyrics. His first album was released that year and instantly shot to the top of the charts. The first of his many films, *Love Me Tender*, appeared in 1957. It is impossible to overstate the impact of Presley on the teen culture of the mid-1950s. The reaction of parents, church leaders, and other guardians of morality was equally intense.

According to the Nelson family lore, Ricky, who was sixteen years old at the time, became envious of his girlfriend's enthusiasm for Elvis and boasted to her that he was going to record a song himself. He recorded his own version of a song by the black rock and roller Fats Domino called "I'm Walkin'," an upbeat ballad expressing the singer's hopes that his girlfriend would soon come back to him because "for you, pretty baby, I'd surely die." Ozzie had Ricky perform the song at the end of the show on April 10, 1957. The recording was a major hit, and Ricky was a new recording sensation. The recording of "I'm Walkin'" sold sixty thousand copies in the first three days and some three hundred Ricky Nelson fan clubs sprang up overnight.[17] For the next several years Ricky would typically close every episode of the show with a musical performance. Ricky Nelson went on to become one of the best-selling pop singers of all time, with a top 10 hit every year from 1957 to 1963 and a total of sixty million records sold. In 1958, with Elvis away in the army, Ricky was the top selling rock-and-roll artist in the country.

Ricky's performance style was a far more subdued version of the Elvis experience. He copied the sneer and even a bit of the low growl, but his gyrations were minimal, his rhythms more subdued, and the lyrics relatively wholesome, dealing with the pangs of teenage romance with songs such as "Hello, Mary Lou, Goodbye Heart"; "Teenage Doll"; "Stood Up"; "Poor Little Fool"; "Bebop Baby"; "Waitin' in School"; and simply, "A Teenager's Romance." This was rock and roll for the suburbs, and teenagers loved it.

The episode that featured Ricky's musical début is worth examining in more detail as a quintessential Nelson family "adventure." In its portrayal of the easygoing relationship and the shared interests of Mom, Dad, and the kids, it gave a distinct message to the viewers: rock and roll was simply the latest wave of popular music appealing to young people and, if parents and children could just communicate respectfully with one another, even this latest onslaught on American decency could be absorbed into respectable family life.

The program begins with all of the family sharing their excitement about the band that is scheduled to perform for the dance at the country club that the whole family will be attending. Both the parents and teenagers are major fans of Tommy Jackson, whose dance band offers a version of the big-band sound of Tommy Dorsey and Glenn Miller. David and Ricky have all of Tommy Jackson's albums. Indeed, 1957 may have provided some of the final days of an era when everyone in the family went to the same dances and enjoyed the same recording artists.

Harriet finds out, through a slightly confused message, that the band needs "somebody for the drums" that night. Ricky has been practicing the drums for some time, so she volunteers him as a substitute for their drummer. The conversation at the family dinner table that night is filled with excitement as Ricky gets advice from the former bandleader Ozzie about what to wear and how to play with the band. When Ozzie suggests that Ricky wear a tuxedo to play in the band, Ricky objects that bands are wearing new styles of clothes. Ozzie quickly contradicts Ricky, saying that "the basic principles don't change" and advises him to wear the tuxedo. That statement might well serve as the theme of the entire series.

They subsequently discover that the bandleader only needed someone to carry the drums for the band, not to play them. But because Tommy Jackson recalls a time years earlier when Ozzie had given him a chance to play, Tommy lets Rick sit in for a while and even do a drum solo. Ricky's solo turns into a combination of jazz and rock-and-roll percussion.

Then Ozzie himself suggests to the bandleader, "How about Rick singin' a rhythm-and-blues tune and the rest of us'll give a little moral support?" Ricky goes into his performance of "I'm Walkin'," causing some young women in the audience to swoon, a far milder version of the typical teenage hysteria that greeted Elvis's performances. Ricky then dances a jitterbug with one of the young ladies. When he finishes, his parents and David join Ricky for a barber-shop quartet version of an old song from turn-of-the-century vaudeville, "My Gal Sal." This is another crowd-pleaser, especially for the older folks. One of Ozzie and Harriet's friends starts snapping his fingers to the music, telling his wife, "This is my kind of music!" The choice of "My Gal Sal" is thematic. The song, which became popular over fifty years earlier, praises a young lady whom people called "frivolous Sal, a peculiar sort of a gal." She is described as a "wild sort of devil, but dead on the level." In other words, as the Nelson family tells their listeners, naughty, even "wild," behavior did not begin with rock and roll, and popular music often sang the praises of such loose behavior. But through it all, family values always managed to survive. A family such as the Nelsons, literally joined in such close harmony, could certainly handle the threat of Elvis on the American home and its values.

It was a very reassuring message to American parents, but it was also a shrewd business move on the part of Ozzie Nelson. He understood that television watching was something done by the family as a group. As Hal Himmelstein has described it, the television set was becoming the "kitchen window as we curiously peeked at the goings-on of our next-door neighbors, the Nelsons."[18] And what families saw through that window was serving a normative function, showing both parents and children the way to the good life. Ozzie figured out that, if Ricky could embody the perfectly wholesome teenager as well as his Mom and Dad exhibited perfect parenting, the show could maintain a solid spot in the ratings. And so it did, for nine more years.

Of course, Ozzie 's message was not true to the facts of the situation, and nowhere was this better expressed than in the very profession that had brought Ozzie and Harriet to national attention, the world of popular music. Up into the mid-1950s the musical hit parade was dominated by middle-of-the-road singers such as Perry Como, Patti Page, Johnny Mathis, Doris Day, Eddie Fisher, and others, smooth performers who appealed to both young and old listeners and record buyers. With the arrival of Elvis, Bill Haley and the Comets, and Jerry Lee Lewis, not to mention the crossover of black music into the pop mainstream with Chuck Berry, Fats Domino, Little Richard, and others, records began to be marketed specifically to teenagers. Radio stations, whose formats were changing over into all music all the time, started featuring disk jockeys who appealed exclusively to teenagers. Other elements of the mass media followed suit. A multitude of "teen" magazines began to appear in the drugstores and newsstands. To a lesser extent Hollywood started marketing movies directly to the teenage audience. This was, of course, about money: the teen dollar.

The impact of this development is best understood with some historical perspective. In eighteenth- and nineteenth-century America, the term "teenager" would have had no meaning. In the largely agricultural economy, children began to take on their share of the farm work as early as possible, and they tended to marry and begin raising their own families before they reached the age of twenty. Children in towns and cities also found jobs as soon as possible, seldom seeing any need for a college education, and marrying early as well. After World War I, with the increase of college education among young men and women, the phenomenon of "flaming youth" captured the public imagination, with "flappers" in short skirts and bobbed hair and their collegiate boyfriends in raccoon coats, automobiles, and all the misconduct of the Roaring Twenties. While such behavior was actually available only to the privileged few, the flapper and the collegiate showed up regularly in the popular short stories and novels of F. Scott Fitzgerald, on the covers of *Vanity Fair*, in the Broadway musicals, and in the silent pictures as further examples of the carefree, even reckless, youth of the 1920s.

The Great Depression brought such frivolity into general disfavor and sent most adolescents back into the workplace whenever possible. The model teenager was the boy who took on a newspaper route or the girl who learned dressmaking or other employable skills to help out the family's dire financial situation. The unselfish ideal was captured in the pages of popular novels such as *A Tree Grows in Brooklyn* and *The Human Comedy*, in films such as the Andy Hardy series and the Mickey Rooney–Judy Garland musicals, and in the popular radio series *Henry Aldrich*, well up to the end of World War II.

And then came the baby boom. The year of Ricky Nelson's musical début— 1957—marked the entrance into puberty for the first wave of post–World War II babies, and by then the American adolescent was a major segment of the population. The teenagers—and there were so many of them—had more disposable income and leisure time than ever before. In 1957 the typical teenager was no longer helping out with the family farm or business; the breadwinner-father was supporting the family single-handedly in some mysterious occupation at a factory or office that did not involve his wife or children. This arrangement provided the teenage son or daughter with a new amount of leisure time and an allowance to spend as he or she wished. If the teenager had a part-time job at the local supermarket, gas station, or drugstore, instead of helping out the family's finances, that money would more likely go into the teenager's pocket or savings. It might be going toward the purchase of the teenager's own automobile or college education. There was a good deal of dating and "going steady," but few teenagers planned on getting married until after high school or college or a solid start in an occupation. In short, with spending money, a good chunk of leisure time, the mobility of the automobile, and many years of extended adolescence before settling down into a career and marriage, the teenagers of mid-twentieth-century America were coalescing into a distinct "youth culture," which at first mainly represented a large market demographic to which merchants and advertisers were eager to appeal.[19]

Hollywood reached out to the teenage audience with some attempts at realistic portrayals of teen angst and rebellion in films such as Marlon Brando's biker-gang drama, *The Wild One* (1953); *Blackboard Jungle* (1955), a drama of juvenile delinquency in an inner-city high school that introduced the song "Rock around the Clock"; *Rebel without a Cause* (1955), a portrayal of teenage confusion and unrest in the apparent tranquillity of the suburbs, starring the teen icons Natalie Wood and James Dean; and in more daring depictions of adolescent sexuality in rebellion in highly regarded and popular films such as 1955's *Picnic*, 1959's *A Summer Place*, and 1960's *Splendor in the Grass*. These were accompanied by a flood of teen fantasies such as the "beach-blanket" movies of Frankie Avalon and Annette Funicello and the assembly-line production of Elvis Presley musicals throughout the 1960s. Even Broadway theater showed a new interest in teenagers, with the gang warfare of *West Side Story*, the teeny-boppers of *Bye Bye Birdie*, and the adolescent protagonists of *The*

Diary of Anne Frank; Look Homeward, Angel; The Miracle Worker, and other critically acclaimed theater of the late 1950s, which were all made into popular films in the 1960s.

As the fifties moved into the sixties, all the attention that teenagers and their money were receiving from the merchants of popular culture began to create a distinct self-awareness, an aura of importance surrounding their issues, problems, and ideals. The youth movement began to articulate its own vision of the world. The freedom, sexual and otherwise, expressed in rock and roll and acted out on the movie screens of America became the rallying cry of the baby-boom generation. By the mid-1960s the urban beat of Motown and the psychedelic rock of the Beatles and the Rolling Stones dominated the world of popular music. Teen dancing moved from the traditional ballroom steps and jitterbugs of the senior prom into the free-form, often drug-enhanced, response to the electric guitars and drumbeats of sixties rock. The folk music of Joan Baez, Bob Dylan, and others added an element of social protest against racism, poverty, war, and the other injustices that the young perceived as the legacy of the older generation.

The year 1957 gave us Ricky Nelson singing rock and roll at his parents' country club dance. The year 1967 gave us the "summer of love" with flower children on drugs making love, not war. Such a transformation of the youth culture and American society at large in the space of one decade was encouraged and guided by the omnipresent influence of popular music, an industry that had once included Ozzie Nelson.

However, while the rest of the entertainment industry fought to capture the hearts and pocketbooks of this new generation, television remained something of a holdout, especially during the years that the Nelsons inhabited television land. There were many children's shows coming into living rooms in the 1950s and 1960s, especially on Saturday mornings and after school. Only a few "teen" shows emerged, however, mostly in the after-school and Saturday "dance-party" format of shows such as the very popular *American Bandstand* and sometimes in the performances of the older contingent of kids on *The Mickey Mouse Club.*

If one observes the television fare that accompanied *The Adventures of Ozzie and Harriet* during its 1952–1966 run, one will find quite a few teenagers. Since *Our Miss Brooks* (1952–1956) took place in a high school, the cast included several teenagers, most notable the squeaky-voiced student Walter Denton. Both *The Life of Riley* (1953–1958) and *The Danny Thomas Show* (1953–1964) featured an adolescent son and daughter; the teenagers Betty, Bud, and Kathy were important in most of the plotlines of *Father Knows Best* (1954–1960). They were succeeded by Mike, Robbie, and Chip, the teenaged children of Fred MacMurray on *My Three Sons* (1960–1972); Wally Cleaver and his buddy Eddie Haskell on *Leave It to Beaver* (1957–1963); and, of course, Opie on *The Andy Griffith Show* (1960–1968). The teenaged children on *The Donna Reed Show* (1958–1966) even managed a mild repeat of Ricky Nelson's singing success. In 1962 Paul Petersen, who played the teenage son, Jeff, performed a song called "She Can't Find Her Keys," which became a major hit, followed by several other successful recordings. Shelley Fabares, who played the daughter, Mary, was even more successful; her recording of "Johnny Angel" was #1 on the music charts that same year, selling more than one million copies.

However, each of these adolescents was presented within the context of their family, as supporting characters in the domestic drama and never as the central consciousness of the show and certainly never in opposition to their family, as was the case with so many of the adolescent characters on the Broadway stage and in Hollywood films. In the entire period only two prime-time television shows succeeded with teenagers as the main characters, *The Many Loves of Dobie Gillis* (1959–1963) and *The Patty Duke Show* (1963–1966). *Dobie Gillis* at least featured Dobie's buddy, Maynard G. Krebs, a self-professed nonconformist who habitually questioned the system and, in his beatnik-rebelliousness, offered a glimpse at the restlessness of adolescents in the Kennedy years.

Prime-time television was being targeted not toward teenagers but toward the family at large. Television viewing was, and still is, largely an activity shared by the entire family. Of all age groups measured by the Nielsen people, teenagers consistently rank as the lowest users of television.[20] The teenagers of the 1950s were no exception to this pattern. They spent their leisure time in part-time jobs and on extracurricular activities and social engagements outside the home. They listened to their radios in their bedrooms and cars, and they spent their money on records, movies, and dances. In their search for role models or codes of conduct, they were not turning to television.

They would certainly have had a difficult time finding any images or voices of the rebellious new generation on television. Elvis appeared only a few memorable times before he was inducted into the army in 1958, and a few other folk singers and rock and rollers would appear on the musical-variety shows of the period. Only Ricky Nelson showed up on a weekly basis, as the unofficial star of his own show, playing one or another of the songs that were turning him into a "teen idol." However, thanks to the show business savvy of his father, Ricky was sending a message not of rebellion but of reassurance. As Halberstam has surveyed the situation, he has seen that Ozzie Nelson was

> shrewd and intuitive, with a fine instinct for how the rest of the country wanted to see itself in terms of a middle-class family portrait; if he did not like and did

not understand the increasingly sharp divisions beginning to separate the young from their parents in America, then he understood how to offer a comforting alternative to it. American families, he understood, did not want at that moment a weekly program to reflect (and, worse, encourage) teenage rebellion. There was too much of that already.[21]

Of course, whether or not Ozzie saw it or wanted it, there was much more teenage rebellion waiting to happen. And a lot of it would be televised.

·6·

LOOKING OUT THE
PICTURE WINDOW

In the early 1960s television brought into the homes of America two eloquent expressions of the nation's hopes for the rest of the twentieth century. In his inaugural address in January 1960, President John F. Kennedy announced that "the torch has been passed to a new generation of Americans—born in this century," and he called upon his fellow citizens to "ask not what your county can do for you—ask what you can do for your country." In the summer of 1963, from the steps of the Lincoln Memorial during the Great March on Washington, the Reverend Dr. Martin Luther King, Jr., proclaimed, "I have a dream . . . that one day this nation will rise up and live out the true meaning of its creed: 'We hold these truths to be self evident, that all men are created equal.'" Both of these expressions of American idealism were delivered live to the entire nation and recorded for posterity through the medium of television. Throughout the rest of the decade, however, television would transmit more disturbing images, replacing the American Dream with a national nightmare of political and social upheaval.

One of the defining events in television history occurred in November 1963 when, for the first time, all regularly scheduled programming stopped so that Americans could witness the horror and share in the grief surrounding the assassination and burial of President Kennedy. For four unforgettable days all normal activities seemed to stop as the entire nation stayed glued to their television sets. Meanwhile, the networks dispensed with regular programming and commercials and combined their camera crews to offer live coverage of the chaos surrounding the shooting in Dallas, the arrival of the president's coffin accompanied by his widow in blood-stained dress and the newly sworn-in President Lyndon Johnson, the capture and vigilante killing of the president's suspected assassin, and the solemn funeral procession to Arlington National Cemetery, with an unprecedented gathering of world leaders and a simple salute from the president's three-year-old son as his coffin passed by. As Steven D. Stark has observed, "TV was now more than the medium of choice; it was the only medium anyone could envision capturing an event. In one weekend, America had gone from a print-and-radio-nation (we read and heard the news) to a television nation (we saw the funeral)."[1] All of this on that small screen in offices, schools, and other public gathering places, but mainly in the home.

As the decade progressed, more and more disturbing images would be delivered into American living rooms. Even in the comparatively complacent years of the Kennedy administration, considerable ferment grew around the issues of racial discrimination and civil rights as well as early resistance to the military buildup in Vietnam. These and other issues would grow into a fireball of social unrest by the end of the decade, and the networks would be the bearers of considerably disturbing news on a nightly basis.

While the news may have been growing more and more unpleasant, television entertainment struck out in the opposite direction. A schizophrenic pattern developed in the relationship between the network's nightly news programs and the prime-time entertainment that followed. Both drama and comedy engaged in a deep escapism, expressing itself most often in nostalgia for the simpler worlds of the Old West and rural life. The most popular shows of the early 1960s were the adult westerns. At the start of the 1960s *Gunsmoke* was continuing its run as the #1 show in the Nielsen ratings for four years in a row (1957–1961), with *Wagon Train* in 2nd place until it became the 1st place show in the 1961–1962 season. Throughout the decade television drama continued to go west, presenting a slew of popular cowboys and lawmen from the American frontier. Among the many westerns that made it into the top rung of the Nielsen ratings were Have *Gun Will Travel, Wanted: Dead or Alive, Rawhide, The Rifleman, Cheyenne, The Lawman, The Virginian, Branded, Daniel Boone*, and the phenomenally popular tale of the Cartwright ranching family on *Bonanza*. Meanwhile, the star of *Gentle Ben* was a black bear who lived with a family in the Everglades, while Lassie, the heroic collie, performed his heroic deeds for a farm family.

This same escapism was evident in many of the most successful comedies of the period with their whimsical approach to rural or small-town life in series such as *The Andy Griffith Show, Green Acres, The Beverly Hillbillies, Mayberry R.F.D., The Real McCoys*, and *Petticoat Junction*. Other comic "escapes" from contemporary life were enacted in *The Flintstones* (1960–1966) and *Gilligan's Island* (1964–1967). Stark maintains that *The Beverly Hillbillies* and similar rural comedies "hit a nerve" with viewers for a variety of reasons.

First, he suggests that, in the wake of the Kennedy assassination, "the nation turned to utter escapism to bury its grief."[2] In fact, as Stark points out, the seven episodes of *The Beverly Hillbillies* immediately following the assassination of President Kennedy became the most widely watched half-hour shows in television history. In the nostalgic settings, issues of racial injustice, urban chaos, or youth rebellion were not part of the picture.

These rural comedies and melodramas, however, were not simply nostalgia for some viewers. At a time when the cracks in the national cultural consensus began to show in the mid-sixties, a portrayal of simple, good-hearted cowboys, farmers, and small-town folk could be seen by the older generation as evidence of the abiding worth of traditional values that were being challenged by the political protestors of the time. Stark maintains that these shows appealed to the values of people Richard Nixon would soon be referring to as "the silent majority," who disapproved of much of the political and social changes taking place in the country and were frightened or angered by the radical activity of civil rights and antiwar protestors.

Meanwhile, there could be a third interpretation of the rural lifestyle presented on these shows. The protestors themselves could point to *The Beverly Hillbillies* as an emblem of the very anti-technology-return-to-nature movement that they were espousing and trying to live out in their own rural communes. The issues raised by the counter-culture were too raw for television to process directly; they could be approached only through elaborate codes. Were the shipwrecked inhabitants of *Gilligan's Island* actually a case of (accidental) "dropouts" from the modern society that had forced them into certain roles and expectations appropriate to a millionaire, a professor, and others? Could *The Flintstones* have been about the survival of a family without the help of modern technology or other benefits of Western civilization? Could the Clampetts and the good people of Mayberry serve as a protest against the elitist establishment behind the Vietnam conflict and other evils of American life? In this sense perhaps the rural shows were not so escapist after all.

However, escapism certainly seemed to be the mode of discourse in the unusually high number of 1960s military comedies. At a time when the Vietnam conflict was becoming more complex and unpopular, the networks responded with several comedies set in military environments where words like "Vietnam," "napalm," or "Tet offensive" were never spoken. One of the most popular in this genre managed to combine the country-life motif with the military. *Gomer Pyle, U.S.M.C.* (1964–1970) took a popular character from the Mayberry world of *The Andy Griffith Show* and placed him in the Marines at Camp Henderson, California, during a peacetime period. (To a great extent, the concept for the series was imitating the popular novel *No Time for Sergeants*, which, in its incarnations as a Broadway play and a movie, had launched the career of Andy Griffith a few years earlier.) *Gomer Pyle, U.S.M.C.* managed to show up among the top 10 shows five out of the six years of its run, which ironically parallels the period of escalation of the Vietnam War. *Hogan's Heroes*, which also enjoyed a six-year run (1965 to 1971), followed the zany escapades of prisoners in a Nazi POW camp. While the Allied prisoners engaged in numerous plots and adventures to disrupt the order of the camp, their Nazi captors, especially Colonel Klink and Sergeant Schulz, were portrayed as inept bunglers. *McHale's Navy* (1962–1966) was an exercise in military nostalgia, starring Academy Award-winner Ernest Borgnine as the play-by-my-own-rules commander of a World War II PT.

Several other light-hearted looks at military life—with a nostalgic glow—showed up on the small screen. *Ensign O'Toole*, which ran for only one season (1962–1963), was set on a Navy destroyer in peacetime, and followed the hijinks of a motley gang of officers and crew. *Rat Patrol*, which ran for only two seasons from 1966 to 1968, took a whimsical approach to the renegade adventures of four World War II commandoes in the North African desert fighting General Rommel. *F Troop* (1965–67) delved even deeper into nostalgia in its farcical portrayal of a Civil War army troop stationed out in Indian territory, thus managing to combine both military comedy and another look at the Old West.

Only one dramatic series focusing on the military met with any success during the 1960s, and it, too, was in its own way an exercise in nostalgia. *Combat* (1962–1967), using actual wartime footage in the background, aimed at a realistic depiction of World War II soldiers moving across Europe after the D-day landing. *Combat* seems to have been the only example of anything approaching a realistic depiction of military life. Wacky military comedies were much more popular.

As the decade came to a close, the country and western–tinged nostalgia and escapism were still the dominant tone. Even the variety shows of the period had a rural feel, with such popular offerings as *The Glen Campbell Good-time Hour, The Johnny Cash Show, The Jim Nabors Hour,* and the ultimate in country corn, *Hee Haw.*

Many studies of the period also point to the prevalence of "magicoms" in the 1960s. Several situation comedies indulged in fantasies, particularly in their approach to family comedy. *Mister Ed* (1961–1965), a popular comedy about a talking horse, was followed by the even more popular *My Favorite Martian* (1963–1966), the story of a young newspaper writer in Los Angeles who "adopts" a Martian whose spaceship had crashed on earth and tries to pass him off as his uncle. *My Favorite Martian* was #10 in the Nielsen rankings in its first season. Both *The Munsters* and *The Addams Family*, which ran simultaneously for two seasons, from 1964 to 1966, presented the home lives of monster-families who thought of themselves as normal but terrified the rare outsider who encountered them. From 1966 to 1968 a live-action version of the comic strip *Batman* was an overnight sensation with its grotesque portrayals of super-villains such as The Penguin, The Joker, The Riddler, and Catwoman. It only lasted two seasons in prime time, but it gained a large cult following, particularly by use of the gimmick of playing two nights a week, with the first show of the week ending in a cliff-hanger to be resolved the next night, and in its use of phrases such as "Pow" or "Thud" that would flash on the screen during the fight scenes. Fantasy reached new heights in 1967 with the arrival of Sally Field as *The Flying Nun* (1967–1970). Inspired perhaps by the runaway popularity of Julie Andrews's portrayal of an irrepressible novice in the 1965 film version of *The Sound of Music,* this series followed the misadventures of an effusive young novice who spent a lot of time flying through the blue skies of San Juan, Puerto Rico, where her convent was located. With her diminutive stature and her large wing-shaped bonnet, Sister Bertrille would often be caught up and swept away by a strong wind, with inevitable comic complications involving her sister nuns or neighbors.

The most popular of the magicoms, however, were the two that were set (where else?) in the home, involving wives who possessed magical powers. *I Dream of Jeannie* (1965–1970) told the story of an astronaut, Tony Nelson, who, when forced to abort a space mission, parachuted onto a desert island. Tim Brooks and Earle Marsh describe the show's premise and plotlines concisely:

> While waiting for a rescue team he came across an old bottle that had apparently washed ashore. When he opened the bottle, out popped a 2,000-year-old (but remarkably well-preserved) genie, who promptly accepted him as her master, since he had set her free. Returning to Cocoa Beach, Florida, with the rescue team, Tony found that nobody would believe that he had found a luscious, sexy genie. . . . Complicating the matter, the genie, appropriately named Jeannie, refused to perform magic or ever appear for anyone but Tony. Her efforts to serve him often resulted in rather confusing situations, caused in part by her lack of familiarity with 20th-century American customs.[3]

The series featured many visual gimmicks besides the appearance and disappearance of Jeannie, played by Barbara Eden. Her mostly invisible dog and various relatives popped in and out of view all the time. During the show's last three seasons, Jeannie's wicked twin sister (played by Eden in a dark wig) appeared regularly. And, as if the attractive Barbara Eden did not provide enough visual appeal, the last season introduced another actress to the cast, Farrah Fawcett, destined for major sex–icon status in the 1970s.

The most successful magicom was the other domestic fantasy show, *Bewitched,* which enjoyed an eight-year run from 1964 to 1972. Its main character was Samantha Stephens, played by the charming Elizabeth Montgomery (the daughter of Robert Montgomery, a television actor and host of his own series in the 1950s), a young suburban wife who happened to be a witch but who wanted desperately to fit into the role of a normal housewife. *Bewitched* got better Nielsen ratings than any of the other examples of escapist fare, making it to the #2 spot (right behind the behemoth hit *Bonanza*) in its premiere season and remaining in or close to the list of the top 10 shows for several years of its run. It also managed to take home a few Emmy Awards, for its director William Asher and two of its supporting actresses, Marion Lorne, who played Samantha's Aunt Clara, and Alice Pearce, who played Samantha's nosy neighbor, Gladys Kravitz.

The comedy invites considerable cultural analysis in its depiction of a powerful woman "stuck" in the suburbs in a condition soon to be described and decried so concretely in Betty Friedan's pioneering study of rising female disaffection with the status quo, *The Feminine Mystique*. It is also significant that the unruly woman should be portrayed as a "witch," the very charge that was brought against the uncontrollable women of Puritan New England three hundred years earlier. Endora, Samantha's fabulous mother, played with wizardly glamour by the acclaimed film actress Agnes Moorehead, constantly chided her daughter for abandoning the endless adventures of witchery for the bland pleasures of suburban domesticity. The most symbolic episode of the series may well have been the one in which Endora casts a spell on Samantha's husband, Darrin, that causes him to shrink to a few inches in height. Besides the Freudian implications of such "shrinkage," the tiny Darrin's protestations of mastery over his household, coupled with the condescending treatment he receives from Samantha, obliquely depict the psychic condition of the American male threatened by the emerging women's movement. Gerard Jones makes a case for this on the basis of a coded message in one of the episodes:

There was an odd clue to the underlying dynamic of *Bewitched* in the credits of the first episode featuring Sam's identical cousin, Serena [played by Montgomery]. The role is attributed to "Pandora Spocks." The Pandora's box of the American mainstream was female power. Serena was the Sam-that-might-have-been, the sexy sprite who loved every moment of her own life but brought terror and trouble to poor schmucks like Darrin. (And was Pandora Spocks a cousin to Benjamin Spock? Would her box be opened by the coming generation, the adolescents raised on the psychology of personal fulfillment?)[4]

Some of the appeal of these shows came simply from the novelty of the visual tricks done with film. As long as most prime-time programming was produced on film, why not play with the cinematic techniques? What fun to observe Sally Field in a nun's habit flying around, or to see the sounds of

Batman's punches as we do in the comic strip, or to watch people and objects appear and disappear in the wink of an eye or, in Samantha's case, the twitching of a nose. The episode that showed Darrin shrinking used all sorts of camera tricks, such as double exposure and oversized sets and props, to show his change in stature.

Yet there may well have been some coded messages and unarticulated processing of the social changes of the time happening among the viewers. As Stark has commented, "By packaging troubling cultural shifts in the guise of comic fantasy, these shows made it easier for Americans to come to grips with rapid social change."[5] Stark recounts that one of the writers of *Mister Ed* said that they thought of the talking horse as a rebellious teenager, and *Gilligan's Island* was pitched to CBS as a story of a "social microcosm" of disparate individuals forming a sort of hippie commune. The shows about Martians and monster families hinted at the tensions as Black families were seen as alien outsiders moving into white neighborhoods, while the magical-housewife comedies served as satires of traditional gender roles. In this sense these fantasy comedies, especially the magicoms, were exploring some of the very issues they were being accused of ignoring. As Stark asks, "Who's to say that shows about witches, castaways, and talking horses didn't help tell us, in an age of rebellion and psychedelia, something about who we were and might yet become?"[6] Perhaps even the military comedies were gingerly approaching the topic of the defense-buildup during the Cold War years.

Meanwhile, across the cultural landscape, a lot of comedy was taking a much more direct approach to the issues of the period. Political and social satire was alive and thriving in the coffeehouses, nightclubs, college auditoriums, and the other venues of the 1960s stand-up comedy world, with masters of the art such as Lenny Bruce, Mort Sahl, Dick Gregory, and Richard Pryor. Many of the earliest successes of the emerging Off-Broadway theater scene offered scathing critiques of American life with black humor. Edward Albee's *Zoo Story*, Jean Genet's *The Blacks*, Jean-Claude von Italie's *America Hurrah*, and similar productions at experimental theaters such as La Mama and the Living Theater put Off-Broadway on the cultural map. The 1968 megahit Broadway musical *Hair*'s portrait of the flower children of the sixties combined their celebration of sexual freedom, the drug culture, and communal living with their protests against war, racism, environmental pollution, and other afflictions of American society. Even Hollywood stepped up to bat. Mike Nichols's portrayal of middle-class amorality in *The Graduate*, Arthur Penn's examination of the role of violence in American culture in *Bonnie and Clyde*, and two critiques of the racial divide in America in Stanley Kramer's *Guess Who's Coming to Dinner* and Norman Jewison's *In the Heat of the Night* were the four nominees for the Best Picture Academy Award in 1967.

The cultural climate seemed ripe for a televised attempt at satire, and, given the stand-up and nightclub roots of much of the political humor, the variety-show format would seem to be the ideal venue for such material. The first, and least successful, venture was somewhat of an import. *That Was the Week That Was* (1964–1965), which came to be known as TW3, was based on a British series with the same name. It might best be understood as the television front in the "British invasion" of American culture at the time. The cast of the show was an impressive group of mainly American performers; it included Henry Morgan, a veteran radio and television wit with a leaning toward the intellectual; Bob Dishy and Phyllis Newman, distinguished award-winners from the Broadway theater; Buck Henry, who would go on to write the screenplay for *The Graduate* and become one of the guiding talents behind *Saturday Night Live;* and some other comic performers who would find further success on prime-time television, such as Tom Bosley and Alan Alda. The program was produced live, with sketches, musical numbers, and news reports aimed at topical satire. For most of its run David Frost, who had starred in the series in England, hosted the show.

Highlights of the show were the songs performed by Tom Lehrer, a songwriter-satirist with a Harvard degree in mathematics and statistics, who combined appearances at clubs and concert halls with teaching stints at Harvard and MIT. One of his memorable contributions to the show was the song "National Brotherhood Week," which encouraged everyone to "come on and shake the hand / Of people you can't stand," and ended with the reassuring thought, "It's only for a week, so have no fear. Be grateful that it doesn't last all year." Another number, "So Long, Mom (A Song for World War III)," included the refrain, "So long, Mom, / I'm off to drop a bomb/ So don't wait up for me!" One of the more outrageous numbers, "The Vatican Rag," satirized the Catholic Church's attempts to modernize its teachings and practices in the decrees of the Second Vatican Council held during the early 1960s, portraying the changes as a marketing tool to "sell the product." The Scott Joplin–style piano rag that Lehrer offered as new sacred music began, "First you get down on your knees / Fiddle with your rosaries / Bow your head with great respect / And genuflect, genuflect, genuflect."

The second season of the show coincided with a particularly heated national election. As Brooks and Marsh recount it, "Perhaps by chance, perhaps by design, TW3 was repeatedly pre-empted during the fall and replaced with low-rated political speeches and documentaries paid for by the Republicans. By the time the show reappeared after the election, its momentum was gone, and audiences had switched to the competition."[7]

There may have been other reasons as well for the show's short run. It may have simply shown up too early in the decade for most viewers. As Stark has observed, Americans in 1964 were still in mourning over the loss of a beloved president and awash in memories of the Camelot years of the Kennedy White House. They were also being encouraged to rally around the ideals of Kennedy's successor, Lyndon Johnson, as he envisioned a Great Society of equal rights, jobs, and housing for all citizens and enacted sweeping social legislation aimed at benefiting the nation's poor, especially in the inner cities. Most of the nation still felt strong ties of affection and loyalty toward their national leaders. (It has even been suggested that, especially in the early years of the Johnson White House, the strong Texas twang and mannerisms of the president and his wife, Lady Bird, with their resemblance to the beloved Clampetts, may have served to endear them to the millions of Americans who were watching *The Beverly Hillbillies* every week and turning it into such a popular show.) It would take a few more years of presidential deception and other national shocks to prepare audiences for any major attempts at political satire.

Perhaps there was also a certain American unwillingness to watch a show that had originated in Britain, with its ultra-British host, offering its irreverent views of America. The "British invasion" may have arrived, but not on television. The lack of British presence on the small screen is particularly significant in retrospect when one considers the ubiquity of British talent in every other medium of popular culture throughout the 1960s. The most overwhelming influence was in the world of popular music, with the phenomenal success of the Beatles, The Rolling Stones, and other British rock stars. The fashion scene was falling under the spell of the Carnaby Street styles of "swinging London," followed by the psychedelic outfits and Edwardian attire associated with the flower-child culture and Eastern religion that showed up on the Beatles album covers and musical arrangements (and has been parodied so thoroughly in Mike Myers's *Austin Powers* films). American theatergoers in the 1960s were becoming familiar with the works of outstanding contemporary British playwrights such as Robert Bolt, Harold Pinter, John Osborne, Peter Shaffer, and Tom Stoppard, as well as the productions of the revolutionary British director Peter Brook. Some of the most popular Broadway musicals of the time, *Camelot* and *My Fair Lady*, at least seemed British, while almost every season included some genuine British musical imports, such as *Oliver; Half a Sixpence; Oh What a Lovely War; Stop the World—I Want to Get Off;* and *The Roar of the Greasepaint, The Smell of the Crowd.* One of the most popular and admired comic productions on Broadway, *Beyond the Fringe,* was the work of four brilliant young comic writers and performers from Cambridge and Oxford Universities—Dudley Moore, Peter Cook, Alan Bennett, and Jonathan Miller. The Broadway stage was populated by a host of famous talent from the British Isles, such as Alec Guinness, Albert Finney, Paul Scofield, Alec

McCowen, Julie Andrews, Anthony Newley, John Gielgud, Cyril Ritchard, Eileen Atkins, Joan Plowright, John Mills, Beatrice Lillie, Margaret Leighton, Irene Worth, Roddy McDowall, Vivien Leigh, Nicol Williamson, Glenda Jackson, Angela Lansbury, and a genuine superstar at the time, with two major successes in *Camelot* and *Hamlet*, Richard Burton. It is telling that Burton lost the Tony Award for Leading Actor in a Play in 1964 because he, appearing in *Hamlet*, was competing with two other actors from Great Britain: Albert Finney in John Osborne's *Luther* and Alec Guinness in Sidney Michaels's *Dylan*—three actors and three playwrights from the British Empire.

Meanwhile, Hollywood was also treating American audiences to the British experience. The decade had begun with one of the masterpieces of the British director Alfred Hitchcock, the brilliant thriller *Psycho*. It was followed by an array of Oscar-winners and other hit films with British characters or settings: *Lawrence of Arabia, Tom Jones, Becket, Mary Poppins, Alfie, Georgy Girl, Darling, Doctor Dolittle, The Lion in Winter, Oliver, My Fair Lady, Blow-Up, The Prime of Miss Jean Brodie, A Man for All Seasons*, as well as the Beatles films, *A Hard Day's Night* and *Help*, and, of course, the James Bond films. Some of the biggest Hollywood stars of the decade were imports from Great Britain: Julie Andrews, Audrey Hepburn, Peter O'Toole, Albert Finney, Rex Harrison, Julie Christie, Richard Harris, Lynn and Vanessa Redgrave, Maggie Smith, Peter Sellers, Michael Caine, Sean Connery, Hayley Mills, Alan Bates, to name only a few.

Even in the realm of the gossip columnists, the biggest story of the decade revolved around the adulterous affair and subsequent stormy marriage of two natives of Great Britain, Elizabeth Taylor and Richard Burton. Meanwhile, the media followed the Beatles to India for transcendental meditation and chronicled the wild lifestyles of the fashion model Twiggy and the other habitués of swinging London. The American public was fascinated with all that was coming out of England in the sixties. But practically none of the colorful world of British pop culture showed up in the television programming of the time. And apparently British satire was particularly unwelcome.

By 1967, however, the very medium that had been providing a steady diet of escapist fare was now, by sheer volume of news reports, forcing Americans to face some harsh information from the outside world. The network news, which after President Kennedy's assassination had been expanded from fifteen minutes to half an hour, provided images of violent social disturbance on a nightly basis. From the civil rights struggle came the images of police dogs, fire hoses, and bullets turned on nonviolent marchers and peaceful protestors demanding the right to vote or equal access to schools and other public facilities. From the inner cities came pictures of burning buildings and lootings as the impoverished and unemployed inhabitants cried out for better housing, schools, jobs, police protection, and other goods and services so readily available in the suburbs. On the steps of college administration buildings could be seen mobs of students protesting against the military draft system and joining their fellow students in other countries in questioning the entire capitalistic order. From San Francisco's Haight-Ashbury to the farmland-turned-festival site of Woodstock, New York, the music, drugs, and naked bodies of the counterculture shocked the nation. Even more disturbing was the television footage from Chicago, the arrests and the "shoot-to-kill" order of Mayor Richard Daley as thousands of protestors surrounded the 1968 Democratic National Convention. From Vietnam came the weekly tallies of the rising death tolls of the nation's young men in combat and pictures of children running from their villages with their skin set on fire by the napalm dropped out of the sky. And late in the decade, once again the unthinkable: the assassinations of Senator Robert Kennedy and Rev. Dr. Martin Luther King, Jr. Were America's television viewers finally ready to see a blending of the news and entertainment in a show with topical humor and political satire?

They were certainly ready for something. In the middle of the network season, on February 5, 1967, CBS introduced *The Smothers Brothers Comedy Hour*, in a time slot opposite NBC's blockbuster *Bonanza*, which was currently enjoying its third season as the #1 show on television. The network was willing to go with such an offbeat program figuring that they had nothing to lose by putting it up against the current ratings-and-share giant and hoping that this type of comedy might appeal to the younger viewers. Their risk paid off. *The Smothers Brothers Comedy Hour* captured a huge audience immediately, ending up in 16th place in the Nielsens in its first season and slipping only to #18 in its second season. But the show's regular attacks on the government and many other ventures into offbeat humor offended many viewers and led to battles with the network and an abrupt cancellation at the end of its third season.

The format of the show was the standard comedy-variety formula. It opened with a monologue by the hosts, combining their music with comic banter. The singing and dancing ensembles, accompanied by the Nelson Riddle Orchestra, provided impressive production numbers. Musical and comedy guests appeared regularly. The supporting cast and writers included some major musical talent, such as Mason Williams, Jennifer Warnes, and John Hartford, and up-and-coming comedy talent such as Sally Struthers, Don Novello, Rob Reiner, and Steve Martin.

The hosts of the new variety show seemed innocent enough. Tom and Dick Smothers were clean-cut folksingers in the mold of the currently popular Kingston Trio and the Chad Mitchell Trio. Their previous stand-up performances had not been known for any strong political bent. In the musical duet that always began the show, Tom played the guitar and seemed a bit clueless, frequently making foolish observations, tripping over his words, and forgetting (or changing) the lyrics and melodies of the songs they were singing. Dick played the bass and tried to maintain a calm and pleasant demeanor as Tom kept interrupting each number with inappropriate remarks. Their major running joke was simply a play on sibling rivalry, with each one saying to the other, "Mom always liked you best."

However, these two clean-cut young men were secretly more in the mold of other folksingers of the period: Bob Dylan; Joan Baez; Odetta; Pete Seeger; and Peter, Paul, and Mary, as well as others whose songs arose to announce that "the times, they are a changin'." Folk music, with its long tradition of social criticism, was becoming quite popular in mainstream circles, and, perhaps more than any other technique, *The Smothers Brothers Comedy Hour* used folk music and its practitioners as its primary vehicle for satirical commentary. The Smothers Brothers preferred to invite musical guests who represented the counterculture, groups such as The Jefferson Airplane, Buffalo Springfield, and Simon and Garfunkel, for example.

As the show began its second season in the fall of 1967, CBS generated considerable publicity by inviting on the show the folksinger Pete Seeger, whose antiestablishment songs had caused him to be boycotted from network radio and television since 1950. For the taping of the show Seeger performed his composition "Waist Deep in the Big Muddy," a song about a World War II military leader who led his patrol into a deep river and caused many of the men, including himself, to drown. Seeger intended the song as a parable of what he considered the stubborn and misguided policies of President Lyndon Johnson, who was sending American troops into disaster in Vietnam; the song ended with the refrain, "and the big fool says to push on." CBS Standards and Practices ordered the number cut from the show. Such direct censorship created considerable controversy in industry circles, major publicity in the press, and fierce battles between the Smothers Brothers and the network. In February, as proof of the network's dedication to free speech, Seeger was invited back on the show, where he was allowed to sing an entire medley of antiwar songs, including the one that had been cut earlier. In David Marc's account of the incident, however, one can sense how controversial such a performance remained for many in Middle America:

> Though many reluctant CBS affiliates had been embarrassed into carrying the segment by the publicity that the censorship incident had generated, the network's Detroit affiliate WJBK, owned by the Storer Broadcasting Company, saw fit to turn off the sound during the last verse of "Big Muddy" on the night of the telecast.[8]

Other musical guests created similar controversy. For the first show of their third season, the brothers planned to include a performance by Harry Belafonte (by then a major spokesperson for the civil rights and anti-war movements) of a song called "Don't Stop the Carnival." As Belafonte sang the calypso song, singing, "Carnival's an American bacchanal," the screen showed images of the previous summer's Democratic National Convention, with the violent confrontations between the Chicago police and anti-war demonstrators outside the convention hall and the rounding up of journalists inside the hall. CBS, however, cut the five-minute segment. Hal Himmelstein describes the bizarre outcome of the network's action:

> To fill the dead air created by the CBS cut, Tom and Dick attempted to insert a studio audience "question and answer" segment they had shot, but CBS rejected that plan and instead aired the show in its shortened version. Adding insult to injury, CBS, with the five-minute gap to fill, sold the time to Republican presidential candidate Richard Nixon.[9]

Later in the season, on March 2, 1969, the antiwar activist Joan Baez's performance on the show included a song dedicated to her husband, David Harris, who had recently been sentenced to three years in prison for draft evasion. This incident was recalled at the end of the show's run in a commentary in *TV Guide*, which asked: "Shall a network be required to provide time for a Joan Baez to pay tribute to her draft-evading husband while hundreds of thousands of viewers in the households of men fighting and dying in Vietnam look on in shocked resentment?"[10] Even in an era when matters of major political and moral consequence on a national scale were being examined, the image of the family gathered around the television hearth was once again invoked as the appropriate context for judging the content of television entertainment.

Besides the music, the sketches on the show, from the very outset, were built on the anti-establishment humor of the stand-up comics and avant-garde theater of the times, with special criticism of the Vietnam War. A recurring sketch on the series, called "Share a Little Tea with Goldie," featured a stoned hippie, played by the avant-garde comedian Leigh French, offering her comments about the joys and problems of marijuana and other recreational drugs and some off-color jokes as well. She typically employed terms with double meanings, so that the word "roaches" would have one meaning for the older generation among the viewers and another for the younger viewers. In the second season one of the new breed of hip comedians, David Steinberg, presented a mock sermonette with an irreverent version of the story of Moses and the burning bush, which prompted the highest amount of negative viewer mail in the show's history. One of the most popular features of the show was the weekly satirical "editorial" provided by the comedian Pat Paulsen. During the summer run of the series in the tense election year of 1968, Paulsen announced that he was beginning his presidential campaign, although he also informed everyone, "If nominated I will not run, and if elected I will not serve." CBS, claiming that they feared demands for equal time from all the legitimate candidates, would not let the segment run until after the November elections.

For Tom and Dick the struggle with the network censors became a matter of intense personal and artistic significance. They opened their second season by singing a song entitled "We're Still Here," acknowledging that they had received numerous complaints from viewers and several reprimands from the network censors. By the third season relations between the brothers and the network executives had become severely strained. Eventually Tom and Dick requested a copy of the CBS Standards and Practices policies and demanded that CBS put in writing any objections they had to any of the material to be taped for the show. On its part CBS promised its concerned affiliate stations that they would make the tape of the next Sunday night's show available by the previous Wednesday or Thursday.

By January 1969, in their third season, *The Smothers Brothers Comedy Hour* had dropped out of the top 40 in the Nielsen ratings, and they were in constant conflict with the network officials, sometimes ignoring the objections of the Standards and Practices office and airing unapproved material. Finally, in April 1969, when a tape of the upcoming show did not arrive at CBS's headquarters in time for the affiliate review, CBS used the technical policy violation to cancel the show, which was proving to be too much of a headache. Even though, shortly after the announcement of the cancellation, the program won the Emmy for Outstanding Writing in Comedy, Variety, or Music, the show ended its run in June 1969. CBS replaced it with a comedy-variety program with a distinctly different approach, *Hee Haw.*

The Smothers Brothers sued CBS for breach of contract. The court found in favor of the brothers, declaring that the network's response to the delayed delivery of the tape was merely an excuse to cancel a troublesome series. However, while the court decision seems to indict CBS for censorship, it is undeniable that the show seems to have alienated a large contingent of viewers, as evidenced by the large amount of negative mail and the significant drop in the third season's ratings. Apparently viewers were still not enthusiastic about satire in prime time.

Meanwhile, another variety show with topical satire had shown up in prime time. In September 1967, NBC had run a special presentation of a show called *Rowan and Martin's Laugh-In*, which garnered a huge audience along with considerable critical praise, and, at the end of the season, an Emmy Award for Outstanding Musical or Variety Special. In the following January the show premiered as a regular series and was an instant sensation for the struggling network. (Except for *Bonanza*, NBC had managed to get only two or three shows among the top 20 in the ratings each season throughout the 1960s.) Finally, something with a satirical attitude got the attention of the country's viewers. *Rowan and Martin's Laugh-In* shot to the top of the ratings, enjoying the #1 spot for two seasons and a solid run of five years, during which it was awarded the Emmy Award for Outstanding Musical or Variety Series twice, along with several other Emmys for Outstanding Writing and Directing.

Laugh-In managed to take various elements of *That Was the Week That Was* and *The Smothers Brothers Comedy Hour* and throw them into a daring mix that delighted its viewers while still managing to be topical. It remains a vivid time capsule of the flower-child era, with its psychedelic sets and the hairstyles, miniskirts, and hip-Brit Carnaby Street fashions of the cast. The show's title was a reference to the "love-ins" of the period, the free-form celebrations and protests of the hippies and others in the counterculture, covered extensively in the media, especially in the previous summer in San Francisco, 1967's "summer of love."

The most exciting feature of *Laugh-In*, however, was its brand-new format. The show was filmed and then edited into a frenetic series of quick sketches, one-liners, and cameo appearances that kept viewers in stitches. Even when a routine lasted more than a minute, the pace of the dialogue was rapid. Each show began with a swift comic interchange between the two hosts, Dan Rowan and Dick Martin, which, in its nonsensical format, usually included many sexual double entendres and satirical commentary on political issues. Regularly recurring segments of each episode included "The Party," a minute or two during which the groovy music would pause and a guest would look directly into the camera and deliver a one-liner; a Graffiti Wall covered with other one-liners; and, at the end of each show, the Joke Wall, which featured windows out of which the cast members would pop to deliver yet more one-liners. The subject matter of almost all of these brief sayings would be naughty sexual humor, political commentary, or, sometimes, complete nonsense.

Another distinctive feature of the show—and surely one reason for its popularity—was the talent of the large ensemble. *Laugh-In* introduced many gifted performers to its viewers, including some genuine stars such as Goldie Hawn and Lily Tomlin. Goldie Hawn appeared in the shows as a bikini-clad go-go dancer with messages written on her body with Day-Glo body paint. Often, in her persona as the ultimate ditzy blonde, Hawn would attempt to make announcements that she usually screwed up, or she would ask one of the celebrity guests a particularly silly question. A big hit with the viewers and the critics, Hawn stayed with the show for three seasons and might have stayed longer had not destiny intervened. During the show's second season Hawn appeared in a major Hollywood film, *Cactus Flower*. Her performance was honored with the 1969 Academy Award for Best Supporting Actress, and Goldie began her ascent to Hollywood stardom.

Lily Tomlin was the show's other major discovery. The characters she developed for her one-woman sketches were strikingly original, destined for comic immortality. Tomlin could be Edith Ann, a precocious, spunky, and opinionated little girl who spoke to the audience while seated in a rocking chair that was much too large for her. Or she could appear as the Tasteful Lady, dressed and coiffed for an afternoon of bridge or shopping, complete with white gloves, to express her disapproval of everyone else's lax behavior. Tomlin's most famous character was Ernestine, the telephone operator who relished the power she wielded as a representative of the Bell Telephone monopoly. She answered every inquiry with sarcasm and responded to every complaint with threats. She would listen in on private conversations. One of her chief amusements was to call celebrities, especially President Nixon, whom she addressed as "Milhaus," or Frank Sinatra, to harass them for their exorbitant telephone bills or to flirt with them. Ernestine was a bundle of odd physical quirks, with her high-pitched nasal voice, pinched nose, habits of licking her lips with her tongue or snorting when she laughed, and regularly reaching down into her décolletage to adjust her brassiere. Ernestine became so popular that the Bell Telephone Company actually offered Tomlin a job as their spokesperson in commercials. Tomlin, seeing this as a compromise of her artistic integrity and political views about mega-corporations, turned down their offer. Having joined the cast in its third season, Tomlin stayed with the show until it was cancelled, moving on to a brilliant career in live concerts, television specials, films, and award-winning one-woman shows on Broadway.

There were many guest stars on particular episodes. Some, such as Sammy Davis, Jr., and his fellow "rat packer" Peter Lawford, would be involved in several of the sketches in a given show. The more distinctive feature, however, was the set of brief cameo appearances by major guest stars, who would appear on the screen to utter one sentence, such as "Sock It to Me" or "You Bet Your Bippy" or other nonsensical or naughty phrases. Some of the legends of television comedy—Milton Berle, Sid Caesar, Jack Benny—showed up in cameos, as did some of Hollywood's old-timers—Edward G. Robinson, Orson Welles, George Raft, Otto Preminger—as well as many current celebrities from film and television—Jack Lemmon, Sally Field, Michael Caine, Flip Wilson, Sonny and Cher, Peter Sellers, etc.

On the one hand, the pervasive mood of the show was frivolous and almost childlike, reveling in nonsense and play for its own sake, with some of the oldest shtick in the archives of vaudeville. On the other hand, it could also be naughty, with the sexual humor, references to marijuana, and irreverent approach to religion, government, and other guardians of social mores.

Amid the foolishness, however, the writers inserted a regular dose of political satire. One weekly feature, "Laugh-In Looks at the News," provided commentary on newsworthy political developments of the past week, with particular attention to the civil rights struggle and the war in Vietnam. Another regular feature was the presentation of the Flying Fickle Finger of Fate Award. Rowan and Martin themselves would "give the finger" to a major corporation or the Pentagon, Congress, or other federal agency that had recently committed some outrageous blunder. Many of the graffiti or comments during "The Party" would have a political edge. One particularly memorable episode included an interview with the conservative political pundit William Buckley, who admitted that he had agreed to appear on the show only after they promised to fly him to the taping in an airplane with "two right wings." In fact, a good number of the political figures who made cameo appearances tended toward the right of the political spectrum. John Wayne and Billy Graham joined in the fun, and even Richard Nixon, during his 1968 presidential campaign, came on the show to ask in mock disbelief, "Sock it to ME?"

The show managed to prove the dictum of another icon of the 1960s, Mary Poppins, that "a spoonful of sugar helps the medicine go down." The decidedly anti-establishment tone of *Laugh-In*'s comedy came wrapped in so much silliness that it tasted good to Middle Americans. There was a flower-child festivity about the whole event. The visual trickery and hectic pace of the show also validated the insight of another 1960s pop theoretician, Marshall McLuhan; on *Laugh-In* the medium was indeed the message. As Himmelstein has commented:

> The program became a frenzied hour of tomfoolery that reflected the confusing mosaic of everyday experience of the late 1960s and early 1970s, a period in which events and personal relationships seemed far from the ordered state of things as reflected in the suburban middle landscape of the 1950s and early 1960s.[11]

Were one to look only at these variety shows, one might conclude that political satire was doomed to very limited success in prime time. With one show lasting less than two full seasons, another one cancelled by nervous network executives, and only one show managing to insert some political satire into a hellzapoppin' mix of vaudeville shtick, television did not seem the proper vehicle for political and social commentary. However, as time would prove, television satire had simply not found its proper format. What the variety show could not accomplish, the domestic comedy would provide, and, in the process, it would change television comedy for years to come—perhaps forever.

· 7 ·

KEEPING IT IN THE FAMILY

In 1968 the television producer Norman Lear had produced a pilot for ABC, based on a popular British sitcom, *Till Death Do Us Part*, about a bigot who is constantly at odds with his family, especially his liberal son-in-law. Lear set his comedy in a working-class neighborhood in Queens, in the home of a belligerent dock foreman (and part-time cabdriver) named Archie Bunker and his loveable but dim-witted wife, Edith, who shared their living quarters with their proto-feminist daughter, Gloria, and her liberal-humanist graduate student husband, Mike Stivic. Archie was quite outspoken in his prejudice against minorities, view of antiwar protestors as unpatriotic cowards, and opposition to welfare programs, women's rights, and everything else he saw as destroying the America in which he had grown up. He was also a tyrant in his home, insensitive and demanding toward his wife and loudly critical of the behavior and opinions of his daughter and son-in-law. At first glance Archie Bunker was hardly a laughing matter.

Indeed, when ABC presented the pilot to test audiences in January 1969, the show inspired a good deal of negative response. Lear produced another pilot for ABC, but it met with the same disapproval from sample audiences in March, and ABC, considering the show too controversial, passed on the project. Lear then took the pilot to CBS, whose new president, Robert Wood, was looking for more daring material to attract younger viewers. Accounts of the response at CBS vary. Richard Adler claims that the reactions of the test audiences in March 1970 were "as negative at CBS as they had been at ABC" and that even the network's chairman, Bill Paley, had serious reservations about it; Gerard Jones maintains that the show's pilots tested much more successfully at CBS, while Steven Stark implies that the testing at CBS went better.[1] Jones refers to the remarks of *Variety*'s critic Les Brown who:

... speculated that the difference between the ABC and CBS tests might have been due to the different outlooks of New Yorkers and Angelenos but even more likely to the six months [sic] that had passed between tests. As the Nixon Administration wore on and the Vietnam War showed no signs of ending, as ethnic movements grew more militant, as Spiro Agnew began sounding off, as feminism hit mainstream America, the national debate kept getting louder.[2]

Whether or not the test audiences or other CBS executives liked the show, historians agree that Bob Wood was the show's most enthusiastic supporter and ordered it to be added to the prime-time schedule in mid-season as a replacement for *To Rome with Love*, a situation comedy with unsatisfactory ratings. The show premiered at 9:30 on Tuesday night January 12, 1971. Expecting considerable complaints from viewers, the network assigned extra operators at the switchboard and suggested to all the affiliates that they do the same. As it turned out, not that many people watched the show and there was very little viewer response of any kind. As the weeks went along, the show's ratings and shares offered no significant improvement on *To Rome With Love's* performance for the network. The new series seemed headed for cancellation.

Robert Wood, however, refused to give up on the show. *All in the Family* came along just when he was revamping CBS's prime-time philosophy. Wood had started his television career in sales for the radio and television stations owned by CBS in Los Angeles and then moved on to run CBS's five owned-and-operated television stations in Los Angeles, New York, Chicago, Philadelphia, and Saint Louis. His sales research revealed that while CBS continued to enjoy its perennial position with the best overall ratings in the country, its local stations and affiliates were not the #1 stations in the major cities. And while they enjoyed a very loyal following among the 50-year-old-and-older demographic, they were not the favorite of the 18 to 49-year-old viewers, who were more valuable to advertisers. Other research confirmed this analysis; NBC had already figured this out and was targeting the young, urban viewers more aggressively. For the 1970–1971 season Wood took the bold move of canceling certain highly rated shows that research showed were appealing primarily to the older, rural, and less affluent viewers, including the long-running (but expensive) variety shows of Red Skelton and Jackie Gleason and popular rural sitcoms such as *Petticoat Junction* and *Gomer Pyle, U.S.M.C.* He was eager to replace them with shows that would be big hits for the younger, more educated, consumers.

All in the Family also came along at a critical time in American political history. Richard P. Adler describes the national mood at the beginning of the 1970s:

This was, above all, the time when the country's agony over the Vietnam War was at its height. The withdrawal of U.S. combat troops had begun in the summer of 1969, but the pace was far too slow to appease the growing number of Americans opposed to the war at home. In November more than a quarter-million protestors gathered in Washington, the largest antiwar demonstration in U.S. history. The following spring, President Nixon announced the invasion of neutral Cambodia. In the demonstrations that followed, four Kent State students were killed by National Guardsmen and more than 100 colleges and universities across the country were shut down. As 1970 came to a close, Lt. William Calley's court martial for the My Lai massacre was about to begin; while out in California, the murder trial of Charles Manson and his followers was coming to an end.[3]

Other issues that would emerge within a year or so would be the leaking of the Pentagon papers to the media, the Watergate hearings, Nixon's trip to China, the aftermath of the Stonewall riots that brought the gay liberation movement into the public eye, the Attica prison riot with its revelation of racism and violence in U.S. jails, the rising tide of feminism represented by the publication of *MS* and other feminist journals, and the eventual resignation of President Nixon. There was much to talk about in 1971. But could it be funny?

In the opinion of many experts the answer was "yes" and "no." Unlike the viewers, the critics paid a great deal of attention to the show immediately. As Jack Gould wrote in *The New York Times*, "rarely has a series set so many reviewers . . . dashing to the memo pads to record their feelings."[4] But critical opinion varied considerably. Gould called the show an "attempt to bring the disease [of bigotry] out into the open with the aim, one hopes, of applying the test of corrective recognition and humor."[5] But another critic for *The New York Times*, Stephanie Harrington, said that the show was "kind of like wishing for a little more frankness in political dialogue and getting your wish in the form of Spiro Agnew." She asked, "Just what social purpose is being served? By making the expression of hostility more commonplace, do we really exorcise it? Or do we, in fact, make it more acceptable?"[6] An early review in *Variety* called the show "the best tv comedy since the original 'The Honeymooners.' It's the best casting since Sgt. Bilko's squad. It should be the biggest hit since 'Laugh-In.' . . . Prime element is audacity, generally a benchmark of really imaginative work."[7] The reviewer in the *Christian Science Monitor* praised it as "the first major social departure for this commercial genre."[8] Critics from the black community, who might be expected to be concerned about white bigotry as comedy, offered differing opinions as well. Whitney Young, writing in the African American publication *The Los Angeles Sentinel*, described the show as "filling the public airwaves with hate-filled epithets" and considered it "irresponsible to air a show at a time like this when our na-tion is polarized and torn by racism.[9] His colleague in the same publication, Pamela Haynes, however, offered a positive appraisal:

> The paramount thing about "All in the Family" is that for the first time, instead of trying to pass off an expensively groomed and immaculately coiffed Doris Day as "the typical American housewife" and a distinguished, suave and ever so toler-ant Robert [Young] as everyone's father, they have presented a fat, ignorant, angry middle-aged pig who swears at his wife, belches at the table and gets choked up over sugary tributes on greeting cards. In other words, Archie Bunker is real.
>
> Far from protesting, members of the minorities slandered by Archie should rejoice at this non-cosmetized portrait of the "master race."[10]

The reaction of the industry, however, was undividedly enthusiastic. In May, after less than four months on the air, All in the Family was awarded Emmy Awards for Outstanding Comedy Series, Outstanding New Series, and Outstanding Actress in a Comedy Series for Jean Stapleton, who played Edith.

It was the viewing public that still needed to be convinced. The show's rat-ings near the end of the first season were around 17 or 18, compared to the 27–29 points for the top-rated shows of the season. Janet Staiger's accounting is even more vivid. As she describes it, "the estimated number of homes view-ing All in the Family was 10,800,000" while a "typical most-viewed show in early 1971 ran around 20,000,000. Thus, All in the Family secured a viewing audience of only about one-half of the typical most-viewed program."[11] The Emmy awards, however, gave the show some major publicity, and people started watching it during the summer reruns. It became the #1 show in the major markets during the summer months. When the fall season began the first episode came in at #12 in the Nielsen ratings. With the second episode the show moved into 1st place, where it remained for the rest of the season.[12] Throughout the 1971–1972 season All in the Family garnered a 50 share on av-erage, sometimes even 60. It would remain in first place for a record-breaking five seasons in a row.[13]

While it was clearly a major hit, much controversy continued to swirl around the character of Archie as a "lovable bigot." Were the viewers watch-ing because they enjoyed seeing someone so clearly prejudiced and stubbornly ill informed get his comeuppance? That certainly seemed to be the intent of the liberal creator of the series. Jack Gould articulated such an interpretation in his summary statement that "the larger lesson is that [Archie] is continually a loser, always a bit more frustrated than he was before" and reported that "some sensitive community groups involving blacks, whites and the clergy" had approved of the program.[14] Carroll O'Connor, who played Archie, also defended the show as an attempt to "exorcise' bigotry. As he put it, "you bring a thing out in the air and look at it and laugh at it, you'll destroy it."[15]

The most public criticism of the show came at the beginning of the second season, in the form of a lengthy article by Laura Z. Hobson, the author of an acclaimed novel about anti-Semitism, *Gentleman's Agreement*. While Hobson recounted many of the negative reactions the show was receiving for its racial and ethnic slurs, she maintained that, in fact, the writers were not allowing Archie to be bigoted enough. Hobson argued that the show, by avoiding the really worst ethnic slurs, actually was sanitizing prejudice, portraying Archie as "your friendly neighborhood bigot" and making such bigotry acceptable. Hobson ultimately declared, "I don't think you can be a bigot and be lovable."[16] Four weeks later Lear responded to what he called Hobson's "novella" in his own article in *The New York Times*. Adler has offered a concise summary of Lear's counterargument:

> He rejected her contention that there is no such thing as a lovable bigot. Most prejudice, he argued, comes not from villains motivated by irrational hatred, but from otherwise good people whose bigotry springs from ignorance and fear. It is Archie's complexity and inconsistency which makes him recognizably human and, therefore representative. . . . Lear also pointed out that Archie's expressions of prejudice were carefully balanced with rebuttals from other members of his family, most often his son-in-law, Mike. It is Mike's statements that consistently make sense, while Archie's convoluted logic is inevitably shown to be false and foolish.[17]

The controversy raged on, only making the series more of a "must-see" for viewers of every ideological stripe. Over the years, while the show's shock value diminished, the series continued to deal with social issues and formerly taboo topics, remaining a viewer favorite for twelve years. The secret of such long-running success cannot lie simply in its topicality and daring satire. Many elements of comic artistry conspired to achieve such popularity. These many features are worth further examination.

The Comedy of Argument

The show's premise allowed for a pattern of dialogue that was often loud and angry, creating a new type of humor in the sitcom genre: the comedy of argument. Or perhaps it is more accurate to say that *All in the Family* returned to the early days of television situation comedy, to the husband-and-wife fights of the Ricardos and the Kramdens that had been replaced by the argument-free discussions and group decision making on *Father Knows Best*, *The Adventures of Ozzie and Harriet*, *The Donna Reed Show*, and the other suburban family sitcoms that were such a prime-time staple in the late 1950s and 1960s. Oddly enough, the only other regular presentation of such comic argument at the time was the "Ed and Eunice" segment on the otherwise congenial *The Carol Burnett Show* (1967–1979). Ed and Eunice, a small-town working-class couple, engaged in frequent sessions of name calling, insults, and screaming matches with each other or with Eunice's Mama, who lived with them. Similarly, on *All in the Family* the patriarch, Archie, played by Carroll O'Connor, regularly berated and belittled his wife, Edith, played by Jean Stapleton, criticized and corrected his daughter, Gloria, played by Sally Struthers, and insulted and argued with his live-in son-in-law, Mike, played by Rob Reiner. The arguments—and the laughs—were constant.

The Blue-collar World

The crowded blue-collar setting of the Bunker household also represented a return to some of the early days of television comedy and the working-class families seen on *The Honeymooners*, *The Life of Riley*, *The Goldbergs*, and *Mama*. The middle-class households of the 1950s suburban comedies had all been headed by professional, college-educated fathers who worked in offices or, in the case of Ozzie Nelson, did not seem to work at all. The networks had found that the comfortable homes of middle-class suburban families—with their up-to-date kitchen appliances and laborsaving devices; the fashionable clothes, jewelry, and hairstyles; and the lawnmowers and automobiles in the garages—provided more appropriate environments for the sales pitches for those very products in the accompanying commercials. Such a portrayal of the suburban domestic paradise inherently precluded any critique of the American way of life.

David Marc's study of *All in the Family* maintains that a return to the lower economic environment was a crucial factor in developing a family sitcom into an instrument for social criticism. The show's drop in social status was accompanied by a distinct discontent on the part of blue-collar Archie Bunker. The earlier working-class families were not as angry as Archie. Marc, for instance, argues that even the hot-tempered Ralph Kramden, with his continuous attempts to get lucky financially, lacked the social resentment of Archie:

> If Ralph Kramden's obsession with get-rich quick schemes at least implied an active faith in the American Dream, Archie Bunker seemed to harbor no such illusions; he just watched television. . . . Whereas the Kramdens were merely the playthings of cruel and ironic gods, the Bunkers were citizens of a neurotic industrial

state. As such, they were caught in a hopeless tangle of social corruption: economic exploitation, racism, sexism, xenophobia, and worse. Gleason's bus driver did not complain that blacks were getting what was rightfully his. Ralph Kramden lived in an atemporal vacuum where it was just him, the money, and Fate; now if only Fate would finally give him a break. In contrast, Archie shlepped the baggage of mass man through an incomprehensible clutter of social contexts.[18]

As a blue-collar worker, Archie Bunker could be immediately identified as a member of the group President Nixon was calling "the silent majority," those loyal Americans who were not raising their voices in protest against the war in Vietnam or demonstrating to achieve their "rights" as women, gays, or ethnic minorities. They were people with a firm, even if somewhat unreflective, belief in the American way and the value of hard work. But had their time passed? Marc describes Archie as one of those whom social progress has passed by:

> Archie, the enemy of liberal secular humanist values, emerges as a pathetically displaced person. Everything he knows to be right is wrong. . . . He has worked hard and has done what was expected of him. But where is his reward? Being given away by the government to racial strangers, sexual deviants, and ideological insurgents.[19]

Classic Foolishness

The comic presentation of a strongly opinionated man whose attitudes could be so easily contradicted by factual information taps into some of the most classical satire of the theatrical tradition, readily found in the works of Aristophanes, Plautus, Shakespeare, Molière, Sheridan, and Shaw. Especially as the show continued from season to season, Archie resembled more and more the stock comic figure of the foolish and tyrannical parent of classical comedy, as becomes clear in Adler's description of the character:

> Although the shock value of Archie's bigotry probably stimulated some of the initial interest in the series, it cannot account for its sustained popularity. In fact, bigotry was never really the primary focus of either the program or the character of Archie. . . . In the hands of a less gifted actor, he could have quickly become grating and tiresome. But the energy Carroll O'Connor brought to the role redeemed Archie, even in his most stubborn and wrongheaded moments. When he is on the screen, it is he who dominates, giving orders, delivering opinions, trading wisecracks, trying—and often failing—to stay in control of what is happening to him. . . . Archie is a conservative in the strictest sense of the word. He not only supports the *status quo*, he longs

to return to a time when things were simpler. He is unable to accept change because he is incapable of changing himself.[20]

The plots of most of the episodes were built around the exposure of Archie's worldview as incorrect. When, for example, a black family, the Jeffersons, moves in next door, Archie's opposition to them is considered by Mike and Gloria to be another case of injustice and ignorance, to be attacked by arguments, while innocent, good-hearted Edith simply finds it contrary to common sense and her own experience when she gets to know them in the practical day-to-day interaction of neighbors. Frequently, it would be the instinctive goodness of Edith's innocent observations, more than the ideological rantings of Mike, that would reveal the error of Archie's ways of thinking. Sometimes the inaccuracy of Archie's attitudes would be shown by the behavior of some of the very people he disliked. His prejudices were contradicted by the obvious intelligence, professional achievements, and personal character of the African Americans and other minorities who visited the house (especially the wicked wit of Sammy Davis, Jr., who, as himself, came to the house to pick up a briefcase he had left in Archie's cab) or by the nonstereotypical demeanor of Mike and Gloria's gay friends or the courage and honesty of the draft resister invited by Mike to the Bunker family's Christmas dinner, whose antiwar views were defended by Archie's buddy whose son had died in battle. In such regular revelation of his foolishness, Archie joins the company of Shakespeare's petty-official Malvolio and the melancholy philosopher Jacques or Molière's misers, misanthropes, and hypochondriacs—trapped in their illusions and resisting all efforts of their loved ones to liberate them.

Visual Comic Technique

All of this verbal buffoonery was delivered with facial expressions and tics that added considerably to the comedy. Carroll O'Connor had come from the world of the theater, but he had a face that was made for television. His wincing and groaning at the mention of any liberal public figure or progressive idea; his whining when he had to "explain" anything to Edith or "Meathead" (Mike); his bug-eyed and clenched-teeth countenance when angered; his nose in the air when he was convinced of the righteousness of his views—all were part of O'Connor's comic arsenal, and they worked to his distinct advantage in televised close-ups. (O'Connor won the Emmy Award for Outstanding Lead Actor in a Comedy Series an unprecedented four times.) If his words did not reveal him to be a fool, his excessive emotional reactions made the point.

Transgressive Comedy

All in the Family's writers introduced a new element into television comedy that took the art of satire into the realm of the transgressive. The most shocking feature of the show was the number of racial epithets that sprinkled Archie's conversation. As might be expected, such language led Lear into frequent confrontations with the network's Standards and Practices people and prompted many letters to the show. (Actually, Lear has said that he found the censors even more upset about the sound of the flushing toilet, a frequent occurrence in the Bunker household where one bathroom served all.) Archie would matter-of-factly refer to "jungle bunnies," "spades," "colored," "spics," "chinks," "Japs," "micks," and "hebes," as well as "pansies" and "queers." Mike and Gloria would always protest, while Edith would writhe in discomfort or simply appear not to notice the slur, but Archie persisted in applying terms that had been considered standard titles in the all-white blue-collar world of his younger days. And viewers would giggle like naughty schoolchildren at the forbidden behavior.

Lovable Characters

However foolish, shocking, or outrageous he may have been, Archie Bunker was also the object of enormous affection, on the part of his wife and daughter and even, begrudgingly, from his son-in-law. The frequent displays of affection from Edith and Gloria inspired a certain degree of warm feelings for Archie among the viewers. In fact, Archie could be likeable, even lovable. He took his responsibilities seriously and worked hard to put food on the table and a roof over their heads. Marc observes that Archie's breadwinner role was

> a relevant reminder to any high-minded middle-class viewers who may be watching that a contempt for hardhatism does not change the fact that workers like Archie are the people who make civilization and culture possible. We do not see Archie punching the clock or hoisting boxes, day-in and day-out, expending his life. We do, however, see Mike reading and otherwise preparing for an academic career under the roof that Archie has been paying off for so many years with his sweat and diligence. Mike's notorious energy at the dinner table comically epitomizes the situation, as Archie watches his wages . . . disappear into the bottomless pit of his "Meathead" son-in-law.[21]

Archie also loved his wife and daughter. Even though he habitually ignored Edith, found her conversation inane, and frequently ordered her to "stifle" herself, it becomes gradually clear to the viewers that Archie was at a loss in the face of the unfamiliar demands of husbandly affection and duty, especially in times of crisis in Edith's life, such as her discovery of her breast cancer, the onset of her menopause, and her experience as a victim of an attempted rape in the family living room. And Edith was clearly in love with Archie. Marc points out that Edith was "devoid of the resentment and rage that gave Alice Kramden the courage to withstand and combat the insufferable bluster of Ralph."[22] Instead, dedicating herself to Archie's every need, Edith seemed content, blissfully dismissing Archie's tantrums, and, at times, almost idiotically cheerful—a downscale mix of Gracie Allen and Harriet Nelson. And yet, thanks to her daughter Gloria's instruction and encouragement and her own hidden brainpower, Edith emerged over the years as a woman who frequently stumbled onto the very truth that seemed to be eluding Archie. Many episodes also concluded with Archie and Gloria embracing and, with all their disagreements, professing their love for one another.

Moreover, as Adler points out, viewers were given plenty of opportunity to see "the vulnerability beneath the bravado so that we recognize that Archie's tirades and put-downs are, as Lear claimed, motivated not by hatred but by a need to maintain his identity in a relentlessly changing world.[23]

Complex Characters

The satire was especially effective and appealing because of the balance of the admirable and the ridiculous in each of the characters. Archie was a bigot but he was also hardworking, patriotic, and a responsible husband and father. Edith was good-hearted but a bit of a doormat. Gloria's feminist protests often morphed into whining, and her desire for self-determination was often at odds with her cherished status as Daddy's Little Girl. Mike's idealism had a way of turning into hostility and self-righteousness. These combinations of character traits often colored the presentation of their opinions and influenced viewer reception. Brooks and Marsh ascribe much of the popularity of the show to this spectrum of viewer reactions:

> Part of its appeal was based on the fact that it could be interpreted in several different ways. Liberals and intellectuals could cite it as an example of the absurdity of prejudice, while another large segment of the viewing audience could agree with Archie's attitudes and enjoy him as their kind of guy.[24]

The Family Setting

Finally, all of these elements worked so well because the show was about a family. In fact, Norman Lear had originally become interested in developing

the show primarily because of his own family background. Lear once described the impetus for the show as follows:

> What inspired me was simply reading that somebody had done a show in which
> a father and son-in-law were arguing, were totally apart—not just a generation
> gap, but were divided on every ideological issue, and fought about race, religion,
> politics, economics, up and down the line. That was all I need to excite me, be-
> cause I had lived that with my father.[25]

And, as Adler maintains, the approach to all of the controversial issues on the
program—not just bigotry but many other topics (homosexuality, impotence,
menopause, cancer, rape, unemployment, etc.) that had not been treated in
television comedy before—was to treat them "not as abstractions, but in terms
of their meaning for the lives of a recognizable American family."[26]

Moreover, the setting was a particularly appropriate one for the portrayal of
such politically and socially explosive topics. The hot issues of the 1970s were
literally coming home, and television needed to portray that the urgency of
these issued stemmed directly from their impact on the family. As Adler ex-
presses it:

> Prior to *All in the Family*, social problems were portrayed as something that hap-
> pened "out there" in the public arena. By contrast, home was a refuge and the
> family was sacrosanct, the realm of the purely domestic. Lear ignored these con-
> ventions and portrayed the family as a political area—as *the* political arena. The
> conception was audacious and powerfully dramatic. But it was also true to life:
> the crises of the 1960s were acted out in living rooms across the country. Perhaps
> not since the Civil War had America experienced a conflict that had cut through
> families in such an intimate way.[27]

One issue that increased the fervor of the debate over the program's social
impact occurred when, at the beginning of its second season in September,
1971, *All in the Family* was moved to 8:00 on Saturday nights, a traditional time
for family viewing, including a lot of children in the audience. One study of
the show showed that *All in the* Family had the largest child audience of any
regular TV show.[28] Hobson emphasized this point among her many objections to the show, berating the producers for exposing millions of viewers "and
their children, week after week to bigotry . . . particularly since more children
than ever will be watching this season."[29] Later, in 1975, the show was moved
to 9:00 p.m. in accordance with a new policy called Family Viewing Time.
Under considerable pressure from the FCC at the time, broadcasters agreed to
follow a policy in which programs broadcast before 9:00 p.m. should be suitable for viewers of all ages. Since Lear refused to "tone down" the program, it

was moved to a later time slot. However, in the fall of 1978, after the federal courts had ruled that such a policy was illegal, *All in the Family* returned to its 8:00 p.m. spot for the rest of its run. In any case, as millions of parents and children watched the show together, Lear and his writers wrapped their presentation of taboo subjects and their satirical comments on social issues in an ultimately reassuring message about the family. As Adler describes it:

> The series repeatedly demonstrated that no matter how great the strain, how heated the argument, the family's bonds of love are stronger. The idea is old-fashioned but appealing. In the final analysis, the series represented an affirmation of the power of the family to endure.[30]

All of these comic techniques worked together to create a rich vehicle for satire. Indeed, many critics hailed it as the first significant attempt to blend satire with the domestic comedy genre. Where the variety show format, for various reasons, had failed, the situation-comedy framework, in this case at least, proved to be a surprisingly successful vehicle for social commentary. In the ongoing story of the Bunker family, Archie emerged as a vivid individual, a recognizable and believable character who embodied and upheld a traditional American political and economic system that included racism, militarism, sexism, and the many other forms of ignorance and injustice that the other televised attempts at satire had also tried to ridicule. As such, he offered a more visible and closer target for comic criticism.

All in the Family ran for eight years (1971–1979) under its original title. At the beginning of the 1979–1980 season, with Sally Struthers and Rob Reiner having left the show, the format of the series changed to something more of a workplace comedy as Archie went into business with a friend, took over his favorite tavern, and named it Archie's Place. With the death of Edith, announced at the beginning of the 1980–81 season, the program became even less of a family comedy. Like other workplace comedies with their ensemble casts, the redesigned show allowed Archie to interact with a wider spectrum of characters with more diverse ethnic backgrounds. *Archie Bunker's Place* ran until 1983, giving Archie a total of twelve years of life on the small screen. During all that time the show continued to enjoy excellent ratings and received numerous awards. Besides O'Connor's four Emmys for Outstanding Lead Actor in a Comedy Series, Jean Stapleton won three Emmys for Outstanding Lead Actress, Rob Reiner won the Outstanding Supporting Actor award twice, and Sally Struthers won Outstanding Supporting Actress once. The show also won numerous Emmys for directing and writing and garnered the Emmy for Outstanding Comedy Series four times. Norman Lear went on to produce many other controversial television comedies. *Maude* (1972–1978) and *The Jeffersons* (1975–1985) were direct spin-offs of *All in the Family*. *Maude*, chronicling the life of Edith's cousin Maude Finley, a liberal suburbanite, was the most daring in its treatment of previously taboo topics such as abortion, menopause, alcoholism, nervous breakdowns, as well as Maude's frequent expressions of ultraliberal political opinions. *The Jeffersons* got considerable comic mileage out of George Jefferson's reverse racism against "Whitey." Lear developed several other successful but less satirical sitcoms featuring mostly African American casts such as *Sanford and Son* (1972–1977), *Good Times* (1974–1979) and *Diff'rent Strokes* (1978–1986), as well as several other experimental comedies. In March 1975 one cultural commentator, describing the omnipresence of Lear's "jokey topicality" in prime time, estimated that one hundred and twenty million Americans watched Norman Lear comedies each week, a total of roughly five billion viewers every year. Clearly Norman Lear had discovered that comedy was the most effective means of exploring diversity, engaging in controversy, and introducing avant-garde attitudes into the homes of America.

Hence, through a decade of trial and error, beginning with the early attempts at social commentary on *That Was the Week That Was*, network producers and writers eventually discovered the formula for political satire that worked in prime time. If America had problems and challenges, most television viewers preferred that they not be addressed by the quasi-intellectual wits, especially the British ones, on *That Was the Week That Was*. The networks, perhaps reflecting a viewer consensus, preferred that the questions not be raised by left-wing folksingers and stand-up comedians on *The Smothers Brothers Comedy Hour*. Social and political criticism became more acceptable when it came wrapped in innocent lunacy and delivered at a rapid-fire pace by the colorful zanies and flower children of *Laugh-In*. But, finally, satire seemed to work best when it was domesticated. Instead of presenting a "Fickle Finger of Fate" award to a prominent politician or an impersonal bureaucracy or corporation, Norman Lear preferred to attack the failures of the American system by illustrating its results in a very specific family who became familiar and beloved guests in American homes. In the usual pattern of all television comedy, even the most important problems facing the nation—and perhaps their solutions as well—were, in fact, "all in the family."

·8·

THERE'S NO PLACE LIKE WORK

Comedy set in a workplace environment had a modest beginning in the early days of television comedy, but it has evolved into a complex genre that has provided some of the most inventive and beloved comedies of their era. Two of the longest running and critically acclaimed series in television history have been workplace comedies. *M*A*S*H* (1972–1983) chronicled life and death in a mobile surgical unit in wartime Korea, while a Boston bar "where everybody knows your name" was the setting for *Cheers* (1982–1993). Even the breakthrough domestic comedy *All in the Family* transformed itself into a popular workplace comedy set in a tavern, called *Archie Bunker's Place*, for its last four seasons (1979–1983). Bob Newhart, Mary Tyler Moore, Candice Bergen, and other major figures in television comedy have found the workplace setting particularly congenial to their talents.

In the early 1950s, when the big hits on the new medium were variety shows and domestic situation comedies, only a few workplace comedies captured much attention, and in retrospect they come across as relatively formulaic. *Our Miss Brooks* (1952–1956) starred the well-known radio and film comedian Eve Arden as a wisecracking high school English teacher constantly threatened by her disgruntled principal while eagerly pursuing the handsome but shy biology teacher. Another sitcom with a high-school setting, *Mr. Peepers*, centered on a shy but loveable science teacher, played by Wally Cox. Besides Cox, the cast also included the notable talents of Jack Warden, Ruth McDevitt, and Arthur O'Connell, and a couple of actors who would go on to major success in television comedy, Tony Randall (*The Odd Couple)* and Marion Lorne (*Bewitched)*. The show enjoyed a three-year run from 1952 to 1955. *Private Secretary* (1953–1957) featured another popular film actress, Ann Sothern, as a secretary who was always involving herself in her boss's personal life while she too searched for Mr. Right. Both of these comedies were moderate successes; *Private Secretary*'s relatively higher ratings may have been due to CBS's airing of the show on alternate Sundays with the much more popular *The Jack Benny Show*. Another show that enjoyed a four-year run during the decade was *The Phil Silvers Show* (1955–1959), which starred the former vaudevillian and Broadway comic as Sergeant Ernie Bilko, a con man in an environment that might be considered a workplace setting, an army base in peacetime. The show usually revolved around Bilko's various moneymaking schemes and not the demands of his job, however, and, while critically admired, it achieved only moderate ratings success. When comparing these four modest hits of the 1950s with the runaway popularity of *I Love Lucy, Your Show of Shows*, and stars such as Milton Berle and Jackie Gleason, it can be said that the workplace comedy did not capture the hearts of television viewers in the Eisenhower era.

The American political climate changed when the 1960 election replaced Dwight and Mamie Eisenhower with a younger, more attractive couple in the White House, John and Jacqueline Kennedy, whose combination of personal glamour and political activism energized the nation. David Marc and Gerard Jones both consider it more than coincidence that the most popular couple to emerge on television in the early 1960s resembled the Kennedys, an attractive, cultured, socially liberal man and woman for the "new frontier," Rob and Laura Petrie, played by the television newcomers Mary Tyler Moore and Dick Van Dyke on *The Dick Van Dyke Show* (1961–1966).[1] Laura was an artistic, college-educated housewife who stayed at home in New Rochelle raising their son while Rob commuted into Manhattan to his job as a comedy writer on a television show. The plots of the series took a new approach to situation comedy by combining the settings of the home and workplace. Such a mix of domestic and professional activity was quite a change from the family comedies of the period. *Father Knows Best, Leave It to Beaver, December Bride, My Three Sons*, and other popular domestic comedies of the era hardly ever showed the breadwinner-father at work; *The Adventures of Ozzie and Harriet* never revealed what Ozzie Nelson did to provide so well for his family. While the main emphasis of the show was on the married life of Rob and Laura Petrie, many of the episodes included scenes at Rob's workplace, with numerous conflicts revolving around his difficult relationship with the show's pompous producer, Melvin Cooley, and the show's neurotic star, Alan Brady. In a tweaking of the formula of the domestic sitcom, the "Fred and Ethel" roles of "best friends" were filled by Rob's co-writers at the television studio, Sally and Buddy, who spent a lot of time with Rob and Laura in their home or in other situations and locales in the city or suburbs.

Even this inventive comedy, however, did not spark much interest in the workplace- comedy genre. Its ratings in its first season were not impressive. By

1962 it moved into the top 10 in the Nielsen ratings, but that level of popularity lasted only three seasons. In its fifth year on the air, when it dropped to 16th place in the ratings and Van Dyke and others on the show were eager to move on to new ventures, the show ended its run. The viewing public still seemed only mildly interested in the workplace as a setting for comedy. The major appeal of *The Dick Van Dyke Show* arose from the chemistry between Van Dyke and Moore as a modern husband and wife and not from his adventures at his job.

Further attempts at something like workplace comedy in the 1960s seemed to be even more wary about placing too much emphasis on the job. *The Andy Griffith Show* (1960–1968), in its casual intermingling of scenes at Sheriff Andy's headquarters and his home, might be considered as a bridging of home and office, but the informality of small-town life and the low demands for law enforcement in Mayberry made the workplace look more like an extended family environment. The military base environment of *Gomer Pyle, U.S.M.C.* (1964–1970), like Sgt. Bilko's army camp in the 1950s, could also be considered a workplace situation, but it did not emphasize the hero's professional duties in the way that the plots of *M*A*S*H* consistently centered around the demands on medical professionals in wartime. *Room 222* (1969–1974), set in an inner-city high school, proved to be more of a drama than a comedy, as it focused on contemporary social issues with a combination of humor and dramatic action. In general the television comedy of the 1960s continued to focus on the home, even when the home life became rather fantastic, as in *Bewitched* (1964–1972), *I Dream of Jeannie* (1965–1970), and the briefer appearances of the monster comedies, *The Addams Family* (1964–1966) and *The Munsters* (1964–1966). While family life continued to provide comic material, there just did not seem to be anything funny about going to work.

But on September 19, 1970, when Mary Richards drove to Minneapolis to work at the newsroom of WJM-TV in *The Mary Tyler Moore Show* (1970–1977), the workplace comedy finally came into its own. Contrary to the previous decade's timid balancing act between domestic comedy and some comic involvement on the job, the main setting of the show was the newsroom of the television station. For the first time since *Our Miss Brooks*, the main characters were professional colleagues whose primary interaction occurred at work. Most of the episodes took place exclusively in the newsroom. During the show's run, as Mary's neighbor Rhoda and their landlady, Phyllis, became more important players, Mary's apartment became the scene of more activity, but there were only a few visits to any other characters' homes.

Finally, a hit workplace comedy inspired many popular imitators, set in a variety of workplace environments and urban locales. Many of them became major successes in their original run and have enjoyed long afterlife in syndication. *The Bob Newhart Show* (1972–1978) exploited the comic possibilities of a Chicago psychologist's workday, interacting with his clients, receptionist, and the dentist who worked across the hallway. *Barney Miller* (1975–1982) presented the hurly-burly of life in a New York City police station; *Taxi* (1978–1983) explored the same urban territory from the vantage point of a taxicab garage; and *Welcome Back, Kotter* (1975–1979) detailed the challenges of a teacher of underachieving "sweathogs" in a Brooklyn high school. *Alice* (1976–1985) followed the adventures of a waitress in Mel's Diner in Phoenix, while *WKRP in Cincinnati* (1978–1982) featured the offbeat staff of a radio station in Ohio.

The genre continued to thrive in succeeding decades of television entertainment, going on to produce two series that would turn into major phenomena in their day. After a slow start in the 1972–1973 season, *M*A*S*H* moved into the top 10 of the Nielsen ratings and stayed there for all but one of the seasons during its eleven-year run. It told the story of a troupe of doctors, nurses, and other personnel working in the 4077th Mobile Army Surgical Hospital during the Korean War in an absurdist situation that for most viewers mirrored the Vietnam conflict that was winding down during the early years of the series. The show won a bundle of Emmy Awards over the years for its directing, writing, and the performances of several of the actors. The lead actor, Alan Alda, won three Emmys for his performance as the cynical intellectual Hawkeye Pierce and became something of a poster boy for the new sensitive male so admired in feminist circles. Its final episode, which aired as a two-and-a-half hour special on February 28, 1983, has gone down in television history for capturing the largest audience ever to watch a single television program, with a 60 audience share, estimated at 125 million viewers, more than half of the national population.

The success of the barroom comedy *Cheers* (1982–1993) repeated the pattern of *M*A*S*H* by suffering through a sluggish ratings start in its first few seasons but finally moving up into the top 10 shows for the rest of its eleven years on the air. It surpassed *M*A*S*H* in the number of Emmys it received, winning the award for Outstanding Comedy Series four times and garnering an unusual number of Emmys for its actors. Rhea Perlman, for her role as the acerbic waitress Carla, won Outstanding Supporting Actress four times, setting a record in that category. Its final episode was also one of the most top-rated television shows of all time. Reruns of *Cheers* continue to attract huge audiences as something of a cult favorite in late-night syndication.

Other workplace comedies that succeeded in earning numerous awards and winning the hearts of viewers for runs of five seasons or more include *Taxi* (1978–1983), *Newhart* (1982–1990), *Night Court* (1984–1992), *Designing Women* (1986–1993), *Murphy Brown* (1988–1998), *Empty Nest* (1988–1995),

Wings (1990–1997), *Coach* (1989–1997), *Frasier* (1993–2004), *The Drew Carey Show* (1995–2002), *Spin City* (1996–2003), *Just Shoot Me* (1997–2003), and *Ally McBeal* (1997–2002).

This survey might also include some popular "domestic-servant sitcoms" such as *Hazel* (1961–1966), *Benson* (1979–1986), and *The Nanny* (1993–1999) in the workplace-comedy roster as well, but each of them tends to wiggle out of the category. Although each of these shows was set in the main character's workplace, their comic formulae tended to follow the patterns of domestic situation comedy in a family setting with members of the family or other people who worked in the home as main or supporting characters. *The Nanny*, in fact, tended to become more of a domestic comedy midway through its six-year run, as the main character, Fran Fine, became more romantically involved with her employer and eventually married him and bore twins. The plots and circumstances of *Benson*, in contrast, became less domestic in its third season, as Benson moved from his position of butler in the governor's mansion to state budget director and then continued to rise politically until, in the show's final season, he ran his own campaign for governor in opposition to his former employer.

The workplace offers so many possibilities in terms of settings, characters, and scripts that one is tempted to ask what took television writers and producers so long to arrive at the winning pattern or for viewers to appreciate the genre. The opportunity to move out of the living rooms and kitchens into offices, schoolrooms, police stations, bars, and radio and television studios liberates the shows in terms of designs and realistic possibilities for a wider variety of comic encounters, schemes, and mishaps. The specific urban locales offer a framework for comic plots involving the local customs and personalities. *Cheers* included cameo appearances by Boston Red Sox players, the mayor of Boston, and story lines about hockey players and trips to the Cape. *Murphy Brown* included many real-life national politicians and media personalities in its story lines.

In workplace comedy the cast of characters becomes immediately wider than a realistic family situation could provide, even with the help of neighbors. Characters can come from a greater variety of backgrounds. It is easy to introduce additional characters who join the workforce (Murphy Brown's numerous short-term secretaries, for example) or to have certain characters appear as visitors or customers at the workplace or as romantic partners or spouses of the employees (Latka's wife, Simka, on *Taxi;* Frasier Crane's long list of girlfriends and the equally numerous boyfriends of his producer, Roz Doyle, on *Frasier*). Characters are allowed to be more eccentric and even unlikeable (Carla Tortelli on *Cheers,* Louie DePalma on *Taxi)* because of the presumption that they need to be tolerated only during the workday.

If one actor leaves the show, his or her character can be replaced more easily than a family member can on a domestic sitcom, and the arrival of the new character can change the balance in the relationships among the ensemble. On *M*A*S*H*, the uptight commanding officer, Colonel Blake, played by McLean Stevenson, was replaced by the more lovable and wise World War II-veteran Colonel Potter, played by Harry Morgan with such success that he received the 1979–1980 Emmy as Outstanding Supporting Actor in a Comedy. When Wayne Rogers, who played Hawkeye's sidekick, Trapper John, left the show in a contract dispute, his role was easily taken on by Mike Farrell as B. J. Hunnicut. *Cheers* also finessed this critical casting arrangement twice. When Shelley Long decided to leave the cast, her character, the graduate student Diane Chambers, was replaced by Kirstie Alley's Rebecca Howe, a beautiful young woman suffering from a massive case of low self-esteem but whose sexual chemistry with Sam Malone kept that comic motif alive. When Nicholas Colasanto, the actor who played the bartender Coach, died, his character was replaced by a younger bartender, Woody Boyd, played by Woody Harrelson, whose farm-boy naïveté brought a new strain of comic characterization and plot to the show. Long, Alley, and Harrelson would all be honored with Emmy Awards for their performances.

The genre also offers opportunities for exploring new boundaries in verbal comedy. Many of the workplace comedies take place in white-collar environments with main characters who are generally well-educated or well-trained professionals: psychologists, physicians, educators, politicians, designers, lawyers, journalists, or broadcast media professionals. The dialogue therefore can be more sophisticated and witty. A few of the comedies take place in more blue-collar settings, where, instead of the sophisticated banter of the professionals, the conversation is more directly hostile, which can generate equally clever dialogue, as was well illustrated in the award-winning scripts for *Taxi*. Some series managed to mix the wit of educated professionals with working-class hostility. The underachieving students on *Welcome Back, Kotter* and the spectrum of clients at the police station on *Barney Miller* regularly required the high school teachers and law enforcement professionals to engage in less sophisticated conversations. The setting for *Cheers* offered perhaps the best framework for such a mix, as it could combine the witty repartee of the graduate student–waitress Diane Chambers and the therapists-customers Frasier Crane and Lilith Sternin with the working-class humor of the bartenders Ernie "Coach" Pantusso, the former pro-baseball player Sam Malone, the country bumpkin Woody Boyd, the waitress Carla Tortelli, and the perennial customers, Cliff the postal worker and Norm the sometime accountant.

A closer look at two of the most successful workplace comedies reveals the range of possibilities for the genre and the high level of comic writing and performance that can be achieved at either end of the workplace spectrum. *Taxi*, which aired on ABC and then on NBC from 1978 to 1983, followed the lives of blue-collar workers struggling to survive amid the urban problems of New York City in the 1970s and 1980s. *Murphy Brown*, airing on CBS from 1988 to 1998, featured well-dressed and well-coiffed professionals at a fictional television news magazine in Washington D.C., dealing with the demands of high-stakes media power plays and political pressure in the high-tech 1990s. Whether their workers were blue-collar types engaged in part-time jobs or high-level professionals, both of these comedies exhibited witty dialogue and dead-on comic performances, and both were honored with numerous Emmy Awards and other accolades for their outstanding achievements.

In its first three seasons *Taxi* was the Emmy winner for Outstanding Comedy Series, a rare achievement that has been matched so far by only three other series: *All in the Family*, *The Mary Tyler Moore Show*, and *Frasier*. The star of the show, Judd Hirsch, won the Emmy for Outstanding Lead Actor in a Comedy Series twice, and other actors in the show—Danny DeVito, Christopher Lloyd, and Carol Kane—each won two Emmys apiece during the show's five-year run. It also garnered two Emmy Awards for Outstanding Writing of a Comedy Series and two Emmys for James L. Brooks for Outstanding Directing of a Comedy Series. *Taxi* also won the Golden Globe Award for Best Musical or Comedy Series three years in a row. It was praised as a "bright, brisk, urban beacon of grown-up comedy" with "television's slickest repertory company this side of the incomparable *M*A*S*H*."[2] John O'Connor praised the show for its "first-rate repertory company" and its clever scripts that helped "to lift the series . . . into the special niches accorded to 'All in the Family,' or, not surprisingly, 'The Mary Tyler Moore Show.'"[3]

Taxi was inspired by a 1975 *New York Magazine* article "Night-Shifting for the Hip Fleet," which had described life at the Dover Taxi Garage #2 in Greenwich Village, focusing on the "shape-up time" at the garage from 2:00 to 6:00 p.m. as the night-shift drivers waited around for the day-shifters to bring the cabs back in. The writer, Mark Jacobson, had been a cabdriver at the Dover. One of the article's points of interest was the fact that the disparate group of people who drove the cabs, like the author himself, had other career plans and saw driving a cab as a temporary occupation. In early 1978 the comedy writer-director Jim Brooks and others from his newly formed production company met with Jacobson in New York City and spent some time hanging out at a New York taxi garage. Sitting there, they observed that the center of the group was a young man who, unlike the others, seemed content simply being a cabdriver; he provided the basis for the show's main character, Alex Rieger. They also spotted a dispatcher who was not averse to taking bribes from the drivers, and the Louie DePalma character was born.[4] The creators, as they painstakingly cast the show, developed a motley crew of other characters: Tony Banta, an aspiring boxer; Elaine Nardo, a young divorcée with two children who also worked as a receptionist at an art gallery; Bobby Wheeler, a struggling actor; Latka Gravas, a mechanic from an unidentified Eastern European country; John Burns, a college student; and the Reverend Jim Ignatowski, a survivor of the sixties drug culture who had founded a religion as a means of helping fellow hippies avoid the military draft.

Taxi is one of those rare comedy shows where the talent behind the camera may be even more impressive than the excellent cast. The creative team behind *Taxi*, a collection of exceptional talent who formed something of a superb workplace ensemble themselves, took a firm hand in the shaping of the show. Jim Brooks was already the winner of multiple Emmy Awards and other honors for his achievements in "quality" television. Early in his career he had served as a writer for Marlo Thomas's *That Girl* (1966–1971), which was admired for its portrayal of an "independent" career woman. Brooks had experimented with a more serious, socially relevant, comedy drama, *Room 222* (1969–1974), set in an inner-city high school, and he had served as producer, director, and writer for *The Mary Tyler Moore Show* and its spin-offs *Rhoda* and *Lou Grant*. After so much success at MTM productions, Brooks was ready to create his own production company. To do so he recruited three others from the MTM operations. David Davis was a veteran television writer and associate producer who had worked with Brooks as a fellow producer on *The Mary Tyler Moore Show* and had gone on to produce *The Bob Newhart Show*. Ed Weinberger and Stan Daniels had both won awards for their work on *The Mary Tyler Moore Show* and had gone on to create and produce several other comedies for MTM. Weinberger would eventually go on to create and write for *The Cosby Show*. The four of them formed a new production company, The John Charles Walters Company, a name taken from a sign for an English pub that Weinberger had bought in a Los Angeles antique store. Producing credit for the show went to Glen and Les Charles, also veterans of the MTM studios, and almost all of the episodes of the show's first three seasons were directed by James Burrows, who had directed various episodes of *The Mary Tyler Moore Show*, *The Bob Newhart Show*, *Rhoda*, *Phyllis*, and *Lou Grant*. During the run of *Taxi*, Burrows and the Charles Brothers formed their own production company to create and produce *Cheers*. Burrows has gone on to direct episodes of many of the outstanding comedy shows on television, including *Night Court*, *The Tracy Ullman Show*, *The Simpsons*, *News Radio*, and *Friends*, while Brooks has directed or produced various award-winning feature films (*Terms of Endearment*, *Broadcast News*, *Big*, *As Good As It Gets*) and capped his television career as the producer of *The Simpsons*.

The handpicked acting ensemble, most of whom would go on to considerable success in films, television, or theater, came from diverse professional backgrounds. The central character, Alex Rieger, would be played by Judd Hirsch, the most established actor of the group, who had already made a name for himself primarily as a serious actor on television as the star of a gritty made-for-television movie, *The Law* (1974), which inspired a short-lived series, and another police series, *Delvecchio* (1976–1977). Hirsch could also boast of a successful career in theater, which had culminated in his starring role in Neil Simon's 1978 autobiographical comedy *Chapter Two*. Christopher Lloyd, who would play Rev. Jim, had considerable experience as a character actor in off-Broadway theater, television series, and film, but was not well known at the time. Danny DeVito, who would play Louie DePalma, had worked in off-Broadway theater and film, most notably as one of the asylum patients in both the stage and film versions of *One Flew over the Cuckoo's Nest*. Tony Danza was a newcomer to television, with an interest in acting as well as a boxing career in New York City when he was asked to audition for *Taxi* and landed the role of the young boxer, Tony Banta. Andy Kaufman was an outrageous performance artist who had appeared on *Saturday Night Live*, presenting, among his many diverse routines, a shy, heavily accented, and low-talented performer called Foreign Man, who would form the basis for his character of Latka Gravas on *Taxi*. Marilu Henner, who would play Elaine Nardo, had already appeared in several Broadway musicals, including the long-running hit *Grease*, and had done a lot of work in television commercials and feature films. Jeff Conaway, who would leave the series after three years, began the show as perhaps the "hottest" actor, having just played a major role in the hit film musical *Grease*. He had been a child actor on Broadway, a member of a successful rock group, and a student of Martha Graham at New York University. His character of the struggling actor-cabdriver, Bobby Wheeler, was marginal to most of the plots, however, and it was eliminated in the show's fourth season. Conaway's subsequent acting career has not been as successful as those of the other members of the *Taxi* crew, which eventually would include Carol Kane as Latka's wife, Simka, and Rhea Perlman as Louie DePalma's girlfriend.

One unusual feature in the contracts with the cast occurred in the case of Andy Kaufman. Kaufman was reluctant to join the cast; he was much more eager to become a regular member of *Saturday Night Live*'s ensemble. But when *SNL* producer Lorne Michaels refused to offer him any such deal, Kaufman negotiated an arrangement with *Taxi*'s producers that limited his participation in the show. He would be scheduled to appear in only thirteen of the twenty-two episodes the first year, and he was required to be available for only two days a week instead of the usual five. While this created resentment among the other cast members, they had to admit that he was the best prepared member of the ensemble and he never blew a line in rehearsal or performance.[5]

The show's setting was notably darker than the usual workplace-comedy environment. In contrast to the bright offices of the television studios or professional offices of earlier MTM shows, the Sunshine Cab Company garage was dreary, cluttered, and unkempt. The office of the tyrannical dispatcher, Louie DePalma, was a "cage" created by metal fencing, from which he would bark orders, threats, or insults through a microphone. Alex Rieger and most of the other drivers sat around a bare table playing cards as they awaited their assignments. The mechanic, Latka Gravas, would appear periodically from among the cabs he was repairing, and the spaced-out Rev. Jim Ignatowski would emerge from the darkness of the garage's corners to offer eccentric observations and bizarre reactions. The infrequent glimpses of the cabbies' apartments revealed living arrangements ranging from Alex's modest but neat one-bedroom dwelling to the almost-homeless condition of the Reverend Jim. The lower-income living arrangements of the characters on *Taxi* differed dramatically from the cheery Victorian apartment house of Mary Richards in Minneapolis or the upscale high-rise apartment overlooking Lake Michigan on *The Bob Newhart Show*.

The wider urban setting of *Taxi* was even darker than the workplace environment itself. This was New York City in the late seventies. The show débuted only a year after the Son of Sam murders and the city's electrical blackout-cum-lootings of the summer of 1977. New York City had come close to declaring bankruptcy, and the city was viewed by many as dangerous, fiscally troubled, and heavily populated by minorities, immigrants, drug addicts, and criminals, not to mention the sexual adventurers who populated Studio 54, Plato's Retreat, and the gay bars and clubs of Greenwich Village. Television comedies at the time based much of their humor on a view of life in New York City as chaotic, even frightening. Archie Bunker regularly articulated his anger at the changes taking place in his neighborhood in Queens as well as the activity he witnessed as a part-time taxi driver in the city. Other shows set in New York City (*Rhoda; The Jeffersons; Barney Miller; Welcome Back, Kotter; The Odd Couple*) often included references to muggings, robberies, traffic jams, overcrowded subways, power outages, litter and grafitti, and other urban ills. One of the grimmest portrayals of New York City's urban decay had appeared only two years earlier in Martin Scorsese's film, *Taxi Driver*, with Robert Niro's menacing performance as the title character, Travis Bickle. While none of the characters or situations on *Taxi* would match the Scorsese-DeNiro portrayal of life in the urban hellhole of Manhattan, the premise of developing a show around New York City cabdrivers certainly hinted at a darker than usual situation comedy.

Indeed, the spectrum of characters on *Taxi* was broader and allowed for more diverse character comedy than previous workplace settings had offered. Judd's Hirsch's role as Alex Rieger repeated the familiar pattern of the central, mimetic character with whom the viewers could identify, providing a moral-psychological core for the work family.[6] Mary Tyler Moore and Bob Newhart had established the pattern of the main character as the island of normalcy in the midst of workplace lunacy on their shows. Linda Lavin's character served a similar function in the diner setting of *Alice*, and Hal Linden did likewise in the chaotic police station of *Barney Miller*. The writers of *Taxi* established the viewers' rapport with Alex in the premiere episode of the show, which revealed his status as a divorced father who had not seen his daughter in fifteen years and has a chance for a brief, poignant reunion with her just before she boards a plane to attend college in Europe. Throughout the series Alex is the character to offer advice, lend money, accompany other characters into challenging situations, support them in the occasional lie, and referee their arguments. The other relatively normal character was Elaine Nardo. While her sexual attractiveness, clearly established in the premiere episode with the lascivious expressions and comments of Louie DePalma, was a frequent catalyst for the comic plots, she also managed to fit into the predominantly male world of the garage.

In the formula of workplace comedy most of the coworkers or other characters surrounding the central figure tend to be flawed, neurotic figures, whose various obsessions allow them the liberty of more hostile or inappropriate behavior. On *The Mary Tyler Moore Show*, Sue Ann Nivens (Betty White), the sexually predatory "happy homemaker"; Ted Baxter (Ted Knight), the clueless, egotistical news anchor; the cynical head newswriter Murray Slaughter (Gavin MacLeod); and the gruff producer Lou Grant (Ed Asner) provided an array of neurotic behavior. The staff at the police precinct headquarters on *Barney Miller* included Harris (Ron Glass), a wisecracking African American; a hypochondriac officer waiting for retirement named Fish (Abe Vigoda); and a slow-on-the-uptake hulk named Wojo (Maxwell Gail). The station population was also enhanced by a continuous flow of streetwalkers and other criminals, street people, outraged citizens, and variously disturbed characters who wandered in and out of the station. The diverse ethnic heritage of the station house (Japanese, Puerto Rican, African, Jewish, Polish) also offered material for the occasional barbed comment or hostile observation. Dr. Bob Hartley's array of clients, especially when they interacted in group therapy sessions, allowed *The Bob Newhart Show* to engage in the "sick comedy" that the "button-down mind" of Newhart had popularized in his stand-up comedy routines and albums. There was a similar collection of hostile and neurotic coworkers and customers in the diner of *Alice*.

Taxi, however, upped the ante on hostility and neurosis. The diminutive dispatcher Louie DePalma gave new meaning to the term "petty tyrant," dispensing constant invective and insult with impunity, regularly addressing the drivers as "you losers." He was positively gleeful as he created his own rules for the workplace, charged fees for phone calls, and withheld or revealed information to the workers under his iron control. Danny DeVito has remarked that he saw his character as perhaps the only one at the garage who loved his job, with its rich opportunity for control of others' destinies. Only rarely was Louie shown in any sympathetic light.

Louie's hostility was only one element in the mix of neuroses among the coworkers. The Reverend Jim's history of drug usage and subsequent brain damage offered opportunities for positively absurdist dialogue. He frequently intervened in the middle of his coworkers' conversations, misunderstanding their statements or uttering non sequiturs that sometimes served as ironic commentary. Often his remarks seemed to be part of an ongoing interior dialogue. His puzzling remarks and behavior, however, often served as nostalgic reminders of the virtues of the hippie generation, with his gentle disposition, lively imagination, impaired but lofty intelligence, appreciation of the beauty hidden in the ordinary, tendency toward mysticism, and his lack of concern for material goods. To add to the absurdity, despite his unkempt appearance and general lack of mental focus, many women found Jim attractive.

Because of his unfamiliarity with the culture of the United States and his general naïveté, the character of Latka Gravas, the garage mechanic from an unnamed Eastern European country, was given opportunities for the same misunderstandings and non sequiturs as Reverend Jim. Meanwhile he provided another level of nonsense in his frequent unintelligible speeches in his native language and his practice of his native customs, particularly after his courtship and marriage to another immigrant from his country, Simka Dabhlitz (Carol Kane). Latka was the innocent fish-out-of-water whose sincerity often served as a rebuke to the mood of hostility and cynicism prevailing in the garage environment.

There was a similar comic simplicity in the character of the dim-witted but good-hearted young Tony Banta, who cherished a dream of a boxing career. With his compact athletic build and his baby-faced Italian good looks, Tony also brought some sex appeal to the situation, which was only occasionally brought into comic play. The sex appeal was generally provided by the vivacious Marilu Henner.

A further development of the absurdist strain of the show was provided by the other character that Andy Kaufman played on the show. In his stand-up act Kaufman had developed the character of an over-the-hill Las Vegas entertainer named Tony Clifton, who was so arrogant and rude that he usually elicited boos, severe heckling, and even threats from audiences. While the producers and writers planned to include the Tony Clifton character in early episodes of the show, the arrangement never worked out, probably because Clifton's level of unpleasantness was too intense for the television context. Instead, Kaufman played a milder version of the character, another slick, conceited lounge singer named Vic Ferrari. Even though his repellent character was toned down, Ferrari was still conceited and obnoxious enough to represent the very opposite of the gentle, simple soul of Latka Gravas.

As the show's many awards clearly indicate, *Taxi* succeeded in exploring the potential for a workplace comedy to go where domestic comedy could not: the diversity of characters, the darker atmosphere inside and outside the shop, the neurosis, hostility, and outright absurdity of situations and dialogue in a low-end section of a part-time employment situation. The drop in its ratings in its last two seasons suggest that the show's grimy locale and gritty tone may, in fact, have become a bit too dark for viewers' taste. The late-night ambience of the show's popular reruns seem a more appropriate venue for this downscale vision of the modern workplace.

At the other end of the spectrum in several ways, the award-winning comedy *Murphy Brown* followed the personal and professional life of the star reporter for a successful television news magazine show, F.Y.I., in Washington, D.C. One major contrast with *Taxi* can be seen in *Murphy Brown's* focus on its central character. Instead of offering an assortment of comic misadventures starring different characters in each episode so that each actor had his or her moment at the center of the screen, *Murphy Brown* fixed its viewers' attention firmly on its central character. The series would succeed or fail on how funny Murphy herself would prove to be. As the center of the comic action, however, Murphy would depart from the tradition established by her sitcom predecessors. Unlike Mary Richards, Barney Miller, Bob Hartley, or Alex Rieger, she would not function as the voice of common sense and emotional balance for the workplace ensemble. In fact, Murphy turned out to be perhaps the most volatile personality in the place. As a divorced recovering alcoholic with a cynical view of the world that she had been reporting on for twelve years at F.Y.I., Murphy was an emotional minefield. Her fits of temper, sarcastic rejoinders, blunt observations, and generally gloomy approach made life difficult for her coworkers. Her dissatisfaction with every secretary assigned to her became a running joke throughout the series. But she was a great reporter, at the top of her game professionally.

The show did feature the familiar ensemble of quirky coworkers, however. The executive producer of F.Y.I. was Miles Silverberg (Grant Shaud), who always seemed a bit too young, inexperienced, and insecure for the job. Jim Dial (Charles Kimbrough) was the news program's pompous anchor, and Frank

Fontana (Joe Regalbuto) was the show's investigative reporter, whose friendship with Murphy went back many years. The newest member of the team was Corky Sherwood (Faith Ford), a former Miss America with no journalistic experience or skills other than her good looks and cheerful personality, which, of course, Murphy found particularly irritating. Even with this assortment of characters, *Murphy Brown* was designed to depend less on the ensemble's chemistry and more on the appeal of its star. The choice of actress to play Murphy was crucial, and the credit for the inspired casting of Candice Bergen must be given to the show's guiding spirit, Diane English.

Diane English had already gained industry credibility as the producer of two smart situation comedies at CBS. *Foley Square*, a comedy starring Margaret Colin as an assistant district attorney in Manhattan, lasted only a few months in 1986 but garnered much critical praise. *My Sister Sam* (1986–1988) starring Pam Dawber (from *Mork and Mindy*) as a freelance photographer living in San Francisco whose teenaged sister had moved in with her, followed the same pattern of spotlighting an independent career woman dealing with the usual challenges of the urban-singles lifestyle. English and her producer-husband, Joel Shukovsky, had moved to Hollywood from New York City from positions at the PBS station WNET. They both shared an interest in the news business, and they had earlier conceived an idea for a sitcom about an "underdog woman working for a very low-roller cable station, trying to worm her way in and get the stories"[7] The basic premise evolved into something quite different. As Shukovsky describes it:

> Diane wanted to do something about a woman who broke the rules. . . . But we didn't want to do another show about a woman struggling to make it. Things have changed for us, and we wanted to do something with more edges. Murphy doesn't have a best friend next door. She doesn't rely on any one guy for her social life. . . . She's a loner. She chooses to set her life up in a way so that she's busy all the time with her career.[8]

With the main character clearly distinguished from Mary Richards and other struggling career women, English and Shukovsky faced another challenge, the perennial sitcom issue of "likeability":

> The thing that would make Murphy interesting to us would be to make her someone who was this world-beater individualist, someone who had made it. Most half-hour shows take the side of the underdog. The network rationale usually is, "Can you really root for someone who is rich, famous, and beautiful?"[9]

English described the development of the main character as the central element of *Murphy Brown*. She envisioned Murphy as "a woman facing a certain number of milestones in her life," recovering from alcoholism, facing forty, an idealist from the sixties, who, as she has gotten older, has become more of a hard-bitten realist, coming back to her job after a stint in the Betty Ford Clinic, a lot more vulnerable.[10]

After considering many other actresses for the lead, English was firmly convinced that Candice Bergen was the ideal choice to play Murphy Brown. Bergen herself was eager to take the role. There was, however, some serious hesitation at CBS about the casting. A strikingly beautiful woman, Candice Bergen had enjoyed a very successful career in modeling and films, but she had no proven record in television situation comedy. She was, however, the daughter of the great comedian Edgar Bergen, she had appeared frequently as a guest host on *Saturday Night Live*, and her film career included comic turns in several well-regarded films, including *Carnal Knowledge, Starting Over,* and *Rich and Famous.* But whether her talents would fit into television's situation-comedy framework was yet to be seen.

Murphy Brown also took workplace comedy into an unfamiliar territory: political humor. Using the opportunity provided by the show's setting in a Washington, D.C. newsroom, the producers and writers frequently offered political commentary, articulating a liberal critique of Washington politics and gender issues, especially during the early years of its run under the Bush-Quayle administration. Such comic criticism would eventually explode in the real-life controversy with Vice President Dan Quayle that has gone down in the television history books. At the end of the 1991–1992 season it was disclosed that Murphy was pregnant. It took an entire season for Murphy to complete her pregnancy, and in May 1992 she delivered the baby. Resisting the marriage proposals of the baby's actual father and another suitor, Murphy decided to raise the child on her own. The day after the heavily watched episode, during a campaign speech about family values, Quayle made headlines with his comment that "it doesn't help matters when prime-time TV has Murphy Brown, a character who supposedly epitomizes today's intelligent, highly paid professional woman, mocking the importance of fathers by bearing a child alone and calling it just another lifestyle choice."[11] During the next season a special episode of the program responded by ridiculing Mr. Quayle in a highly promoted hour-long episode that garnered huge ratings. The controversy helped keep the show in the top 10 for several seasons.

Murphy Brown arrived on the crest of a wave of situation comedies produced by women that injected a dose of feminist humor into American television. Another hit comedy of the decade, *Roseanne* (1988–1997), had reshaped the family situation-comedy formula along the lines of Roseanne Barr's stand-up comedy act that chronicled her life as a blue-collar "domestic goddess." Roseanne was both the star and executive producer of the show. Her character on the series was an outspoken, overweight wife and mother of four children, and much of the show's comedy sprang from a woman's view of family life, the job market, and other challenges of working-class life in Middle America. For perhaps the first time in television situation comedy, a large majority of the show's main characters were female: Roseanne, her two daughters, her mother, her grandmother, her sister, and several of her friends and neighbors. Another popular situation comedy, *Designing Women* (1986–1993), produced by the husband-and-wife team of Susan and Harry Bloodworth-Thomason, followed the lives of four women who ran an interior decorating business in Atlanta. The characters' repartee, more philosophical discussions, and most of the conflicts were built around their struggles for financial and romantic success on feminist terms. *Ellen* (1994–1998) followed the same formula as *Roseanne*, mining its humor from the stand-up comedy of its executive producer-star, Ellen DeGeneres, and generating even more controversy than *Murphy Brown* when, in the show's third season, Ellen DeGeneres came out as a lesbian in both her personal life and the story line of the show. For several seasons CBS ran *Murphy Brown* and *Designing Women* on Monday nights as counter-programming to ABC's *Monday Night Football*. Of all these successful series, *Murphy Brown* came to symbolize the new era of feminist discourse in television comedy, meriting a cover story in *Newsweek* (March 13, 1989) during its first season and cover stories in several issues of *TV Guide* and other magazines during its ten-year run. Its newsroom locale seems to have served as the ideal environment for feminist issues in the workplace and the political arena.

With the opportunity for cast departures and arrivals provided by the workplace-comedy format, the producers and writers of *Murphy Brown* also managed to keep the show fresh by the addition of new characters over the years, many of whom represented some of the actual changes occurring in the world of television news. Among the most notable additions to the cast was the veteran television director Garry Marshall, who from 1994 to 1997 appeared on the show as the irascible new network president Stan Lansing. Lansing's overriding concern for the stockholders in the mega-corporation that had bought the network, coupled with his general opposition to anything Murphy proposed, only served to strengthen Murphy's anti-authoritarian streak. The 1996 season introduced Lily Tomlin as Kay Carter-Shepley, the new executive producer of F.Y.I., a stylish, high-living executive who thrived on the power and perks of her job and generally viewed the news department as a branch of the network's entertainment division. A number of real-life news personalities made appearances on the show as themselves. Linda Ellerbee, Irving R. Levine, Connie Chung, Larry King, Paula Zahn, and even the venerable Walter Cronkite showed up in cameo roles. Paul Reubens, famous for his portrayal of Pee Wee Herman on television and film, appeared for two seasons as Andrew J. Lansing III, the syncophantic and scheming nephew of Stan Lansing, who forced Murphy to take him on as her secretary. In the show's final episode, the last of the ninety-three secretaries hired by Murphy was played by Bette Midler.

Many production elements distinguished *Murphy Brown* from the workplace-comedy pack. In contrast to the coziness of *Cheers* or the downscale funkiness of *Taxi*, *Murphy Brown* went for glamour and an upscale professional brightness in its environment. The art director, Roy Christopher, has commented that the pilot script of the show had reminded him of films such as *His Girl Friday*, the 1940 screwball comedy that starred Rosalind Russell as a fast-talking newspaperwoman unintimidated even by her former husband and co-worker, played by Cary Grant. The film's "stylistic impulse toward sparkle, heightened glamour, extra punch" set the tone for the look of the television series. The set for the show, based partly on the new Washington, D.C. offices of *USA Today*, was described by Christopher as "very upscale . . . a real maze, with lots of angles and depth. . . . Yet it has great lightness and movement and dynamics."[12] The series was filmed instead of taped to capture the nuance of light and shade at the F.Y.I. offices as well as Murphy's elegant Georgetown townhouse. And it did not hurt that the show's star was a Hollywood beauty playing a character who could afford the latest fashion in professional attire.

Murphy Brown broke new ground in workplace comedy with its glamorous and intelligent star, unprecedented controversy generated by its topical humor, continuous stream of guest appearances from among the A-list of politicians and media personalities, and its habit of introducing new characters to the workplace environment who generated their own comic conflicts to enliven the plot. The show enjoyed a ten-year run on CBS, from the fall of 1988 to the late summer of 1998. For four of those years the show made the top 10 rankings in the Nielsen ratings and was almost always included in the top 20. The industry honored the series with an Emmy Award for Outstanding Comedy Series twice. (The competition for the title was fairly stiff; when *Murphy* Brown did not win the Emmy, it lost to such standout comedies as *Cheers*, *Seinfeld*, or *Frasier*.) The show was noteworthy for the number of Emmys awarded for Outstanding Guest Actor/Actress, given twice to Colleen Dewhurst for her role as Murphy's mother and to Darren McGavin and Martin Sheen in other years. It also won several Emmys for directing and writing. But the most impressive record was achieved by Candice Bergen, who won the Emmy for Outstanding Lead Actress in a Comedy Series five times before taking herself out of the competition for the 1995–1996 awards, opening the way for Helen Hunt to become the next serial Best Actress winner for *Mad About You*.

Since the departure of *Murphy Brown* in 1998, workplace comedy has faded into the more varied landscape of the outstanding comedies of the decade. Only a few new shows have been set in the workplace, and they have taken a turn towards the fantastic. Perhaps the specific elements of the workplace situation—variety of locales, spectrum of coworkers and clients, possibilities of hostile humor and romantic entanglements—have been explored as thoroughly as possible for the time being. While many of the characters and settings of workplace comedy may have approached the bizarre, the genre cannot stray too far into the realm of the outlandish. The essential humor of the workplace comedies over the years was grounded in the tension between the unruly personalities of the workers and the Puritan work ethic that demands some degree of responsible behavior and a sense of duty. The comic squabbling, schemes, love affairs, and personal disasters were all played out in the context of ongoing professional demands: customers needed to be served, deadlines had to be met, the operation was supposed to make money, and they all wanted to hold on to their jobs. The famous final episode of *The Mary Tyler Moore Show*, when the entire crew, except for the clueless Ted Baxter, was fired, illustrated the threat of economic reality hanging over the temporary "family" that reside in the workplace. All of these scenarios played out in a common context of realism and practicality.

Not so the recent workplace comedies, which have tested the limits of realistic characters and plots. Within the law offices of *Ally McBeal* (1997–2002) and the hospital setting of *Scrubs* (2001–present) the series creators have inserted visual depictions of their character's fantasy lives, various bizarre personality traits, and a good deal of sexual taboo-breaking that moves into the realm of the fantastic. Most episodes of *Life with Bonnie* (2002–2004), an attempt to combine domestic and workplace comedy à la *The Dick Van Dyke Show*, were built around one day in Bonnie's life as a television morning show host in Chicago, usually beginning in her home with her husband, her three children, and their nanny, as the family grab breakfast and head off to work or school, and ending with everyone heading off to their respective bedrooms for a night's sleep. Moreover, the script for the workplace interaction on the set of Bonnie's television show is developed through improvisational humor that is a televised version of breaking the fourth wall. Only *Good Morning, Miami* (2002–2004), set in the familiar workplace confines of a television studio, seemed to represent a return to the standard patterns established by *The Mary Tyler Moore Show*, *WKRP in Cincinnati*, and other shows set in media environments. These few examples of workplace comedy in network prime time, however, have not met with the sort of success enjoyed by the best of the genre. Judging by the Nielsen ratings and industry awards, they have been lost in the mix of a few popular family comedies (*Everybody Loves Raymond*, etc.);

urban-singles comedies (*Friends, Will and Grace*, etc.); animated comedies (*The Simpsons*, etc.); and the more transgressive comedies on the cable channels that are exploring the boundaries of sexual humor (*Sex and the City);* hostility (*Curb Your Enthusiasm*); and otherwise daring language and behavior (*South Park, The Osbournes*, etc.).

For almost thirty years, from the WJM-TV studios in Minneapolis to the F.Y.I. studios in Washington, D.C., the workplace has provided a rich collection of comic characters and stories. Those myriad offices, bars, classrooms, police stations, taxi garages, and other professional and working-class locales have faded away from prime time to live on forever in syndication. Meanwhile, television comedy seems to be heading into even more clever and imaginative directions. On many of the most successful new comedies, work does not occupy much time or attention. Perhaps the workday is over. Perhaps it is time to play.

·9·

PLAYTIME FOR THE GROWN-UPS

The wide viewership sought by the advertisers in prime time requires that the programming appeal to every demographic, but especially the 18- to 49-year-old viewers, who are considered the major consumers of goods and services. One recent survey showed that prime-time programming is often watched by the whole family, including the younger children, and that television watching ranks second (behind family meals) in the list of activities a family does together.[1] The comedy offered during prime time on the broadcast networks, therefore, generally conforms to the domestic ethos with a certain understanding of acceptable content and desirable format, found mainly in the half-hour situation comedies that continue to dominate the evening television schedule. The later hours, however, have been open to more experimentation, and early in television's history one of its most creative minds developed a format for late-night comedy that has persisted for half a century. Sylvester "Pat" Weaver, the head of programming at NBC in the late 1940s and early 1950s, was convinced that the new medium could offer programming that would appeal to an educated, adult audience with the attention span that could accommodate longer segments of programming. Accordingly he developed *Today* as a daily two-hour package of news and entertainment airing live every weekday morning. Hosted by the mild-mannered but whimsical Dave Garroway, who was often accompanied by a chimpanzee named J. Fred Muggs, the show premiered on January 14, 1952, and has never left the air. Its format was essentially the same as it is today, with news, weather and sports reports, and interviews. It even included crowds on the sidewalks looking through the studio windows. Under Weaver's supervision NBC also offered other "long-form" programs, including memorable presentations of live theater and musical performances such as the popular and oft-repeated television version of *Peter Pan* starring Mary

Martin and the 1952 Christmas Eve broadcast of Giancarlo Menotti's *Amahl and the Night Visitors,* the first opera commissioned for television.

Weaver then turned his attention to the nighttime schedule, offering *The Tonight Show* as another long-form program aimed at the adults who were still awake at those hours. *The Tonight Show* premiered nationally on NBC on September 27, 1954. It had already been airing as a local show on NBC's flagship station, WNBT-TV, in New York City since the previous June. When it went nationwide it ran for an hour and a half. (The show's time length over the years has varied somewhat, from one hour to an hour and forty-five minutes and finally settling into a one-hour format in 1980.) The program was aired live, with a studio audience, from the Hudson Theater on Forty-third Street in the Times Square district. The show's first host was Steve Allen, who brought a combination of intelligence and off-beat experimentation that was emerging in the coffeehouses and nightclubs of Greenwich Village and San Francisco and the Off-Broadway theaters at the time. Robert Metz offers a concise description of the tone and content of the show under Allen's leadership:

> The show was a free-form vehicle with bits in which Steve played straight to the regular company of comedians, music from pianist Steve and the singers and from Skitch Henderson and the band, short interviews with strange New Yorkers and members of the audience. . . . The two writers [Stan Burns and Herb Sergeant] recognized Steve Allen for the zany character he was and found all kinds of silly things for him to do. Some of it was physical. Steve would dive into a vat of Jell-O, and on another occasion was dunked in hot water with thousands of tea bags tied to his clothes. . . . It was that kind of show—zany, improvisational, and fun.[2]

The show typically began with Allen sitting at his piano, offering musical selections and presenting his informal comic chatter to the studio audience and television viewers. He would then move to the host's desk and preside over the rest of the show, employing a lot of ad-lib humor and regular sketches with his resident cast of talented comedians. Some of the best skits occurred when Allen, acting as a roving reporter, would engage in "live-remotes" featuring "man-on-the street" interviews with a very nervous Don Knotts, the preening Madison Avenue professional played by Louis Nye, or the bumbling, forgetful Tom Poston. The show also included a nightly news-and-weather update from the announcer, Gene Rayburn, which sometimes provided its own comic material.

As David Letterman would do many years later, Steve Allen and crew ventured out of the theater and into the streets for many impromptu bits. The crew would open the back door of the theater and aim a camera outside. Passersby would stare into the camera as Allen ad-libbed some voice-over. Metz also recounts the times that Allen would don a police officer's uniform, head out into the passing traffic, and stop motorists. Once, Allen flagged down a taxi, shouted "Take this to Grand Central, and hurry," threw a giant salami in the back seat, and watched the taxi speed away.[3] Tim Brooks and Earle Marsh describe an even more outlandish bit of mischief that occurred when the show was doing some telecasts from Miami. Allen somehow talked a contingent of U.S. Marines into staging a nighttime landing on Miami Beach, panicking the tourists in nearby hotels.[4]

During the last few months of Allen's run as host, Ernie Kovacs substituted for him on Monday and Tuesday nights with a similar format and even more far-out sketches, including Kovacs as the effeminate poet Percy Dovetonsils and the popular Nairobi Trio, three musicians in gorilla suits with a conductor using a banana as a baton. Kovacs also experimented with visual tricks. Once, with the use of two cameras and two different sets, Kovacs made it appear that he was standing behind a guest on the show and peering through her head, with his eye showing through a spot in the middle of her forehead.[5] If anything, Kovacs's version of the show was even zanier and more experimental than Allen's.

In January 1957, when Allen left to star in his own prime-time variety show, NBC executives used this opportunity to experiment with a significant change in the show's format. Renamed *Tonight: America after Dark*, the show was hosted by Jack Lescoulie, a news anchor imported from the morning show, *Today* , and was converted into a late-night counterpart to the morning show, featuring news reports, human interest stories, commentaries, and interviews. In line with its "after dark" theme the show attempted to "capture the flavor of America's nightlife through segments from a variety of locations throughout the land."[6] This was done by remote linkups to various newspaper columnists in New York, Chicago, and Los Angeles, with occasional reports from other cities. Musical interludes offered some variety. This programming experiment failed with critics and audience alike, lasting only until July.

NBC returned immediately to the comedy format with a new host, Jack Paar. Paar was a comic in the mold of Steve Allen—witty, intelligent, and nonconformist—and he brought a lively presence to the sketch comedy that was a regular feature on the show. He would open the show with a monologue that he wrote himself, usually built around his personal life with his family and his interactions with his coworkers. Paar moved away from Steve Allen's format of sketch comedy, preferring instead to interact with his regular panel of cast members, a motley crew of eccentric comedians, Cliff Arquettte in character as the folksy Charley Weaver , scatterbrained Dody Goodman, and outlandish personalities such as Zsa Zsa Gabor, Elsa Maxwell, and Hermione Gingold. Paar proved particularly effective, however, as an informed and provocative interviewer, with particular interest in the political issues of the early 1960s.

Paar interviewed Fidel Castro within days of his overthrow of the dictator Batista in Cuba. He telecast live from the newly constructed Berlin Wall, and he hosted presidential candidates John F. Kennedy and Richard M. Nixon—on separate shows. Other guests included Mrs. Eleanor Roosevelt and U.S. Attorney General Robert Kennedy.

Paar's emotional outbursts and displays of temper, however, made him problematic for the network executives. His emotional unpredictability—and perhaps the possible controversy generated by his interviews with political figures—caused the show's production to move away from live telecast to a taped program shortly after Paar took over as host. At the same time, his volatility gave the show an added appeal. Metz offers the observations of Dick Cavett, a writer for Jack's show at the time, about the fascination such behavior had for its viewers:

> Even for those who didn't like it, it was compelling, and you had to admit that it appealed, if only to a voyeur instinct. There was always the implied possibility in his manner that he would explode one day, and you might miss seeing a live nervous breakdown viewed from the comfort of your own bedroom. . . . He instinctively asked and said things that you yourself, if you were not inhibited, would like to ask and say. . . . Here was someone who went through with things that many self-respecting people denounced as somehow "not done." Yet these same people watched him nightly and loved seeing him do those things.[7]

Paar had running feuds with several prominent industry people and was not above airing his on-camera opinions about the columnists Walter Winchell and Dorothy Kilgallen and the editor of *TV Guide*, Walter Annenberg. One of Paar's most emotional moments came on February 10 and 11, 1960, when he objected to the network's editing of a joke he had told during the taping of the show, which was subsequently removed before the show was aired. The joke, made up of several double entendres revolving around the British term for a bathroom, "WC," was quite mild, but NBC decided to remove it from the taped version of the show. Paar felt that the implication would be that he had told a "smutty" joke. Paar was proud of the fact that he never told off-color stories and frequently asked guest comedians to refrain from such material. Seeing this as a personal slur, on the following night he began his show by explaining to the audience what happened and he started crying. Then he walked out of the studio and, as he put it, "turned the program back to the censors."[8] The announcer, cast, and crew, taken completely by surprise, had to continue for the rest of the hour without Mr. Paar. The network talked Jack into returning, and on March 7 he returned and continued hosting the show until the spring of 1962, when he left to star in a similar show in prime time.

After Paar's departure NBC continued the show for several months with an array of hosts, as they waited for the new host, Johnny Carson, to be contractually available. The list of temporary hosts provided by Brooks and Marsh suggest that NBC may have been using the interim period to get a sense of viewer comfort with a wide spectrum of personalities: an assortment of outright comedians from the zany Jerry Lewis and Soupy Sales to the classic Groucho Marx and the politically provocative Mort Sahl as well as more laid-back hosts such as the avuncular Art Linkletter and Hugh Downs and the husband-and-wife team of Peter Lind Hayes and Mary Healy. Interestingly, the list includes only one female individual host, the popular television "personality," Arlene Francis, who had carved out quite a successful career in television as a mistress of ceremonies and a quiz-show panelist on numerous shows (most notably for fifteen years on *What's My Line?*), but she could hardly be considered a comedian. What did the show need: a gifted comedian (Jerry Lewis) or a comfortable television personality (Arlene Francis)? In Johnny Carson the show got both.

Born in 1925, Johnny Carson began his career in show business as a fourteen-year-old magician in his home town of Norfolk, Nebraska, billing himself as 'The Great Carsoni." After a stint in the armed services during World War II, during which he often entertained the troops with his magic act, Carson returned home, where he attended the University of Nebraska and started working at a local radio station and, for his senior thesis, wrote an analysis of the best radio comedians at the time. He eventually moved to California where he continued at various jobs in radio and television. Carson's big break came in 1954 when, during his time as a writer for Red Skelton, he was asked to go on in place of Skelton, who had injured himself in rehearsal. By the time *The Tonight Show* came calling in 1962, Carson was hosting a daytime quiz show on ABC called *Do You Trust Your Wife?* The program's quiz-show format, like Groucho Marx's prime-time show *You Bet Your Life*, was merely a vehicle for a good deal of Johnny's double entendres, physical stunts, and witty repartee, all of which would become part of his performance later on as the "king of late-night television."

Johnny Carson began his reign on October 1, 1962, and he would continue to rule the late-night world for the next thirty years. He brought a unique persona to the role, an unflappable attitude that combined the common sense of his Nebraska roots with a worldly air of a "swinger" at home in the bright lights of New York and the glamour of Hollywood. His good looks and charm made him something of a role model and style setter for a generation or two of American men. With impeccable timing and subtle facial expressions—in imitation of his idol Jack Benny—Carson was the consummate monologist, who could make even a failed joke funny. His spontaneous repartee with his sidekick-announcer, Ed McMahon, and his dapper bandleader, Doc Severinson, gave viewers a certain sense of intimacy with "Johnny."

In his shaping of the standard late-night format, Carson dropped the comic ensemble used by Steve Allen and Jack Paar. Like his predecessors, Carson opened with a stand-up monologue, usually consisting of topical humor and mild political commentary as well as some off-handed chat with his bandleader and the announcer. Then, having moved to his desk, Carson would engage in some short sketches or routines, often involving McMahon, which eventually featured familiar Carson characters such as the psychic Carnack the Magnificent; the flag-waving patriot Floyd R. Turbo; and, with the help of a wig, spectacles, and a modest lace-collared blouse, Aunt Blabby. He would then proceed to interview his guests for the evening, who would sit on the couch next to the host's desk, where the conversation centered on the guest's current activities or witty observations and, almost always, the promotion of the guest's upcoming film, television show, or book. Eventually, most shows would include a guest comedian, often making his or her first national television appearance. Musical performances also became a regular feature of the show.

As *The Tonight Show* settled into this clearly defined formula, it emerged as basically a low-key reformulation of the "vaudeocoms" of Milton Berle, Sid Caesar, and the other variety shows of an earlier era, most of which had also included opening monologues, genial announcers and bandleaders, guest appearances by musical and comedy stars, and sketches performed by the stars with perhaps a resident company of supporting players. But, instead of 90 minutes a week, *The Tonight Show* offered as much as 105 minutes every weeknight until it was shortened to one hour in 1980. The difference introduced by late-night television was the more casual atmosphere of the program, which no longer required elaborate sets, production numbers, or any of the other attempts to re-create the feel of a "night on the town," a Broadway show, or a Las Vegas extravaganza. (The relatively low production expense, in fact, helped make the show a major moneymaker for NBC.) The late-night show's laid-back atmosphere allowed for a lower level of viewer attention. Just as *Today* was aimed at the viewer who was having breakfast, feeding the kids, or getting dressed for work, *The Tonight Show* could be enjoyed by the viewer who was going through the day's mail, eating a late-night snack, talking on the telephone, or, as Johnny often mischievously remarked, lying in bed—alone or with someone else. He was famous for his description of the show as "NBC's answer to foreplay."[9]

The late-night hour guaranteed that the viewers would be primarily an adult demographic, to which Pat Weaver had always hoped to appeal. These adults, however, were in a specific emotional state, tired from their day's activities and ready to relax. The earlier versions of *The Tonight Show* had established that late night was not a suitable venue for zany comedy, lengthy news reports, or human-interest stories, and network executives—and perhaps the viewers as well—were uncomfortable with a host whose personal life or political opinions were too controversial. They seemed to want the television equivalent of milk and cookies, or perhaps scotch and soda, as their day came to an end. For the grown-ups, it was time to play.

Carson was the ideal companion for such relaxation. His agent once said of him, "He looks good in all fifty states. He's an All-American guy," and a reviewer described him as an "engaging fellow, quick of quip, with a modest, mild manner that lets him get off irreverences and double entendres which might seem crass from less boyish comics."[10] He was naughty, but he was safe.

Not that Johnny Carson's personal and professional life did not offer some drama. During his tenth season on the show, in 1972, *The Tonight Show* moved to the NBC studios in Burbank, California, and Carson moved into a million-dollar beachfront estate in Malibu, adopting a more freewheeling and adventurous public persona. His partying, divorces, alimony battles, and regular fights with network executives over his impressive salary demands and other perquisites provided fodder for the tabloids as well as material for his monologues and banter with sidekick McMahon.

But public issues were another matter. While his private life seemed to verge on the scandalous at times, Carson kept a low profile in the political and cultural tumult of the 1960s and 1970s, maintaining a middle-of-the-road stance in the midst of political assassinations; the psychedelic drug culture; civil rights demonstrations; the opposition to the Vietnam War; the Watergate scandals; and the crusades for the rights of women, gays, migrant farm workers, and others that filled the front pages of the daily newspapers. There seemed to be an implicit agreement that the issues that were turning America's college campuses and inner cities into war zones and were provoking bitter dinner table arguments in America's homes were not allowed into the controversy-free zone of the adult playtime hour of late-night comedy. If any elements of the cultural revolution in the outside world entered the late-night arena, they were greeted with Carson's typical observation that "this is some wild and wacky stuff." Perhaps this attitude was best symbolized in Carson's bemused interaction with the sexually ambiguous flower-child troubadour Tiny Tim, whose wedding to Miss Vickie was performed on *The Tonight Show* on December 17, 1969, and witnessed by forty million viewers from coast to coast, including a good segment of "the silent majority" of Middle America.

Carson's retirement from *The Tonight Show* in May 1992 sparked a major battle for his successor. An article in *The New York Times* a few months later presented a long list of possible candidates for the job, including Joan Rivers,

Dick Cavett, Pat Sajak, Whoopi Goldberg, Dennis Miller, Chevy Chase, Arsenio Hall, Jay Leno, David Letterman, and even Rush Limbaugh.[11] Jay Leno had already served as the exclusive guest host for Johnny for quite some time. His feel-good style and his everyman demeanor appealed to an older-American viewership, and his ratings were equal to and sometimes better than Carson had averaged during his tenure.[12] David Letterman's own late night comedy show, emanating from Rockefeller Center in New York City, had been airing right after *The Tonight Show* on NBC for ten years. His post-modern irony and cynicism were more hip and youth-oriented. The fact that Leno was willing to work for less money was also a factor in the decision. When NBC chose Leno, Letterman perceived the decision as a professional snub and quickly accepted CBS's lucrative offer to move his show to their network and air it in competition to Leno.

The choice of Leno as host demonstrated NBC's desire to maintain an atmosphere of congeniality and good-natured conversation with the celebrity guests, whose presence on the show increasingly seemed to be aimed at promoting their newest project. Leno has preserved the Carson format with some variations. Early on in his tenure, Leno moved the locale for his opening monologue closer to the studio audience, even shaking hands with the front row crowd as he came onstage. He blended the function of sidekick and bandleader in the personage of the urbane Branford Marsalis and later, the laid-back Kevin Eubanks. Over the years Leno has regularly beaten Letterman in the ratings race, but his show's one Emmy Award does not match the five that the *Late Show with David Letterman* has accumulated.

The profile of the successful late-night host as white, gentile, and male also seems to be well defined, mostly by the attempts of other comedians to enter the game. Arsenio Hall's syndicated late night show enjoyed a five-year run (1989 to 1994) on the fledgling FOX network, which was willing to settle for some unimpressive ratings as part of its attempts to lure minority viewers. Hall's syndicated show offered a new urban version of the late-night formula. The studio setting featured a sitting area instead of a desk. The audience surrounded the playing area rather than sitting in a theater audience arrangement and greeted Arsenio with a wild "whoop, whoop, whoop" chant and a swinging arm salute. The interviews with the guests, who usually came from the black community or other marginalized groups, were more hard-hitting and aggressive. Hall offended a large number of his viewers with some of his more controversial guests, such as Louis Farrakhan, the leader of the Nation of Islam, who was considered by many to be strongly anti-Semitic; and Andrew Dice Clay, whose stand-up comedy often included sexist, racist, and homophobic material. One of the highlights of the show's run was Arsenio's interview with presidential candidate Bill Clinton in 1991, who treated the studio audience and folks at home to an impressive performance on the saxophone. The show was well received among the black and Latino viewers and the MTV crowd, but it ended its run after five years. Another African American comedian, Keenan Ivory Wayans, lasted only one year (1997–1998) on the FOX network, while Chris Rock has had only moderate success with his entry into late-night programming on HBO.

Female comedians have not fared any better. The biggest surprise was the failure of Joan Rivers, who had been a frequent and very popular substitute host during the last decade of Carson's tenure on *The Tonight Show*. She had been the only substitute for Johnny from late 1983 to 1986, but, buoyed by her success, she made the mistake of competing with Johnny with her own late-night show on FOX in 1986. Partially because of Carson's angry reaction and open opposition to this move, Rivers's show lasted only one season. Even more surprising, considering the success of Milton Berle, Jack Benny, Jerry Seinfeld, and so many other Jewish comedians on television, is the absence of any Jewish comedian-host on the major networks in this genre. Likewise, in a medium that proved so well suited to the talents of Lucille Ball, Mary Tyler Moore, Carol Burnett, Roseanne Barr, and many other female comics, it seems odd that no woman has succeeded in the late-night arena. Is the ethnic or female comedian still considered too unruly or marginal to offer end-of-the-day reassurance? Is this yet another indication of the Puritan character and function of television entertainment coming into the American home, where relaxation can take place only under the custody of the mild-mannered, dependable father figure guarding the home and assuring the inhabitants, watching in the darkness, that all is well in the city on a hill?

The success of David Letterman has both confirmed and tweaked the formula of late-night comedy. Letterman continues the pattern of the host as a white male from Middle America: Steve Allen was born in Chicago; Jack Paar was born in Canton, Ohio, and grew up in Jackson, Michigan; Johnny Carson was born and raised in Nebraska, while Letterman came from Indiana. Letterman's format on both the NBC and CBS incarnations has also followed the traditional pattern, with Dave's bandleader, Paul Shaffer, serving also as the comic sidekick, the same mix of opening monologue, a few skits and routines, conversations with guests, and a nightly performance by a musical guest.

However, as Brooks and Marsh have described the earlier NBC version of the show, "*Late Night with David Letterman* was to TV talk shows as Salvador Dali was to traditional painting. It was a real talk show, the elements were all there, but something was a bit off."[13] His CBS program, *Late Show with David Letterman*, has only upped the ante of absurdist-cubist comedy. Letterman's comic reaction to the passing scene is similar to Carson's evaluation of "wild and wacky stuff," but it is colored by a more sardonic and ironic attitude. His nightly "Top Ten List" offers hip observations on current events, embarrassing comments about celebrities, and mild political satire. In the area of sheer mindless fun, Letterman has offered "Stupid Pet Tricks" as well as the occasional segment of "Stupid Human Tricks" and has revived the "Stump the Band" segment developed by Johnny Carson. He even sent his own mother to cover the Winter Olympics in Lillehammer, Norway, in 1994.

His unique blend of mock-seriousness has been enhanced especially by his self-referential use of the television medium itself, well described by Bernard Timberg:

> Carson's camera was rooted in the neutral gaze of the proscenium arch tradition; Letterman's camera roamed wildly and flamboyantly through the studio. Carson acknowledged the camera with sly asides; Letterman's constant, neurotic intimacy with the camera, characterized by his habit of moving right up to the lens and speaking directly into it, represented a new level of self-consciousness about the medium. . . . Letterman represented a movement from what has been called a *transparent* form of television (the viewer taking for granted and looking *through* the forms of television: camera, lighting, switching, etc.) to an opaque form in which the technology and practices of the medium itself become the focus of the show. Letterman changed late night talk forever with his post-modern irreverence and mocking play with the forms of television talk.[14]

When, in the switch from NBC to CBS, the production of the show moved to the Ed Sullivan Theater located at the northern edge of the Times Square area, Letterman used the move to the new location to expand the program's self-referential tomfoolery. He transformed the neighborhood surrounding the theater into a virtual playground. It became common practice for the camera to reveal the man holding Letterman's cue cards, the lobby of the theater, the roof of the building, and the staff offices, exposing the underbelly of the show. Letterman incorporated telephone calls to production staff in other parts of the building. Not content with such self-revelation, the camera crew, on almost a nightly basis, was sent outside the building into the surrounding vicinity to visit, among other spots, the telephone booth on the corner, restaurants and stores in the area, an adult-entertainment theater across the street, and, most prominent, the souvenir shop of the Mideastern vendors Sirajul Islam and Mujibur Rahman and the Hello Deli, managed by the genial Rupert Jee. The block of Fifty-third Street, which abuts the studio building, has often been roped off as a space for elaborate stunts, races, bowling competitions, the dropping of objects from the building's rooftop, and similar mischief. The Times Square neighborhood is thus transformed into a sandbox for the irreverent antics of Dave and his fun-loving guests and audience.

The cameras have also taken Dave or others to various locations where, in candid camera fashion, Dave might go from door to door to pose absurd or embarrassing questions to unsuspecting homeowners, concoct elaborate or nonsensical food orders from drive-in windows, or romp through shopping malls in New Jersey. Much more use is made of filmed segments of people on the street, excerpts from other television shows, and other visual material that explore the possibilities of video cameras, hidden microphones, and other communications technology as toys. For Letterman the world has become a playground, which can be visited by his viewers in a far more self-conscious and active mode than earlier late-night comedy had enjoyed.

For his part, Jay Leno has attempted to move his program's camera out into NBC's neighborhood in "beautiful downtown Burbank," but without the pedestrian traffic and dense collection of delis, restaurants, and shops that populate Broadway, Leno has not been able to turn the surrounding streets of Burbank into the urban feast of fools that Dave has found in New York City. While Letterman begins each show with views of the Statue of Liberty, Grand Central Station, and other exciting sites of Manhattan, Leno cannot use the sites of the less familiar Los Angeles cityscape to evoke a similar sense of urban playfulness. Yet they both attempt to enter into the same discourse: the function of the talk show as spontaneous, present-tense conversation that aims at relaxation and is hosted by a personality that viewers feel safe about bringing into their home late at night for some playtime.

But the playtime is definitely for adults. Indeed, over the years, the late-night shows' mood of spontaneity and relaxation have frequently allowed more adult humor in the host's monologues and the double entendres and ad-lib remarks of the guests, which network censors allow to remain on taped presentation of the show. Late-night comedy lore has developed around the remarks Johnny Carson made about Jayne Mansfield, Zsa Zsa Gabor, and other sexy guests. Unscripted moments include the time on *The Tonight Show* when Ed Ames, who played Daniel Boone's Indian companion, Mingo, on NBC's adult Western *Daniel Boone*, demonstrated his method of throwing a tomahawk at a male-silhouette target and landed the weapon in the groin-crotch of the figure, prompting one of the most sustained periods of studio audience laughter in television history. Madonna made even Letterman uncomfortable with her free usage of the F-word in their conversation, and Drew Barrymore prompted a similar response when, her back to the camera, she stood on Dave's desk and revealed her naked breasts to him.

The roster of late-night comedy programming expanded in the 1990s into the later hours, with the likes of Conan O'Brien, Carson Daly, Dennis Miller, and Craig Kilbourn, who also continue the pattern of white gentile males as hosts on late-night network television. Only with the arrival of cable has the genre found a successful Jewish host-comic, *The Daily Show*'s Jon Stewart. Generally, these "later-night" shows, scheduled well after the midnight hour, engage in sharper political satire and more extensive conversations with their guests, in keeping with the smaller and more devoted viewership they serve in the very early morning.

The success of these Monday-through-Friday shows played a part in the emergence of one of the most successful examples of late-night comedy in television history, the phenomenon of *Saturday Night Live*, which made its début on NBC on October 11, 1975, and remains on the air with no signs of stopping. *The Tonight Show* and its imitators demonstrated that there were some distinct advantages about the late-night timeslot. The audience for such a show was a narrower age group. The 55-year-old-and-older demographic had probably turned off their sets by 11:30 p.m., and younger children were presumably no longer watching either. The comedy could be aimed at older teenagers and baby-boomer adults. Also, the program did not need to achieve the level of prime-time ratings to be considered successful. However, this would not be the laid-back talk-show format of *The Tonight Show*; it would attempt to offer sketch comedy in a late-night environment. This would be playtime for the nearly-grown-up.

Actually, *The Tonight Show* was even more causally connected to *Saturday Night Live*. For several years NBC had offered its affiliates the option to air reruns of *The Tonight Show* on Saturday or Sunday nights. However, in 1974 Johnny Carson told NBC to discontinue this policy because he wanted to start airing those reruns on weeknights to give himself more nights off. As they started planning for the new show, NBC appointed a comedy writer from Canada, Lorne Michaels, to be executive producer. Having worked on *Rowan and Martin's Laugh-In* and some Lily Tomlin specials, Michaels's sensibility was edgy and tuned in to the baby-boomer generation that had grown up with television. Dick Ebersol, the NBC executive charged with finding a show to fill the Saturday night time slot, has described why he chose Michaels:

> Lorne just took my breath away in the way he talked about things, how he wanted to have the first television show to speak the language of the time. He wanted the show to be the first show in the history of television to talk—absent expletives—the same language being talked on college campuses and streets and everywhere else.[15]

Following this vision, they recruited writers who had soaked up the Ivy League frat-boy attitude of the Harvard Lampoon, the alternative feel of the Village Voice, and the inventiveness of some of the "smart" sitcoms, such as *The Mary Tyler Moore Show*. Cast members were recruited from the Harvard

Lampoon shows and the Second City improvisational troupes in Chicago and Toronto. From its premiere show on October 11, 1975, this fresh, outrageous show signaled a new era for late-night comedy:

> With the arrival of *SNL*, the TV generation, at least for ninety minutes a week, could see television not just as a window on the past or a display case for the fading fantasy figures of their fathers and mothers, but as a mirror—a warped funhouse mirror perhaps, but a mirror just the same, one reflecting their own sensibilities, values, and philosophies. Television, which had shown them the world, had heretofore neglected to show them themselves.[16]

Michaels's first step into new territory was actually a return to television's early days. Like *Your Show of Shows* and other comedy-variety shows of the golden age, the show would be aired live. As Tom Shales and James Andrew Miller have described it, when the show went on the air, "the audience at home watched and laughed, thrillingly aware that 'this is happening now' and that there was thus an element of daring and peril to what otherwise amounted to mere entertainment."[17]

They had probably also learned a lesson or two from the problems encountered by the Smothers Brothers, whose antiestablishment satire had angered many prime-time viewers and caused their abrupt cancellation by the network. The creators of *Saturday Night Live* correctly intuited that late night was the safer venue for the type of irreverent sketch comedy that would characterize the show. *Saturday Night Live*'s brand of edgy, countercultural comedy, with its frequent references to the drug culture of the time, would not be welcome in most family environments. Instead, the program would aim at a younger, baby-boomer audience who would appreciate its more rebellious tone, its daring return of sketch comedy to a live presentation, the hip guest hosts and musical performers, and, most of all, its nutty ensemble of Not Ready for Prime Time Players. It was the sort of niche programming that would underlie the strategy of the cable networks which would be arriving in the 1980s, with MTV for the younger viewers, Lifetime Channel for women, ESPN for male sports fans, Nickelodeon for children, etc. This particular niche, however, was comprised of the 18- to 49-year-old demographic most sought after by advertisers, and most advertisers were happy to pitch their product on a show that was aiming even more directly at this younger group.

From its earliest days the program has been a storehouse of comic talent, showcasing the top tier of new performers who were destined for greater fame in film comedy. The original group included Chevy Chase, John Belushi, Dan Ackroyd, and Bill Murray, who would eventually star in some of biggest box office successes in the history of film comedy. Over the years *SNL* has continued to introduce viewers to talented performers who would move on to film stardom: Eddie Murphy, Billy Crystal, Martin Short, Mike Myers, Robert Downey, Jr., Chris Farley, Adam Sandler, Janeane Garofalo, and Will Ferrell, to name a few. Others in the casts have continued to enjoy successful careers in other television shows. Jane Curtin, Paul Shaffer, Julia Louis-Dreyfus, Phil Hartman, David Spade, Dennis Miller, Chris Elliot, Jim Belushi, Chris Rock, and Damon Wayans have all reappeared in successful television comedies since their days on *Saturday Night Live*. One trio—Christopher Guest, Michael McKean, and Harry Shearer—have made something of a career by collaborating in a number of "mockumentary" films (*This is Spinal Tap*, *Waiting for Guffman*, *Best in Show*, and *A Mighty Wind*). Some of the cast members have appeared in films based on characters first developed on *Saturday Night Live*. The most successful transitions were Belushi and Ackroyd's film based on their Blues Brothers characters and Mike Myers's and Dana Carvey's stoner characters, Wayne and Garth, who starred in the hugely popular *Wayne's World* and *Wayne's World II*. Julia Sweeney's sexually ambiguous character, Pat, starred in her own film; as did Molly Shannon's Catholic schoolgirl, Mary Katherine Gallagher; and Al Franken's self-help counselor, Stuart Smalley, in *Stuart Saves His Family*. No television program has had anything close to the impact on the direction of Hollywood comedy as *Saturday Night Live*.

The tone of the comic discourse on *SNL* was established immediately by the show's early stars. As the first host of the program's mock newscast, "Weekend Update," Chevy Chase greeted the viewers with the words, "Good evening. I'm Chevy Chase . . . and you're not." Hip, self-assured, and ironic, Chase set the tone for the rest of the cast. He could also regress to a fourth-grade level of humor. When a guest commentator on the newscast would offer an opposing viewpoint, Chase would typically lean back behind the guest and mock the commentary with facial expressions or a silent but disdainful mouthing of the guest's remarks. In an ironic commentary on his preppy good looks and athletic build, Chase could also be the master of the pratfall and the pie in the face. Meanwhile, John Belushi was the frat-boy slob who engaged primarily in loud and hostile physical comedy, dressing up as Killer Bee or, arrayed in Samurai warrior attire, engaging in various occupations as Samurai Salesman, Samurai Waiter, Samurai Bellhop, Samurai Psychiatrist, etc. In general, as the resident id, Belushi personified his generation's rebellion against bourgeois repression. Gilda Radner was the childlike, rubber-faced class clown/nerdy girl. One of her regular characters, Lisa Loopner, complete with facial blemishes, continuous postnasal drip, and thick eyeglasses attached with a chain, dated Bill Murray's Todd, the classic nerd with the high belt line, pocket penholder, and the habit of giving "noogies" to Lisa by rapping his knuckles on her forehead. Radner was also a gifted mimic, imitating a spectrum of personalities that included Lucille Ball, Jacqueline Onassis, and Annette Funicello. Radner's most devastating impersonation was Baba Wawa, a spoof of Barbara Walters's peculiar speech patterns and attitude. She appeared regularly on the "Weekend Update" segment of the show as Emily Litella, an older woman who quietly protested against ideas that she had heard incorrectly, wondering, for instance, why there was so much fuss about "violins on television," "Soviet Jewelry," or "presidential erections." Bill Murray was generally the supercool rebel who suavely defied the rules that lesser mortals had to follow, an attitude perfectly expressed in Murray's character, Nick the Lounge Singer. Dan Ackroyd played a wide array of characters. He appeared regularly as the Rovco Salesman, offering the television audience incredible deals on the Bass-O-Matic and Bat-O-Matic blenders; as Leonard Pinth-Garnell, the pompous host of a BBC series, "Bad Playhouse"; and in classy drag and a high-pitched voice as Julia Child. One of Ackroyd's most popular comic performances was his creation, along with the show's frequent guest Steve Martin, of the "wild and crazy guys," two nerdy Eastern European immigrants who fancied themselves to be "swinging American bachelors." Laraine Newman was the spaced-out featherhead and sometime sexy babe. Jane Curtin was the most conventional of the group, pretty and refined, who was regularly embarrassed and humiliated by her association with the others, most unforgettably when, in the "Point-Counterpoint" debate during the "Weekend Update" segment, Dan Ackroyd would respond to her comments by addressing her as "Jane, you ignorant slut."

The running thematic of the ten or so sketches that made up each week's *SNL* was that the ideal of human behavior was to be cool and hip and the mortal sin was to be a nerd. It may be more than mere coincidence that the show began the same year that the severely un-hip Richard M. Nixon was forced to resign in disgrace from the presidency. The connection between the nerd-like qualities of "Tricky Dick" and the evidence of serious wrongdoing in the Nixon White House would not have been lost on the viewers in 1975. The first season's running joke about Nixon's successor, the incumbent Gerald Ford, centered on his physical awkwardness, especially his habit of slipping and falling, impersonated with perfect slapstick skill by Chevy Chase. In a sense, the Puritan interest in the "elect," those whose guarantee of salvation is manifested in their godly behavior and attention to duty, was turned upside down by the attitude informing *Saturday Night Live*. According to the *SNL* ethic, the truly successful and fulfilled people were those who were self-confident enough to break the rules, the Nietzchean *über*men and *über*women who could exempt themselves from the rules of conventional society. Even the show's set was designed to look like a sort of basement recreation room where, away from parental supervision, the overgrown adolescents could indulge in forbidden behavior or at least talk about it.

So the truly blessed people, the objects of everyone's envy, are found in the in-crowd of the cool and the hip who are misbehaving in the basement.

Over the years the *SNL*'s comic discourse has continued to foster the cult of hipness. Each show is hosted by a different celebrity, chosen because he or she somehow personifies the peak of the cultural wave at the time: the star of the hot new movie or television show, the off-beat politician, the glamorous ath-lete, the latest rock star. The premiere show, for example, was hosted by the countercultural comedian George Carlin. Other hosts in the first five seasons included Paul Simon, Lily Tomlin, Candice Bergen, Steve Martin, Madeline Kahn, Jodie Foster, Ralph Nader, Julian Bond, Fran Tarkenton, Ray Charles, Carrie Fisher, Milton Berle, Bill Russell, and even O. J. Simpson. Likewise, every week features a musical performance, usually by a cutting-edge new rock band or solo artist or one of the acknowledged deities of pop or rock music: Paul Simon, Mick Jagger, Aretha Franklin, The Grateful Dead, James Taylor, Deborah Harry, or Bruce Springsteen. Over the course of thirty years the array of musical guests has served as a chronicle of every younger generation's musical tastes.[18]

As an exercise in satire, *Saturday Night Live* has never been as direct as *The Smothers Brothers Comedy Hour* or *All in the Family*. The code of late-night tele-vision generally seems to permit only the sort of mild political potshots of Carson's, Leno's, or Letterman's opening monologues. Moreover, the ironic stance of *Saturday Night Live* precludes the sort of ideological commitment— and the anger—that inspires true satire. The truly hip are beyond any earnest involvement in the messy details of politics or social protest. Rather than ob-ject to Ronald Reagan's deceptions and his administration's illegal behavior in the Iran-Contra scandal, for example, *Saturday Night Live* would prefer to comment on his dyed pompadour hairdo or his liberal use of face rouge. The most frequent occasions for political satire on the show have been the opening segment that comes on-screen unannounced before the show's credits. Some-times the segment resembles an address from the Oval Office, a press confer-ence from the White House or the Pentagon, or a campaign speech. And it al-ways ends with the camera closing in on the speaker as he or she enthusiastically announces, "Live . . . from New York. . . . It's Saturday Night!" The other constant piece of satire comes somewhere in the middle of the hour-and-a-half show. The "Weekend Update" newscast presents a roundup of the past week's political issues, celebrity gossip, and latest scandals. While the introductory segment sometimes attacks the political positions of an of-ficeholder (George Bush's promise not to raise taxes, Clinton's health-care proposal), it more often pokes fun at his or her personal foibles (Jimmy Carter's piety, Clinton's sexual misbehavior, George W. Bush's inarticulate-ness). The "Weekend Update" segment tends even more toward avoidance of serious political criticism and veers towards mockery of an official's social gaffes or physical clumsiness (George W. Bush's choking on a pretzel, Hillary Rodham Clinton's changing hairstyles). Thus, in marketing itself to younger, presumably more politically disaffected viewership, *Saturday Night Live* maintains a relatively apolitical viewpoint. For true political satire a viewer must go to someplace other than late-night network television, more often to the print medium of a publication such as *The Onion* or the political cartoons of Garry Trudeau or to cable television for the faux newscasts of *The Daily Show*.

While *Saturday Night Live* may not make very direct attacks on the political powers that be, it has developed a knack for exploring the dark side of American life, a sort of running commentary on our national foibles. It might even be said that the show's comedy explores the shadow side of contemporary American life, the issues that everyone knows are operative in our culture but are not discussed in polite company: greedy business practices, sexual misbehavior, political chicanery, racial tensions, religious hypocrisy, dysfunctional families, to name just a few. One of the longest-running features of the show has been the mock commercials, takeoffs on well-known advertisements incorporating sexual or scatological humor or drug references. One commercial, modeled on the Total cereal ads, claims it would take over thirty thousand bowls of oat bran to equal the fiber content of one bowl of high-fiber Colon Blow. Their domestic answer to Evian bottled water is a brand called Swill. Dredged from Lake Erie, it's "everything you always wanted in a mineral water. And more." Their solution for the problem of male-pattern baldness is Chia Head. Instead of taking Nytol for a good night's sleep to cure your cold or flu, Hibernol lets you sleep through the entire flu season, usually for two and three months. "You can't find stronger medication—in this country." One mysterious product, called Shimmer, was advertised as a floor wax and a dessert topping in one. Some of their mock public service ads have carried a political edge. The White Guilt Relief Fund was advertised by the black cast member Garrett Morris, who announced, "If you would like to relieve your guilt, I'm willing to accept money as a representative victim of four hundred years of repression." Their PSA for the Navy proclaimed, "It's not just a job, it's $96.78 a week." By tapping into the television generation's experience of their hyper-comercialized environment and their resentment of business and government hypocrisy, these mock-advertisements have offered perhaps the show's most direct connection to any serious critique of the American capitalistic system.[19]

Over the years, while the percentage of cast members that have been African American has remained relatively small, racism and racial stereotypes have been regular topics on the show. Black cast members such as Garrett Morris, Damon Wayans, Chris Rock, Ellen Cleghorne, Tim Meadows, and Tracy

Morgan have carried on the tradition. During his two seasons on the show in the early 1990s, Chris Rock offered perhaps the strongest bit of African American humor in his recurring segment "The Dark Side with Nat X." Wearing a dashiki and sporting an enormous Afro, Nat X hosted his talk show from Compton, California, "a city so bad it has a drive-by shooting lane." A typical comment would be Nat's observations on Black History Month: "Isn't that nice. The Man gives us February because it's the shortest month of the year. It's also the coldest month of the year, just in case we wanted to have a parade." The black *SNL* performer who went on to enjoy the most successful career, Eddie Murphy, contributed his impressions of Buckwheat from the Little Rascals movies, Gumby, Stevie Wonder, James Brown, and a hybrid called Little Richard Simmons. One of his most popular sketches was Murphy's children's show entitled "Mr. Robinson's Neighborhood," in which he played an inner-city scam artist who taught children how to break into homes and automobiles, how to steal money from their mother's purse to send to him, and so on. Mr. Robinson takes the viewers around his neighborhood:

> Oh, look, a bombed-out building! Could you live in it? Could you corner somebody in it and take his wallet? . . . Ooh, look! Mr. Taxicab Driver is driving through our neighborhood. Think he'll pick up one of the people from our neighborhood? No way. Can you say, "throw a coke bottle?" Well, since I have to walk to work—I can't catch a cab—I gotta walk sixty-three blocks, so I'll see you tomorrow.[20]

In "Mr. Robinson's Neighborhood," Murphy managed to combine a send-up of racist stereotypes and a critique of the hyper-segregation in America's major cities that has created such miserable "neighborhoods" along with the subversive suggestion that the original Mr. Rogers, a beloved but ultra-white figure from the viewer's childhood, too nice to be true, represented the hypocrisy of the white ruling class.

Family life has often been the target of the *SNL*'s satire, usually from the viewpoint of the cool hipster stifled by his or her square parents. One of the darkest sketches on this topic, shown on one of the Christmas shows, was an advertisement for a recording of songs entitled "The Dysfunctional Family Christmas," including such popular favorites as "I've Got My Drinking under Control for the Holidays"; "Can't You Let it Drop, It's Christmas"; "What I Want You Can't Buy Me"; and "Fruitcake and Shame." Other bizarre families included the Loopners, a family of nerds; the Coneheads, an extraterrestrial family from the planet Remulak; and the Widettes, who shared a common condition of extremely large posteriors, caused by their incessant eating. The monstrous families played upon the common suspicion of all adolescents (and many adults) that their own families were impossibly and incorrigibly weird.

Religion has provided a favorite target for the *Saturday Night Live*'s humor. During his three seasons on the show (1978–1980, 1985–1986), Don Novello often appeared as the hip Father Guido Sarducci, director of communications for Vatican City. Holding a cigarette in his fingers, Father Sarducci would explain Roman Catholic teachings and church politics in a down-to-earth, highly irreverent manner. But the more memorable character was Dana Carvey's Church Lady, who hosted her own talk show entitled "Church Chat." Enid Strict, the Church Lady, dressed in a prim lady's suit, with a helmet of tightly styled hair and no makeup or jewelry, would peer through her spectacles and comment on the wickedness of the world. Repressed, angry, and severely judgmental, she was particularly obsessed with other people's sexual activities, even given to describing people's genital regions and erotic movements. She frequently referred to the more personal body parts as "the bulbous naughty place" or the "tingly naughty parts" that often got "engorged." She was particularly vigilant against the constant machinations of Satan—aka the Prince of Darkness, the Beastmaster, or the Hairy Host of Hell. She suspected his activity in Halloween, which she referred to as "a night on the town for Satan"; in the Super Bowl, which she re-titled the Satan Bowl, where "large sweaty men collide at a high rate of speed to the apparent delight of onlookers . . . and the fans scream like little Beastmasters, drink beer, and spit up"; and even in Christmas, because the letters that spell "Santa" can also spell "Satan."

A mistress of the pious put-down, Church Lady would berate her guests and threaten them with the hellfire their immoral lives so clearly deserve. Some of her guests included actual celebrities such as Sigourney Weaver, who had played a woman possessed by demons in *Ghostbusters*; Danny DeVito, who was scolded for making a film entitled *Throw Momma from the Train*; and Sean Penn, whose major crime was being married to Madonna. Rob Lowe, whose career was put at risk by the scandalous revelation of a videotape showing him having sex with a prostitute, came on the show and ended up being punished by Church Lady with a very energetic spanking. Cast members appeared in the roles of the spiritual seeker Shirley MacLaine, scandalous women such as Jessica Hahn and Marla Maples, and the televangelists Jim and Tammy Faye Baker and Jimmy Swaggart, who, by happy coincidence, had recently made the headlines for their financial and sexual misbehavior.

Yet, when a genuinely angry gesture of protest against organized religion was expressed by the Irish singer Sinead O'Connor, who, at the conclusion of her musical performance, surprised everyone by ripping up a picture of the

Pope, the producers of the show were deeply distressed and apologetic. Such direct criticism of the establishment was out of place in the venue of late-night television. The comedy of *Saturday Night Live* has often enough been daring and even brilliant in its commentary on political issues and social problems such as racism and commercialism. It has even attacked icons of American culture such as the family and religion. Yet the show has generally remained faithful to the code of late-night comedy. Serious political and social discussion is not to be attempted. It is Saturday night, and, more than any other night of the week, it is playtime for those who are still up watching television. With *Saturday Night Live*, however, television's playground for adults started admitting some younger members. And they have never left.

·10·

MOVIN' ON UP?

It has taken a great deal of time for African Americans to occupy any significant amount of time on the prime-time schedule, and, as the NAACP has pointed out, there is a long way to go before there is proportional representation of the black population on the networks. Nevertheless, the story of African American comedy on television is a lively chronicle of defeat, victory, and controversy that continues to this day.

The early years of television were particularly devoid of any African American presence. In the realm of comedy the only noteworthy programs, *Beulah* (1950–1953) and *Amos 'n' Andy* (1951–1953), did not last very long on the small screen. After their failures, viewers seldom saw any black characters on television. In the comedies blacks appeared only as maids, train porters, and other similar characters throughout the next quarter-century.

Beulah had been a radio show on CBS since 1945. The main character was a hefty, nurturing "colored" maid in the household of a middle-class white couple, the Hendersons. Actually, the part was first played on the radio show by a white male actor. Only in 1947 did a black actress take over the role. Hattie McDaniel, who had made a career of playing mostly comic maids in films but had won an Academy Award for her far more dramatic role as Mammy in *Gone with the Wind* in 1939, was cast as Beulah. When the show moved to television in 1950, the legendary singer-actress Ethel Waters was given the part, with other respected black actors—Butterfly McQueen and, in the second season, Dooley Wilson—in supporting roles. The casting of Ethel Waters in the role, according to Donald Bogle, "lent the series some distinction and a lopsided credibility" and "endowed the show with a subtext that made *Beulah* far more than it appeared on the surface."[1] With a personal history of poverty and family problems, Waters was well known as a blues singer, sophisticated nightclub songstress, major recording artist, star of Broadway musicals and drama, and a film actress who had been nominated for an Academy Award for the film *Pinky*, with a career-crowning performance on stage and in film as Berenice, the cook, in Carson McCullers's *The Member of the Wedding*. Waters had also authored a best-selling autobiography, *His Eye Is on the Sparrow*.

The plots of the series usually showed how Beulah, as something of a wise Earth-mother with her hearty laugh, outspoken demeanor, and natural nurturing skills, would comment upon, and then solve, the latest problem in the Henderson household, with never a thought of her servile condition or any reference to the concerns of black Americans in the 1950s. In fact, there was less anger in the television show than there had been on radio. Mel Watkins has observed:

> If there was any change, it was in the more insistent accord seen between the black characters and the Hendersons. All instances of real strife were excised, and, unlike the radio show, even Beulah's patented sardonic rejoinders were usually toned down. Despite Waters' spicy presence, the show depicted an ideal suburban world in which whites and black servants lived in harmonious acceptance of the status quo.[2]

Not surprisingly, the limitations of the role proved unsatisfactory to Waters, who left the show at the end of its second season. For its third season, the producers brought back the star of the radio version, Hattie McDaniel, to resume the role. But McDaniel was stricken with cancer and had to leave the show after six episodes. She was replaced by another successful film actress, Louise Beavers, who, according to Bogle, turned the role "into an emblem of a budding black middle class":

> Beavers often made Beulah a proper Black matron. Without any trace of a dialect, she was always well groomed, well coifed, and well mannered, looking like a woman ready to go off to church every Sunday. That may explain why, although *Beulah* was criticized, the show was never damned the way *Amos 'n' Andy* was. Beulah seemed capable of dealing with an integrated society, even though she could function only as a servant in that world. She knew how to behave around white people. The contradiction, though—again for the Black viewer—is that this otherwise possibly progressive Black woman has to perform such silly antics.[3]

In any case, Beavers also grew more uncomfortable in the role and, with her departure, despite the good ratings the show was getting, ABC cancelled *Beulah* in 1953.

Watkins's evaluation of *Beulah* is unusually favorable, suggesting that in terms of its domestic comedy formula and depiction of African American life, it may have been ahead of its time:

The program depended on comic situations and cultural assumptions common to the glut of suburban sitcoms which later dominated the airwaves—many of which spotlighted the formula interaction between a white housekeeper or maid and families that were just as exemplary, pristine, and cordial as the Hendersons. Except for Beulah's race, one might have been watching *Hazel* or *My Three Sons*. . . . In its depiction of ordinary black folks who maintained jobs, spoke reasonable English, and had warm cordial relationships with one another, the show was a singular presence on early television.[4]

The other radio show about African Americans, *Amos 'n' Andy*, encountered much more controversy in its transfer to television. Considering the racial tensions in America in the early 1950s, one can say that the television show was doomed from the beginning, unlike its radio predecessor, which may very well be the most popular radio comedy of all time. The radio show made its national début on the NBC network in August 1929, the creation of two white comedians from Chicago, Freeman Gosden and Charles Correll, who played the characters in a Negro dialect. The show followed the misadventures of two Southern black men who had migrated from the South to the North, ending up in Harlem. Within a year the show was a sensation, broadcast every weeknight for fifteen minutes until 1943, when it moved to CBS and became a weekly half-hour show, ending its run on the radio in 1954.

The popularity of the radio program is the stuff of legend. Watkins recounts the stories about the movie theaters that would interrupt the featured film at 7:00 p.m. each evening and bring in loudspeakers so that the audience could listen to that night's episode. Radio spots during the 1932 presidential campaign were carefully scheduled so that they did not compete with *Amos 'n' Andy*. Telephone calls diminished every evening from 7:00 to 7:15, bus lines and taxis had no passengers, and people did not run water or flush toilets during the sacred quarter-hour. Certain events during the program's peak years in the 1930s caused what Watkins has called "a kind of national frenzy."[5] In 1931, for example, in a story that went on for several episodes, Amos was falsely accused of murder and brought to trial. Gosden and Correll were warned by their sponsors that "the Parent-Teacher Association is going to boycott the program if Amos is convicted," and one commentator remarked that "no trial in fact or fiction ever interested the people more."[6] Newspapers carried synopses of each night's show. The great Anglo-Irish playwright George Bernard Shaw summed it up best when he proclaimed, "There are three things which I shall never forget about America—the Rocky Mountains, Niagara Falls, and *Amos 'n' Andy*."[7]

In retrospect, considering the distinctly African American framework of the show, the breadth of its appeal during its radio heyday is remarkable. Watkins attributes its enormous popularity to its appearance at a particular moment in American history:

> It . . . allowed America obliquely to scrutinize and laugh at its own problems. Gosden and Correll [the show's creators] spotlighted two Georgia Negroes whose migration first to Chicago and then to Harlem humorously mirrored the plight of the nation's common man, caught in the transformation from an agrarian society to a complex urban one. . . . Amos and Andy were presented as bona fide Americans (albeit second-class ones) struggling to open their own business—a taxi service—and secure a place in a rapidly changing society that, in a limited manner, was realistically presented.[8]

The audience's identification with these economically challenged characters was strongly reinforced by the hardships experienced so generally after the stock market crash, which occurred only a few weeks after the show's radio début.

At the outset of the series, most of the episodes revolved around the close friendship and extreme contrast between Amos and Andy. While Amos was diligent but slow, Andy was an idle schemer. Although these were familiar stock characters in black minstrelsy, Watkins claims that there was "a veil of propriety" that moderated what could have been stereotypically gullible "Sambo" or trickster "darky" roles:

> The moderation with which Amos and Andy were initially portrayed probably accounts for their huge following. Amos, after all, was such a beloved and trustworthy character that he became a national symbol of thrift and responsibility during the Depression. One newspaper editorial cited him as a model of a sensible response to the nation's economic woes.[9]

Once the economy improved, however, the show's emphasis changed. Many of the plots began to center on the scams perpetrated by Amos and Andy's neighbor Kingfish, who was much more of a schemer than even Andy was. Especially when the format of the show changed in the early 1940s, Kingfish became the star of the show, and most of the episodes followed Kingfish's moneymaking schemes, which often took advantage of Andy, and Kingfish's troubles with his domineering wife, Sapphire, and her mother.

But just as larger social changes had favored the success of the radio show, the social currents of mid-century America militated against the television show's chances of success. CBS had big hopes for the transfer of such a popular radio program to television. They paid the record sum of 2.5 million dollars for the rights to the series. Whereas the roles of Amos, Andy, Kingfish, and others had been played on the radio by Gosden and Correll, it was wisely decided that the television version should feature an all-black cast. The network's highly publicized talent search took two years and involved eight hundred auditions and fifty screen tests. The series was shot on film at the Hal Roach studios at an unusually high budget of $40,000 an episode, directed by a very successful director, Charles Barton, who had directed the popular Abbott and Costello comedies in Hollywood.

Even while the network was planning the television series, however, opposition by black rights groups, especially the NAACP, was forming. Gerard Jones gives a concise description of the mood of the country about racial issues at the time:

> The aftermath of World War II found the power, vocality, and political sensitivity of American blacks hitting a new crest. The black bourgeoisie had been growing for decades in number and strength and pride. Now it was making itself felt. NAACP membership increased ten times over during the 1940s. By 1948 black leaders were making waves in American journalism and entertainment. The Democratic party courted them in the election. President Truman appointed a Civil Rights Commission and declared 1949 a "Year of Rededication" to the principles of racial equality. Hollywood began a series of "message movies" in 1949— *Pinky, Home of the Brave, Lost Boundaries*—and the message was that racial discrimination must end. The liberal concept of full integration—gradual, painless, nonviolent, but inevitable—captured the American conscience.[10]

Amos 'n' Andy made its television début on June 28, 1951. Within a week, at its national convention, the NAACP denounced the series, publishing a list of grievances entitled "Why the *Amos 'n' Andy* TV Show Should Be Taken Off the Air." They complained that all the characters on the show were either clowns or crooks; that even the professional Negroes were shown as quacks, thieves, or cowards; that the women were portrayed as vulgar, screaming shrews; and that they were all shown as dodging work of any kind. The NAACP found this particularly damaging because no other program on television showed blacks in a favorable light. *Amos 'n' Andy*'s demeaning images of African Americans was only furthering the generally negative impression of African Americans held by the white population, most of whom did not encounter any black people in their daily lives.[11]

Thomas Cripps's evaluation of the conflict offers insight into the peculiar problem, then and now, of portraying the African American experience in the established codes of television comedy:

> Television producers had quickly invented a formula that expressed their sentiments as they applied to various ethnic groups—the Jews in *The Goldbergs*, Nordics in *I Remember Mama* . . . and the Italians in *Luigi*. . . . All of them shared a

pool of interchangeable parts: an extended family, crotchety but warmly senti-mental old folks, happy problems happily resolved in twenty-eight minutes of air time, and a division of characters into an older generation encrusted with cul-tural survivals from the old country and a younger group of super-Americans who had assimilated the virtues of the new land.

Unfortunately, *Amos 'n' Andy* was asked to perform similar service for an eth-nic group whose history included slavery, discrimination, and exclusion from the opportunity for easy assimilation implied in the gently comic plots of the Euro-pean ethnic shows. Thus their traits of eccentric manners, dialect, and other cul-tural baggage were perceived not as vestiges of a national culture but as the mocking of racial subculture that was an aberration of white American culture.[12]

J. Fred MacDonald's insightful assessment of the series supports Cripps's opinion that the comedy ultimately belittled Black society. MacDonald presents many arguments from defenders of the show, saying it was comedic caricature firmly in the tradition of American humor and ethnic theater. He notes the middle-class look of the characters' Harlem residences and the por-trayal of Amos's working-class family, as well as the absence of any overt signs of racial segregation.[13] But his bottom-line judgement on the series is negative:

This was a patronizing picture of black society. It depreciated black maturity, rendering most of the adult characters as harmless children filled with pranks and pretensions, but ultimately unthreatening. There were no civil rights ten-sions in this show. *Amos 'n' Andy* was a false interpretation of black reality, un-fairly lulling whites into complacency and unjustly reducing African Americans to a position of inferiority.[14]

Gerard Jones, however, wonders if the reaction to the show was fair and suggests that the NAACP's crusade may have been an overreaction. "Looking back on this hue and cry decades later," Jones writes, "one can only wonder if anyone was really watching the show. Surely it was no 'artistic triumph.' Yet by the same token it seems scarcely insulting enough to justify such a ferocious assault."[15] He documents the changes of characterization, noting that Andy's speech was less dialect driven; that the Harlem shopkeepers, cops, and other neighbors were always positively portrayed; that the home environments were all clean and middle class in appearance; and that it was the first time black professionals had been presented in film or television. The show was also a great opportunity for African American actors, as the cast members and some editorials in black publications were quick to point out to the NAACP.

Jones also illustrates the various efforts of the show's producers and writers to present the characters and situations as more mainstream and middle class, at least in their aspirations. Kingfish and Sapphire are even shown going for marriage counseling, and, in their popular Christmas episode, Andy is shown resisting one of Kingfish's get-rich-quick schemes and getting a part-time job to buy an expensive doll that his daughter desires. The Kingfish character was gradually shown in a more and more negative light. "Through it all," says Jones, "the creators show a drive to dignify and humanize their material . . . they leave little doubt of their basic prosocial position."[16]

Kingfish, however, was the problem, creating a major dilemma for the producers. As Jones points out, Tim Moore's portrayal of Kingfish was socially offensive but artistically brilliant:

> Lying, fleecing, strutting, mugging, wringing dues out of brothers in the preposterous Mystic Knights of the Sea Lodge, nostrils always open for a new scheme to get through life without working, he was still very much the coon. And he stole the show. Tim Moore turned in an expressive, energetic performance that brought to life the tritest plots and flattest lines. As Amos and Andy became duller and more respectable, he became the only sure source of laughs on the show. Since the show's creators had a greater stake in being funny than in being socially correct, he naturally began to carry most of the plots.[17]

It was Kingfish's very distance from the values of the white middle class and the emerging black bourgeoisie that made his character such a comic achievement. Watkins agrees with Jones's assessment of the comic appeal—particularly to black audiences—of the Kingfish character, especially as portrayed by Moore:

> Bombastic, irreverent, stylized beyond belief, Moore's Kingfish was an unbridled example of the ethnic humor that blacks regularly flocked to see in race films and on the stages of black theatres. . . . By virtue of authentic style and the exuberance with which he portrayed Kingfish, Moore projected a character whose jubilant flouting of convention struck a resonant chord with a large section of the black underclass. Moore's Kingfish was not simply the trifling, scheming parasite that he is often made out to be; for many African-Americans, he mirrored an iconoclastic impulse that had lingered since slavery. In many ways he personified the irreverent trickster who refused to be contained or thwarted by a society that merely tolerated his existence. On television, as with his real-life prototypes, he almost never won his battles; but he also never succumbed. His theatrical style, irrepressible nature, and constant twitting of the social norms made him the show's most humorous character and in all likelihood the most beloved by the majority of the black folks.[18]

Iconoclast or embarrassment? Whatever he was, Kingfish was not destined for a long visit in the American home, but not because of any protest activity. The boycott of the program and the program's sponsor, the Blatz Brewing

Company, promoted by the NAACP had little effect. Only one station took the program off the air, and the Blatz company released a poll showing that 77 percent of black people in New York liked the show.[19] However, the show, which had ranked 13th in the Nielsen ratings during its first season, dropped to #25 in its second season. Neither the sponsors nor the network needed the expense and headache of a controversial show with less than impressive ratings, and the show was cancelled, with several unfortunate consequences. For the next twenty-five years there would be no television shows starring an African American, very few black performers showing up as supporting actors or guest stars on any show, and no blacks appearing in any television commercials. The NAACP, accused by many in the black community of "killing *Amos 'n' Andy*," withdrew from involvement in media issues and turned their attention to other aspects of the struggle for civil rights and racial equality.

The television hiatus finally ended in 1968. In September of that year, in the wake of the assassination of Rev. Dr. Martin Luther King, Jr., and the national dialogue about race that ensued, one network took the risk of scheduling a prime-time comedy, *Julia* (1968–1971), with an African American star, Diahann Carroll. The arrival of Diahann Carroll as Julia on NBC—as well as Bill Cosby as Scotty on *I Spy* (1965–1968), Clarence Williams III as Linc on *The Mod Squad* (1968–1973), Lloyd Haynes as Pete Dixon on *Room 222* (1969–1974), and other black characters on regular series—caused a change in perceptions in both African American and white homes. Bogle recalls that throughout the 1960s the nightly news on television had brought into the home powerful images of the Civil Rights struggle's tactics of sit-ins, marches, and protests, with the accompanying pictures of police dogs, fire hoses, and billy clubs turned on the demonstrators:

> Yet much of mainstream America still thought of the new Negro as someone *out there* protesting, not as someone who might be a part of his or her community, someone he or she might actually know. . . . The primetime network series altered perceptions and attitudes by making African Americans a familiar weekly presence in American living rooms.[20]

In the homes of black Americans a parallel change was occurring:

> With the absence of programs about African Americans, Black viewers felt that television was not fully and fairly representing them, not saying who they were and what their lives were like. . . . Only as characters like Scotty, Julia, and Pete Dixon . . . arrived on the tube did African American viewers believe they were seeing some recognizable form of representation of themselves, no matter how idealized or evasive some of those representations ultimately might prove to be. . . . With the primetime series, viewers could see the same Black characters in

the same place with the same expected tangle of relationships at the same time week in, week out. Scotty, Julia, and Pete Dixon and his girlfriend, the high school counselor Liz McIntyre, as well as Linc on *The Mod Squad*, became neighbors of sorts.[21]

For white families the regular presence of African Americans on prime time was something akin to black families moving into the neighborhood, but more manageable and less threatening. For Black families images of African Americans on the small screen served to authenticate their experiences by reflecting them in the mirror of television.

For both sets of viewers the most reassuring television environment proved to be the African American home. As television since 1968 has offered an ongoing but unsteady stream of black comedians starring in various shows in prime time, one pattern of success has emerged. Of all the comic formats the most popular is the domestic situation comedy.

A quick review of the field reveals a limited amount of success in the other genres of television comedy. Only two variety shows, *The Flip Wilson Show* (1970–1974) and *In Living Color* (1990–1994), have enjoyed any sustained presence on the small screen, with *The Flip Wilson Show* faring remarkably well in the #2 spot in the Nielsen ratings two years in a row. In the late-night comedy format, two highly respected comedians, Arsenio Hall and Chris Rock, have done well, but neither one can match the ratings and longevity of Johnny Carson and the other "white giants" of late night. A few attempts have been made to craft workplace comedies, such as *Amen* (1986–1991), which was located in an inner-city church; the short-lived *Frank's Place* (1987–1988), which took place in a New Orleans restaurant; and *Hangin' with Mr. Cooper* (1992–1997) and *The Steve Harvey Show* (1996–present), which were both set primarily in the high schools where the main characters taught. Even Bill Cosby explored the workplace genre early in his television career. *The Bill Cosby Show* (1969–1971) placed the comedian in the role of a high school physical education teacher and coach in a lower-middle-class neighborhood in Los Angeles.

While the other formats of television comedy met with mixed success, the majority of African American comedies—and, over the years, the most popular ones—have relied on variations of the domestic comedy formula that has proven so successful in the mainstream sitcom tradition over the years. Even at the beginning, *Amos 'n' Andy* focused on the home life of Kingfish, his battles with his wife, Sapphire, and his nagging mother-in-law, and the adventures of their Harlem neighbors, while *Beulah* was set in the standard middle-class family environment of Beulah's employers, the Hendersons. In 1968, when African Americans returned to prime-time television with *Julia*, much attention was paid to her character's relatively prestigious career as a nurse in the aerospace industry, but the majority of the episodes featured her home life with her young son, Cory, and her neighbors in her integrated apartment building. *Julia* was followed throughout the next decade by a wave of very popular African American comedies that set their stories in family situations. In *Sanford and Son* (1972–1977), although the main characters were partners in a Los Angeles junkyard, most of the comic conflict came from their family relationships. *Good Times* (1974–1979) chronicled the life of a black family in a Chicago housing project. *The Jeffersons* (1975–1985) followed George and Louise Jefferson as they moved away from Archie Bunker's neighborhood to their "dee-luxe apartment in the sky" on Manhattan's East Side. *What's Happening!!* (1976–1979) featured three black teenagers growing up in an inner-city neighborhood and tended to focus on their family life until the third season, when two of the young men, having finished high school, moved into an apartment together, turning the show into something more like an urban comedy about singles in the city.

An odd variation on the domestic comedy pattern emerged in the latter part of the 1970s, when three popular comedies followed the lives of African American characters who lived in a white family's home. On *Diff'rent Strokes* (1978–1986) two children from Harlem moved into the Park Avenue apartment of a white tycoon because he had promised their dying mother, his housekeeper, that he would look after her children. *Webster* (1983–1987) repeated the pattern. In this case a white former pro-football player had made a similar promise to one of his Black teammates that he would take care of his son, since he was the boy's godfather. When the little boy's parents died in a car crash, Webster Long was taken in by the football player and his wife.

Gimme a Break (1981–1987) began with a similar premise and the reappearance of the sassy black housekeeper figure seen over the years on *Beulah*, *The Danny Thomas Show*, *Maude*, and *The Jeffersons*, but it developed its story into much more complex situations. In this show a white widowed police officer and his three daughters were taken care of by Nell, their black housekeeper. In the show's third season an orphan boy—white like most of the other characters—was taken into the family. During the following season the father died, forcing Nell to become both mother and father to the girls. Meanwhile, the oldest daughter got married and brought her new husband to live with them. Finally, in the most elaborate plot development, the show's final season saw Nell move to New York City taking the orphan boy with her, only to encounter the boy's father and younger brother, who then joined his brother in the housekeeper's new domicile. In all these comings and goings, the various inhabitants changed and even the surrounding locales may have changed, but it was still about the home and, at its heart, the nurturing black woman, Nell.

Then came the Huxtables. *The Cosby Show* (1984–1992), a true television phenomenon, arrived in American homes on September 20, 1984, and, as Bogle says, demonstrated "the unique perspective that could be brought to the primetime series when an African American artist was in control of the material."[22] *The Cosby Show* ranked #3 in the Nielsen ratings during its first season, but it would rise to occupy the #1 spot for the next five seasons, with 63 million viewers (approximately one-quarter of the national population) tuning in at the peak of its popularity. (Ironically, the only other television comedy that can boast the same five-year run at the top of the Nielsens featured another family, headed by the very-white-and-proud-of-it bigot Archie Bunker.) *The Cosby Show* brought NBC back as the number 1 network. It is also regularly credited with reviving the situation comedy genre. The year before *The Cosby Show* premiered, only one sitcom, *Kate and Allie*, was listed among the top 10 shows. Within three years, seven of the top 10 shows were situation comedies, with another seven sitcoms (including *Kate and Allie*) listed in the top 30 Nielsen spots.

The Cosby Show "seemed to pop up out of nowhere. No one in the television industry could have predicted its extraordinary (and rapid-fire) success *and* cultural impact."[23] Bill Cosby had become a familiar face on the television screen since his three consecutive Emmy Awards for Outstanding Supporting Actor on *I Spy* almost twenty years earlier. His various television projects in the intervening years had included one attempt at workplace comedy, *The Bill Cosby Show* (1969–1971); two variety shows, *The New Bill Cosby Show* (1972–1973) and *Cos*, which came and went in two months in 1976; a daytime animated show, *Fat Albert and The Cosby Kids*; several television specials and guest host assignments on *The Tonight Show*; and appearances in a host of commercials, most memorably with giggling little children for Jell-O Pudding.

The impetus for the show came first of all from Brandon Tartikoff, the NBC president, one night when he was watching Cosby host *The Tonight Show*. Taking into account the growth of the African American middle class and a baby-boomer audience that had grown up with Cosby, Tartikoff thought the time was ripe for a new Cosby television venture in prime time. Cosby himself had been pitching his idea for a show about a black family. The show that emerged was a depiction of an upper-middle-class African American family living in a beautifully appointed brownstone in Brooklyn Heights. The father would be a doctor and the mother a lawyer. The number and gender of the children (one boy, four girls) would mirror Cosby's real-life family.

Bill Cosby, as starring actor, co-creator, co-producer, and executive consultant, had total control over the show, approving every script and even helping to design the set. He hired the African American psychiatrist Alvin Poussaint as a script consultant, and eventually invited young African American directors to work on certain episodes. As Bogle remarks, "Not until the advent of Cosby's series was there a program in which the governing sensibility—the absolute first and last word on just about every detail—lay in black hands."[24]

The show's depiction of family life was easy to like, especially Cosby's portrayal of the father, Dr. Heathcliff Huxtable. He was an admirable father figure, as can be seen in Jones's summary of Cosby's characterization:

> "Cliff" is warm, he is funny, he is hip to the ways of the kids, but he is also a traditionalist. He believes in parental authority, male primacy, old-fashioned sexual morals, monetary caution, respect for elders. He is proud of his position as part of the black middle class: He reminds his kids that everything they have is due to their grandfather's hard work as a Pullman porter; he insists that they go to old-guard black universities; he is an aficionado of Harlem Renaissance painting and modern jazz. Yet he is miles away from the sitcom blacks of the '70s, those jolly ghetto dwellers. Cliff is rich, richer than most TV whites.[25]

While in many ways Dr. Huxtable was a traditional figure, as Jones points out, the presentation of a black male assuming his fatherly duties as head of a household had not been seen regularly on television and was therefore, in context, a radical departure.

The character of Cliff's wife, Clair Huxtable, played by Phylicia Rashad, was, in Bogle's words, "an invigorating portrait of a contemporary African American woman."[26] She exuded professional style and intelligence, but she could whip up supper for the kids or a gourmet dinner for guests as expertly as any stay-at-home housewife, and, in fact, Clair was often seen in the kitchen. One episode recounted by Bogle captures perfectly Clair's patented combination of professional, mother, feminist, and nurturer. One of her daughter's well-educated boyfriends rather condescendingly asks Clair if she minds "serving" her husband. Without missing a beat and fixing the young man with her distinct icy stare, she informs him that "'serving' was what someone did in a restaurant. She, however, doesn't mind 'doing for' someone as long as the gesture is reciprocated and there is mutual respect."[27] Answer delivered; questioner put in his place. Rashad's ability to slide from upscale-proper to watch out!-sassy in a heartbeat was a joy to behold.

Cosby and Rashad's sexual chemistry was another novel twist. They were regularly shown flirting with each other, slow dancing or attempting some semi-comic sexy moves, engaging in some serious cuddling in the living room, or getting into some more heavy-duty activity under the covers in the bedroom. As Bogle says, "often Cliff and Clair really looked as if they couldn't wait to have some time alone together."[28]

Time alone was a rare commodity, however, with five children in the house, along with the children's friends, romantic interests, and eventually—in the course of the show's eight years—some spouses and children of their own. Cliff's and Clair's parents—played by the distinguished theater veterans Clarice Taylor and Earle Hyman and the elegant nightclub legends Nancy Wilson and Joe Williams—often came to visit as well.

The atmosphere of the Huxtable home was graced with reminders of African American history and culture, with posters of Frederick Douglass and Martin Luther King, Jr., on the walls, as well as copies of African American paintings from Cosby's personal collection. Many references were made to African American educational institutions and various writers and musicians, especially the jazz artists on the recordings in Cliff's valuable collection, with many artists—Stevie Wonder, Sammy Davis, Jr., Lena Horne, and others—actually appearing on the show.

The history of the civil rights struggle was also recognized and honored in various episodes. Bogle highlights two such moments:

> It's doubtful if anyone who saw it has ever forgotten the episode when pint-sized Rudy sat alone (later joined by the family) quietly spellbound as she watched a television replay of Martin Luther King Jr.'s "I Have a Dream" speech. Then there was the episode in which Theo struggled to write a paper for school. When his grandparents learned that his topic was the 1963 March on Washington, they were flooded with memories. Having attended the march themselves, they reminisced, and Theo experienced living history right there in the Huxtable living room.[29]

Bogle also recounts the controversy that developed when the NBC censors wanted to remove an "Abolish Apartheid" sign that was pinned to Theo's bedroom door and the network's hesitation when Cosby decided that the two new grandchildren on the show would be named Nelson and Winnie as a tribute to South Africa's Mandelas. In both cases Cosby vehemently refused to compromise with the networks, and the South African references remained.

The enormous popularity and the clearly upper-middle-class lifestyle and ideas of the show also prompted considerable controversy. As many critics have pointed out, *The Cosby Show*'s portrayal of the darker side of life for African American families was minimal. Jones accurately identifies the two limitations of the show: the moral uprightness of every character and the isolation of the family from the larger issues facing African Americans, especially those not so financially successful as the Huxtables. Jones offers an insightful summary of the show's weaknesses:

As the novelty of the comedy riffs began to wear off, the stories had to lean on character developments and life lessons. But the characters were too good, too lacking in areas of conflict, to be very interesting. And the life lessons failed to convince. Like *Father Knows Best*, *Cosby* made its lessons easy to demonstrate by keeping its conflicts tiny and its characters virtually without vices. But *Cosby* lacked a cultural context to make its little world plausible or relevant. The Huxtables couldn't venture too far into contemporary urban America—or even the America of the TV imagination—without encountering problems too big for Cliff's little remarks to solve.[30]

Whatever its virtues or failings, *The Cosby Show* remained enormously popular, always showing up in the top 10 shows of every season until its final year, when it dropped to #18. However, for all its popularity and cultural significance, it received relatively little in the way of awards from the industry. Early in its run the show received one Emmy Award for Outstanding Comedy Series in its first season (1984–1985), two Outstanding Directing Awards (1984–1985, 1985–1986), and one Emmy given to Roscoe Lee Browne as Outstanding Guest Performer in a Comedy Series (1985–1986). But no Emmy was awarded to Cosby himself, and no more were given to the show during the rest of its eight-year run.

While it seems odd that such a critically acclaimed and popular series as *The Cosby Show* received so few Emmys, it seems even stranger that such a hit show would not inspire numerous imitators. Many popular black shows on the major networks throughout the 1980s and 1990s, while continuing the trend toward domestic comedy as the preferred genre for African American comedy, did not replicate the sophisticated lifestyle and intelligent family interactions of the Huxtables. The creators of *227* (1985–1990), starring Marla Gibbs, who had achieved popularity playing the sassy housekeeper, Florence, on *The Jeffersons*, chose to return to family life in an inner-city apartment building with eccentric neighbors. While the even more successful *Family Matters* (1989–1998) placed the black family in a suburban setting, the father was a Chicago police officer and the mother was a stay-at-home housewife, hardly the professional equals of the Huxtables, and the family interaction bordered on the cartoonish, devoting much of the comic attention to the antics of a neighborhood nerd named Urkel, who quickly became the star of the show. It should not go unnoticed that *Family Matters* lasted one year longer on prime time than *The Cosby Show*.

Another hit show, *The Fresh Prince of Bel-Air* (1990–1996), took place in a successful African American attorney's mansion in Los Angeles, complete with a butler. But the appeal of the show came from the fish-out-of-water situation of the show's star, a teenager from the projects of West Philadelphia, who had been sent to live with his wealthy relatives in California when life in the inner city had gotten too dangerous for him. Rap star Will Smith, as the transplanted homeboy, did not fit into the upscale lifestyle at the family mansion or the prep school where his uncle enrolled him, and his genuine good nature and benevolence tended to make a mockery of his relatives' pretensions and materialism. The format of another rap singer, LL Cool J's show, *In the House* (1995–1998), began as a quasi-family situation comedy with his character, Marion Hill, a pro-football player (on medical leave), serving as a nanny for the children of a single mother who was renting some rooms in his house. But it morphed into more of a workplace comedy in its second season, when Marion purchased and managed a sports injury clinic. In one noteworthy case the network departed from the domestic comedy format altogether. *A Different World* (1987–1993), a spin-off of *The Cosby Show*, which followed the second-oldest daughter, Denise, as she attended her father's alma mater, Hillman College, was more of a comedy about college life and the adventures of attractive young singles. Its link to *The Cosby Show* disappeared in the second season when the character of Denise Huxtable was written out of the show. While these shows in general did not garner the critical admiration or the spectacular ratings enjoyed by *The Cosby Show*, most of them had long runs and reinforced the dominance of the domestic sitcom as the preferred genre for black television comedy.

In fact, as television enters the twenty-first century, the Cosby formula is having a comeback. On the major networks Bill Cosby even managed a return to prime time on CBS with *Cosby* (1996–2000), another family comedy about a sixty-year-old who, having been downsized out of his job at an airline company, was adjusting to spending his days at home in a neighborhood in Queens, while his wife worked part-time at a flower shop nearby. In 1998 *The Hughleys* appeared on ABC, chronicling the experiences of an upwardly mobile black family who had moved into a predominantly white suburban neighborhood. Damon Wayans, who had begun his television career with some daring sketch comedy on *In Living Color* on the FOX network, entered the world of domestic comedy in March 2001 on ABC as a Cosbyesque patriarch of a well-to-do family on his show, *My Wife and Kids*. And the popular stand-up comedian Bernie Mac has gone the same route with *The Bernie Mac Show* on FOX (2001–present), playing the role of a successful comedian who, along with his understanding wife, takes over the care of his sister's children when she goes to prison. Mac has even revived the George Burns technique of the monologue addressed to the viewers with his comments on the show's plot. The domestic sitcom remains, in African American television comedy as well as elsewhere, the genre that will not die.

Even in the flood of black comedy that has arisen on the new networks in the 1990s, the most successful of them have followed either the tried-and-true formula of the domestic comedy or the friends-as-family variation of the

1990s urban comedy. When the "upstart" networks, FOX, WB, and UPN, emerged in the 1990s and began to shape limited prime-time schedules, they decided to appeal to African Americans as a demographic that was under-served by the three major networks, especially in terms of comedy shows. As a result, throughout the 1990s, the new networks offered a string of comedies of uneven quality that have led to accusations of a "ghetto" mentality: Black co-medians playing to a largely Black audience. FOX led the movement with the sketch comedy show *In Living Color;* a comedy-variety show, *Cedric the Enter-tainer Presents;* and a number of situation comedies: *Roc, Martin, Living Single, Between Brothers,* and the *The Bernie Mac Show.* The WB network followed suit with an array of African American comedies such as *Sister, Sister, The Wayans Bros., The Parent 'Hood, The Jamie Foxx Show,* and *The Steve Harvey Show.* The fledgling UPN network also met with success with the teen comedy *Moesha, Malcolm and Eddy,* and *The Parkers.*

Some of these Black comedies, on the major networks as well as the upstart networks, can be studied as African American versions of the urban-singles comedy like *Seinfeld, Friends, Ally McBeal,* and the legion of imitators that dominated prime-time schedules of the major networks in the 1990s. They were for the most part set in distinctly urban environments and followed the love lives and careers of attractive young African Americans. Most of them also served as effective showcases for up-and-coming African American per-formers who would go on to bigger careers in Hollywood: Martin Lawrence and Tisha Campbell on *Martin;* Queen Latifah on *Living Single;* Shawn and Marlon Wayans on *The Wayans Bros.;* Jamie Foxx on *The Jamie Foxx Show;* Jas-mine Guy, Kadeem Hardison, and Sinbad on *A Different World;* Brandy on *Moesha;* and LL Cool J on *In the House.*

The quality of these shows has varied, and many of the programs on the newer networks have been the particular target of critical scorn, labeled as the "chitlin' circuit" of television programming. Robin R. Means Coleman ex-presses particular contempt for what she calls the "Neo-Minstrelsy" era of tele-vision comedy from 1990 to the present, which, she says, "ridicules Black cul-ture and promotes racial separation and inequality."[31] She provides an extensive list of the features of these shows that she finds particularly demeaning:

> Neo-Minstrelsy comedies are a hodge-podge of inane friendscoms, workplace-coms, and domcoms whose only commonality is that Black culture is presented in a hyper-racialized manner through gross lampooning. Black characters break out in frenzied dancing more often and with greater intensity. The blackvoice has remained, laden with gross malapropisms. This era is also far more nuanced with a heavy emphasis on slang and the language of rap/hip-hop or "the ghetto." The voices seem louder, more shrill, and more bossy and sassy. Dialogue is often

accentuated by ample finger snaps, eye rolling, neck swaying, and tongue cluck-
ing. Physical comedy is now far more prevalent and more ridiculing as characters literally scoot face down across floors, fight with objects such as paper, food,
mops, floor polishers, wiring and cords, wigs, clothes, and nail buffers (and often
lose). The characters' appearance is outlandish as well, with a modernized
Sambo dress. The clothing is worn in excess and gaudy. It is not unusual for
women, for example, to appear wearing stiletto heels, black fish net stockings,
very short satiny shorts or skirts, in a variety of loud, multiple colors.[32]

Means Coleman recounts the 1997 protest of the Beverly Hills/Hollywood
chapter of the NAACP demanding that the upstart networks stop presenting
such offensive depictions, citing popular shows such as *Martin, In the House,
The Wayans Bros.,* and *The Jamie Foxx Show*.[33] She also quotes Bill Cosby in a
1997 *Newsweek* interview, expressing his disapproval of such comedy and its
social effects:

> There is no excuse for those [UPN and WB sitcoms] either, or the lack of intel-
> ligence. We're talking about having an appreciation for a race of people. All they
> found at those networks is a way to say: "This is how these people act and that's
> why we refuse to allow a large number of them to network with us on Wall
> Street or where-have-you." And that keeps us estranged from the rest of the
> country.[34]

Noticing that the FOX network preferred to present shows such as *Martin*
while cancelling more positive portrayals of black life such as *Roc* and *South
Central,* Means Coleman interprets the networks' actions to mean that "racial
ridicule was America's preference for African American portrayals as evidenced by such series' high ratings and longevity."[35]

In her very criticism, however, Means Coleman offers a key to another
interpretation. The high ratings of the shows that Means Coleman considers
examples of Neo-Minstrelsy among black viewers may suggest that something new is happening in African American comedy in terms of audiences
and content. There is a new audience out there in television land for Black
programming, and it is the result of a sharp racial divide. Surveys indicate
that black viewers and white viewers vary a great deal in their choice of favorite shows. In a poll taken in February 1986, in the era when ABC, CBS, and
NBC were the only significant broadcast networks, everyone's favorite series
was *The Cosby Show,* but even then black viewers and white viewers differed a
great deal in their other choices. Two shows featuring black performers, *227*
and *The Facts of Life,* ranked #4 and #6, respectively, in black households,
while they showed up as #16 and #26 among white viewers. White viewers
placed *Murder, She Wrote; 60 Minutes; Dallas;* and *Who's the Boss?* among the

top 10 shows for the 1985–1986 season, while those shows ranked 25, 32, 52, and 54 in black households.[36]

As the 1990s brought many more programs with African American talent into homes, particularly on the newer channels, the racial divide in television viewing grew even wider. According to the Nielsen report issued in December 1998, the #1 and #2 shows for black viewers, *The Steve Harvey Show* and *The Jamie Foxx Show* (both on the WB network), were ranked 118 and 124 among white viewers. The top 3 shows among whites, *ER, Friends,* and *Frasier,* ranked 15, 91, and 93 among black viewers.[37] An April 2003 report showed that the gap between black viewers and white viewers was continuing while occasionally showing an overlap. It also indicated how significant the newer channels such as UPN and Fox had become for black viewers (see table). Meanwhile, the favorite shows among white viewers were *CSI: Crime Scene Investigation; Friends; ER; Everybody Loves Raymond; Survivor: Thailand; Law and Order; Will and Grace; CSI: Miami; Scrubs; and Monday Night Football.*[38] The report noticed more convergence of black viewer and white viewer patterns as the list moved on to rank the top 20 shows for each group. It also observed that the two shows that showed up on both top 10 lists, *CSI: Crime Scene Investigation* and *Monday Night Football,* both showed a racial mix in the casts, players, and announcers. In any case, the report clearly indicated that the most popular shows among the black viewers were comedies featuring African American casts and airing on the newer channels. Meanwhile, these shows did not attract many white viewers.

Given this new situation, the African American comedies on the newer networks can be studied as a new phenomenon, an opportunity provided by the relative narrowcasting of the newer broadcast and cable networks that allows the creators of black comedy to experiment for the first time with African American shows aimed primarily at African American viewers. If this is a "ghetto" situation, it might be likened to the "ghetto" character of the Harlem Renaissance of the 1920s, an opportunity for Black artists to create newer

	Top Shows for Black Households	Network	Rank among White Households	
1.	*Cedric the Entertainer Presents*	FOX	93	
2.	*One on One*	UPN	112	(tie)
3.	*Girlfriends*	UPN	112	(tie)
4.	*Half and Half*	UPN	114	
5.	*The Parkers*	UPN	111	
6.	*My Wife and Kids*	ABC	46	
7.	*The Bernie Mac Show*	FOX	84	
8.	*Monday Night Football*	ABC	10	
9.	*Fastlane*	FOX	85	
10.	*CSI: Crime Scene Investigation*	CBS	1	

forms of art—in this case, television comedy—to celebrate and entertain their own people.

The renowned theater critic, Walter Kerr, in his study of silent film comedy, describes the operation of what he calls "a curious law" governing art forms: "Whenever an entirely new form is let loose on the world," Kerr states, "it must begin at the very beginning. Silent film comedy began as though comedy had never existed, as though Aristophanes had never existed, as though sophistication of the same materials had never been achieved."[39] While the comedy on the upstart networks cannot be accurately described as "an entirely new form," perhaps Kerr's "curious law" is operative to some extent as many of these shows "begin [almost] at the very beginning," returning to earlier television formulas and recycling them in the codes of African American culture.

Perhaps *Martin*, *The Wayans Bros.*, *Malcolm and Eddie*, and other shows that are accused of presenting negative stereotypes of the black community can be better understood as exhibitions of standard buffoonery, encoded in characters, settings, physical shtick, and language that can be recognized and decoded best by an African American audience. In that sense they are simply recycling the history of mainstream television comedy. Can the plots and problems of the Neo-Minstrelsy shows be any more simpleminded than those on *The Flying Nun*, *My Favorite Martian*, or *The Brady Bunch?* Are any of these new "ghetto" clowns any more buffoonish than Uncle Miltie, Ralph Kramden, Gomer Pyle, Archie Bunker, Jethro Clampett, Ted Baxter, Louie DePalma, Cosmo Kramer, or Homer Simpson? Is the physical slapstick any more degrading than what was demonstrated by Lucy and Ethel, Laverne and Shirley, or in the work of John Ritter or Carol Burnett? Do the women dress any more outrageously than Chrissy on *Three's Company*, Elly May Clampett, Daisy Duke, Peg Bundy, or the ladies on *Sex and the City?* Are the facial contortions any more grotesque than those of Sid Caesar, Red Skelton, Robin Williams, John Belushi, or almost anybody on *The Simpsons?* And for sheer idiocy, do these new Black characters come anywhere near the "sweathogs" on *Welcome Back, Kotter;* the brothers Larry, Darryl, and Darryl on *Newhart;* or Beavis and Butthead? Are the finger-snapping and eye-rolling African American characters any more of a stereotype than Fran Fine's gaudy, kvetching mother or feeble but crude grandmother Yetta on *The Nanny* or the campy, flamboyant, and promiscuous homosexual Jack McFarland on *Will and Grace?* Comedy need not always be at the level of Molière or Shaw or even Neil Simon, all of whom will someday find their counterparts in African American comedy on television.

While these newer comedies recycle much traditional comic material, they also exhibit some distinctive features. The relationship between the performers and the studio audience differs from that of the show's white counterparts. While *I Love Lucy* inspired laughter from its live studio audience and comments by the characters on *All in the Family* provoked studio audience applause, many of the Neo-Minstrelsy shows are punctuated by whoops and shouts from the studio audience when a character delivers a put-down or a sarcastic response, a group reaction of "aaawww" from the studio audience when parents and children embrace or friends reconcile, or the occasional squeal when a loving couple kiss. Just as Black preachers differ from their white counterparts by expecting to hear an "Amen" or "Preach it, brother" from their congregations during a sermon, so the comedy of these shows is energized by the frequent audible responses from the audience. The dialogue is usually more energetic with a good deal more street vernacular than most mainstream comedy. And the characters, while more middle class, exhibit some specifically African American quirks, enough that some critics from the Black community consider them to border on offensive stereotypes.

All of this indicates that this experiment in new forms of black comedy is a vibrant one, developing by trial and error, recycling traditional mainstream models while adding their own ethnic content and mode of delivery. And, whether the comic character is admirable or ridiculous, Black viewers seem to tolerate the ignoble and applaud the victorious as has every audience since the satyr plays of ancient Greece. They can enjoy these presentations even more since the primarily Black audience realizes that such characters and situations do not represent the African American community as a whole.

Means Coleman and others compare the Neo-Minstrelsy phenomenon to the degrading images of black culture offered in the days of *Amos 'n' Andy*. The analogy is inexact, however. One of the main objections of the NAACP to the depictions of African Americans on *Amos 'n' Andy* was: "There is no other show on nation-wide television that shows Negroes in a favorable light."[40] This no longer holds true. Both Black viewers and white viewers have much more exposure to a spectrum of portrayals of African Americans on television. Research by the Initiative Media African-American Television Viewing Study found that fifty-one shows introduced for the 2002–2003 television season boasted multiethnic casts.[41] While a closer content analysis might show this figure to be less rosy than it first appears, there is at least solid anecdotal evidence of a variety of African American actors portraying admirable main characters on popular and respected shows such as *ER, Law and Order, The West Wing, The Practice, CSI: Miami, Scrubs, 24, Third Watch*, and others. Black characters can be found on almost every daytime drama. There are many African American news personalities on the local news as well as on *60 Minutes, Today*, and other network news magazines and major sports coverage. Oprah Winfrey rules the world of daytime talk shows. Black athletes and musical performers are a constant presence on television. Whatever else can be said, the population of television land is a lot more diverse—and much more interesting—than it was in 1951.

After the decade or so of testing the formulas of Neo-Minstrelsy, African American comedy is entering another phase in its recycling process. The genre that is currently gaining ground on both the newer networks and major networks, is, of course, the domestic situation comedy, but with a surprising twist. Several of the most popular series—*My Wife and Kids, The Bernie Mac Show, The Parkers*, for example—are shaping their own version of the feel-good era of *The Adventures of Ozzie and Harriet, Father Knows Best*, and other suburban comedies of the 1950s, as well as the wholesome family values of *The Cosby Show*. The home situations on these shows are relatively stable even with the nontraditional parental roles. Most of the characters are financially comfortable, middle-class citizens. The characters are more familiar, likeable, and "normal" than the scheming Kingfish, the outlandish Urkel, or the vituperative George Jefferson or Fred Sanford. They are usually good-hearted and well intentioned, and the stories usually have something of a moral. Husbands and wives usually solve their disagreements by learning something about human relationships. Children and parents regularly learn life lessons. They may look a little different, but they are not that far away from Ozzie and Harriet or the Brady Bunch.

A summary of African American comedy on television should end with something of a montage saluting the many stars of the genre. Donald Bogle, at the beginning of his history of the African American presence on television, observes:

> For African Americans, especially because writers rarely wrote with them in mind, the performers—their individual star personas or sometimes (as was the case with Ethel Waters) their personal stories—took on greater significance. Black viewers might reject the nonsense of the scripts for some episodes of *Sanford and Son* or *The Jeffersons* or *Martin*. . . . But they never really rejected a Redd Foxx or a Sherman Hemsley or Martin Lawrence. . . . What remained consistent throughout television history was that a group of dynamic or complicated or intriguing personalities managed to send personal messages to the viewers. From the days of Ethel Waters in the 1950s to the present, actors found themselves cast in parts that were shameless, dishonest travesties of African American life and culture. Yet often enough some of these actors also managed—ironically and paradoxically—to strike a nerve with viewers by turning the roles inside out.[42]

If, as Bogle says, it is the performers who convey the most significant messages in television comedy, a list of the most outstanding among them is in order. The all-star roster must include Hattie McDaniel, Ethel Waters, Tim

Moore, Eddie "Rochester" Anderson, Diahann Carroll, Redd Foxx, Sherman Hemsley, Isabel Sanford, Flip Wilson, Jimmie Walker, Gary Coleman, Emmanuel Lewis, Nell Carter, Robert Guillaume, Marla Gibbs, Eddie Murphy, Esther Rolle, Will Smith, Bill Cosby, Phylicia Rashad, Charles Dutton, Martin Lawrence, Queen Latifah, LL Cool J, Chris Rock, The Wayans Brothers, Arsenio Hall, Bernie Mac, and many others. Some of them had brief careers on the small screen, while others changed the face of television—and the country—forever. Many of them were awarded Emmys and Golden Globes for their performances. Many have also enjoyed distinguished careers in theater, film, and music. All of them have triumphed over obstacles of prejudice and discrimination that their white counterparts were never forced to experience. All of them have found their way into the homes of Americans both Black and white, provoking considerable laughter and, in the process, changing many people's hearts.

·11·

FUN CITY

The show begins with a black-and-white photograph of the New York City skyline reminiscent of scenes from Woody Allen's film *Manhattan*. In the same Allen style there then follows a photomontage of a happy couple enjoying the city: strolling across a bridge in Central Park with The Dakota behind them, hailing a cab in the rain, walking their dog past a churchyard, ordering food at a deli, browsing through a bookstore, returning from a trip to the corner grocery, buying flowers at a street stand, sharing wine and lunch by the Central Park lagoon, and walking along the East River promenade. Several shots show them engaging in public displays of affection: they are caught snuggling up to each other on that Central Park bridge; the man kisses the woman's shoulder as they wait for the subway train at the Union Square stop; they pause in the midst of a nighttime stroll down a crowded city street to kiss each other once again; and, finally, they commit to a serious kiss as the East River shimmers in the background.

The mood was thus set for *Mad About You*, the popular and award-winning situation comedy starring Paul Reiser and Helen Hunt as Paul and Jamie Buchman, a young married couple living on Twelfth Street and Fifth Avenue in the heart—or is it the belly?—of Manhattan. The funky-blues theme song created a lighthearted romantic atmosphere for these two as they "jump into the final frontier" of romantic love: marriage. And apparently they could not have picked a more likely place to succeed—the big city of the 1990s.

But the Buchmans of *Mad About You* were not alone on their adventure. Throughout the 1990s television situation comedy moved almost all of its most popular characters into identifiable urban areas. *Seinfeld, Friends, The Nanny, Cosby, Spin City, Caroline in the City, Just Shoot Me, News Radio, Veronica's Closet, The Wayans Bros.*, and *The Parent 'Hood* were all situated quite definitely in New York City. Murphy Brown was a major player in the Washington, D.C., media world, while *Suddenly Susan*'s characters put out a magazine in San Francisco; *Frasier*'s opening graphic was the skyline of Seattle; and *The John Laroquette Show* began with the star leaning against a model of the Gateway Arch in Saint Louis. Ellen and Cybill resided in Los Angeles; Drew Carey lived and worked in Cleveland; and Ally McBeal coped with her life and fantasies in a Boston setting. All of these programs made frequent references to their city, and certain ones set in New York City—most notably *Seinfeld*, *Mad About You*, and *Spin City*—made city life essential to the plot.

The urban locale is only one feature that these programs shared. They exemplify many other developments in the situation comedy of the 1990s. A few of them were based on the earlier stand-up material of their stars. For most of them the pace of the dialogue and scenes was more rapid than earlier television comedy. And the family situations, or lack thereof, distinguished them from the pack of television families that have inhabited almost all the situation comedies from the beginning. The scripts for these urban comedies displayed new patterns of comic characters, relationships, plot resolutions and, in their effect on the larger culture, a new code for interpreting life in the 1990s.

To understand the development of television's urban situation comedy, it is helpful to contrast its more fluid shape with the distinct outlines of an earlier strain of situation comedy, what Hal Himmelstein has dubbed the "suburban middle-landscape comedy."[1] In these comedies, television's comic depiction of American life and the actual social ideal of the American family, for a period of almost twenty-five years, matched each other closely.

In the 1950s and 1960s the suburbs became the preferred locale both for situation comedy and the living situation of white middle-class America. Himmelstein describes the era as a time when

> workers found it desirable (and in fact were encouraged by the hegemonic demands of an advanced industrial economy reflected in corporate behavioral norms) to fan out from overcrowded, polluted, multiracial urban industrial inner cities into the overwhelmingly white suburban developments that sprang up to accommodate the rapid family formation in the post–World War II era.[2]

Himmelstein pictures these suburbs as an embodiment of an American archetype, a garden of peace and plenty away from the chaotic wilderness, a sort of paradise:

> The suburb was the mythical space between two untamed rugged frontiers: the wilderness and the chaotic, dangerous inner city. It was a place where sanity prevailed, a place of full employment; conventional white, white-collar corporate families; clean streets, well-kept weedless lawns, neatly trimmed hedges.[3]

The television comedies that these families gathered to watch together tended to display an idealized version of this suburban life, in such long-running programs as *Father Knows Best* (1954–1960), *Leave It to Beaver* (1957–1963), *My Three Sons* (1960–1972), *The Donna Reed Show* (1958–1966), *The Brady Bunch* (1969–1974), and *The Adventures of Ozzie and Harriet* (1952–1966). These popular shows clearly captured the hearts of American viewers with lengthy runs and reruns through the 1950s and 1960s, and eventually they became permanently installed in American popular mythology. Throughout the 1980s reruns of *Father Knows Best, Leave It to Beaver,* and *The Donna Reed Show* were shown at least twice a day on national cable as well as by numerous independent stations in local markets across the country.[4]

Gerard Jones describes the world of Ozzie and Harriet as "the suburban Neverland of family sitcoms, in which details of locale and occupation are intentionally evaded . . . a homogeneous threatless world."[5] The white middle class was eagerly joining the Nelsons in the suburban paradise. With the encouragement of government policies and the practices of home builders and bankers, the suburbs were growing at fifteen times the rate of the rest of the country, isolating the nuclear family in their ranch-style houses and away from their old neighborhoods, extended family, and even from their new neighbors, whose houses were separated from each other by wide lawns, hedges, and fences. The suburbs represented the American Dream of a new start in the new post–World War II era of prosperity, and people seemed eager to learn how to live out that dream from the examples of the Nelsons and other television families. The ideals of suburbia were quite clear:

> Television—especially the sitcom—valorized suburbia as democracy's utopia realized, a place where the white middling classes could live in racial serenity, raising children in an engineered environment that contained and regulated the twin dangers of culture and nature. The American geniuses of Jefferson and Hamilton had at last found each other, producing coast-to-coast tracts of relatively egalitarian single-unit dwellings obtainable at favorable mortgage rates. The media campaign for this burgeoning way of life included the black-and-white nuclear family sitcom that proliferated on television during the late fifties and early sixties.[6]

The values and behavioral norms for such a lifestyle were communicated through the mild humor of these suburban sitcoms. As Himmelstein describes it:

> This was the comedy of the true nuclear family. Sons and daughters struggled to grow up while their parents, who tended to smother them in piety and sociological wisdom, were constantly faced with their children's fantasies and

nonsense, which, while illogical from an adult's point of view, were nevertheless refreshing and adventurous in a world of conformity and of fear of deviation from norms. . . . This universal generation difference defines the basic comedic structure of the genre in its 1950s and 1960s manifestations. It also simultaneously points, albeit indirectly, to a social reality in which the archetypal adult says to us, all children at heart, "When you grow up, you too will find it necessary to conform to the dominant ideology so that you may be successful like us."[7]

Even such a solid ideology was finally forced to yield to the social and economic realities of the 1960s and 1970s, and television comedy also had to recognize the changes. The suburbanized nuclear family has made very few successful appearances on prime-time since *The Brady Bunch* broke up in 1974. The two most successful series during the 1980s, for example, were *Growing Pains* (1985–1992) and *Family Ties* (1982–1989), which offered significant tweaking of the standard formula. The mother on *Family Ties* was an architect, not a stay-at-home Mom, while the father worked at a public television station. The father on *Growing Pains*, a psychiatrist, had moved his office into the home while the mother worked outside the home as a TV journalist. Hardly the Mom, Dad, and the kids arrangement of earlier days.

But television comedy was not ever thus. The earliest situation comedy on television was set in the city. David Marc describes the first sitcom, *Mary Kay and Johnny* (1947–1950), as a "silk-pajamas comedy" that took place in a high-rise luxury apartment house "in the high society environs of a Cole Porter song."[8] But most of us are more likely to remember the two classics of early situation comedy, *I Love Lucy* (1951–1957), which was set in a middle-class apartment on Manhattan's East Side and *The Honeymooners* (1955–1956), set in a decidedly working-class section of Brooklyn. Two highly successful radio comedies that were transferred to television as soon as possible were also set in New York City: *Amos 'n' Andy* in Harlem and *The Goldbergs* in the Bronx. But the classic *Honeymooners* episodes only lasted for one year. In *I Love Lucy's* third season, the Ricardos moved out to Hollywood temporarily, and in the fifth season they moved permanently to Westport, Connecticut. *The Goldbergs's* (1949–1954) and *Amos 'n' Andy's* (1951–1953) legendary popularity on radio did not repeat itself on television for a variety of reasons, but mainly because neither one fit into the homogenized version of American family life that television soon began to portray. Even the two popular comedies of the 1950s that were set in New York City apartments, *My Little Margie* (1952–1955) and *The Danny Thomas* Show (1953–1964), evolved quickly into domestic comedies with very little reference to their urban environment. *The Patty Duke Show* (1963–1966), a moderate success in the following decade, presented its Brooklyn Heights setting as a suburban situation. In visual style and comic content these programs resembled the type of suburban family comedy that would come to dominate television for the next twenty-five years. Television comedy's early residency in the big city was brief.

Television's second era of urban comedy lasted a bit longer, spanning primarily the decade of the 1970s. The pioneer of this era was Daddy's Little Girl herself, Danny Thomas's daughter, Marlo Thomas, in *That Girl* (1966–1971), the adventures of an independent single woman in New York City. She did not, however, prompt a flood of imitators immediately. It took a few more seasons until viewers got to see Mary Tyler Moore as Mary Richards in Minneapolis, Bob Newhart as Dr. Bob Hartley in Chicago, and Archie Bunker in Queens. They also saw Rhoda Morgenstern; the Jeffersons; and "the odd couple," Felix and Oscar, in New York City; Sanford and Son and Chico and the Man in inner-city Los Angeles; Laverne and Shirley in Milwaukee; and J. J. and his family of *Good Times* in the Chicago projects. Often the plots of these comedies included references to urban problems: muggings, city traffic, overcrowded subways, and even the power outages that made New York City in the 1970s the symbol of modern civilization run amok. The October 1974 full-hour episode in which Rhoda's wedding almost never happened because of various urban disasters typifies the pattern.

The 1970s ended with some highly popular ensemble comedies set in clearly identified urban locales: *WKRP in Cincinnati* (1978–1982), *Taxi* (1978–1983), *Barney Miller* (1975–1982), and *Welcome Back, Kotter* (1975–1979). In these urban ensemble comedies an element that had been emerging in the previous sitcoms of the 1970s became more explicit. The characters in these shows were more exotic, often with clear ethnic characteristics and other qualities that identified them as marginalized from the mainstream. For these characters the chaotic urban setting was the appropriate—perhaps the only—environment where their eccentricities could be tolerated, or maybe not even be noticed. One thinks of the Gravedigger's explanation of Prince Hamlet's departure to England, where his madness would not draw attention, for "there the men are as mad as he" (*Ham.* V. i. 155). Perhaps, after seeing so much urban unrest on the nightly news, the television viewers in the suburbs and towns of 1970s Middle America likewise felt that these modern-day madmen and women fit right into the big-city chaos.

The urbanites of 1990s television, however, did not come across, for the most part, as eccentrics but often, even with their quirks, as something close to role models. Most of them were educated young professionals. Their lives revolved around both home and work, and their relationships crossed those boundaries regularly. Influenced by the genre of workplace comedy that began with *The Mary Tyler Moore Show* and evolved so brilliantly into *Cheers,* many of these shows' characters spent a good deal of time on the job or talking about their jobs, and in many cases most of their relationships originated in the workplace. They experienced personal success and frustration, engaged in romantic entanglements and various forms of friendship, and occasionally learned some life lessons mainly at work. These new patterns fit the description once given of *The Mary Tyler Moore Show* as "All in the Work-Family." Mary's last speech, on the show's final episode, could not have been more straightforward: "What is a family? A family is people who make you feel less alone and really loved. Thank you for being my family."[9] In the 1990s comedies the gang in the office or the friends who hung around the apartment became each other's family.

The few shows that were not primarily work-centered were usually not set in traditional home environments. The apartment dwelling of *Mad About You* may have been the most traditional setting, but at least until their baby arrived, the Buchmans seemed to use their apartment as more of a launching pad for their urban experiences. Episodes of the show regularly included scenes in specific New York restaurants and Broadway theaters, hospitals, parks, workout gyms, and famous tourist attractions. Cybill's Los Angeles home, at first glance, may have looked like the set of *The Brady Bunch*. However, Cybill was a twice-divorced career woman, living with a very independent daughter, two ex-husbands frequently visiting, and a best friend who usually arrived with a martini shaker or a fresh boyfriend in hand. The apartments of the characters on *Friends* seem more like the best of all possible college-dorm arrangements with adjacent men's wings and women's wings on the same dorm floor. And the area that served as Seinfeld's living room-cum-kitchen (where, to my knowledge, no dinner was ever prepared) had pretty much of an open-door policy, hardly any more private than the corner restaurant where the odd foursome met for most of their meals. None of these environments enjoyed the locked-door privacy of most American homes.

Family arrangements were also quite changed from the days of *Father Knows Best* and *The Adventures of Ozzie and Harriet*. For the most part these new urban characters were not married, so that children seldom played a part in the shows' comic plots. In contrast to the loving, wise, and mildly authoritarian parents of *Father Knows Best* and the other suburban situation comedies, the parents and other relatives of the 1990s sitcoms were generally problematic, even bizarre. Mel Brooks as Uncle Phil on *Mad About You* and Jerry Stiller as George Constanza's father on *Seinfeld* were two prime examples of the pattern. Given the single status of most of the characters, the plots naturally involved romantic entanglements and explicit sexual dialogue and situations, especially on the most popular of the urban comedies, *Seinfeld* and *Friends*. But why not? All of these family patterns of inconvenient parents and busy sexual lives probably looked as familiar to the 18- to 49-year-old viewers of the 1990s as the picture of Mom, Dad, and the kids did to that same demographic of the 1950s.

The main characters of these urban comedies were generally attractive, well educated and/or well respected in their profession. Yet for all their intellectual or professional superiority, they were often emotionally confused, even childish. They lacked the wisdom and common sense of the adults in suburban comedy. But Ozzie and Harriet and Ward and June, while likeable, had not been a whole lot of fun. Their low-key approach to life's challenges apparently served as a behavioral model to viewers in the Eisenhower and Kennedy eras. The heroes of the new urban comedy, however, replaced common sense with passionate intensity. The nervous stand-up comedian styles of Paul Reiser, Ellen DeGeneres, Jerry Seinfeld, and Drew Carey had set a new emotional tone. Many of the new comic heroes carried personal histories that often set them apart from the statistical middle ground in America: Murphy Brown was a recovering alcoholic: Ellen was gay. Many of the lead characters dared to be unlikable, irresponsible, even hostile. These idiosyncracies, however, were often the consequences of their superior intelligence and emotional intensity. A new synthesis was thus achieved. The eloquent sarcasm of Dr. Frasier Crane, the articulate impatience of Murphy Brown, and the sudden outbursts of Kramer, George, and Elaine were more delightfully off-beat and quirky than mild-mannered Ozzie and Harriet, and yet such behavior was more socially and intellectually respectable than the antics and comments of the sweathogs in Mr. Kotter's classroom. Mix outward respectability with inner demons and you get Ally McBeal.

Plots and dialogue showed a similar development. David Marc outlines the traditional structure of the sitcom episode as follows: Familiar Status Quo—Ritual error made—Ritual lesson learned—Familiar Status Quo. To illustrate the consistency of this pattern, Marc provides examples from such diverse comedies as *I Love Lucy, Bewitched, All in the Family,* and *Cosby.*[10] The plots of the urban comedies of the 1990s, however, were generally more complex. Many of these comedies, especially those with more fully developed ensemble casts, worked with a series of shorter scenes and the interweaving of several situations. *Seinfeld,* of course, offered the best example of this pattern. A typical twenty-two-minute episode could include as many as twenty-five separate scenes. *Seinfeld*'s hectic pace enabled the development of a separate conflict for each of the four main characters, all of them eventually dovetailing or colliding with one another in mutual disaster. *Friends, Frasier, Spin City,* and *News Radio* often employed the same multi-plot structure.

Another pattern, also exemplified best by *Seinfeld,* was the method of resolving these comic conflicts. Typically, the schemes and plots ended in frustration and disaster. Yet unlike the classic schemers, Lucy Ricardo and Ralph

Kramden, the new comic characters were not reconciled to their failure by the loving forgiveness of a long-suffering spouse. No one seemed to gain any new insight, or, as Marc phrased it, no ritual lesson was learned. Unlike Beaver Cleaver or Ricky and David Nelson, Jerry or George or Kramer or Elaine ended up frustrated, unenlightened, unreformed, and quite likely to return soon to the same misguided behavior. Likewise, Joey, Monica, and the others on *Friends*.

However, even though they were doomed to repeat their comic history week after week, television's urban comedians seemed to be having a perfectly wonderful time doing so. Their various hopes and dreams sprang eternal precisely because they lived in an environment that promised endless possibility. This strange combination of cynicism and optimism in the urban-comic viewpoint resembles F. Scott Fizgerald's famous description of driving into Manhattan from Queens: "The city seen from the Queensboro Bridge is always the city seen for the first time, in its first wild promise of all the mystery and the beauty in the world."[11] The comic viewpoint is one of eternal promise; no catastrophe is final. Tomorrow is another day.

The reasons for this new comic perception of the city in the 1990s can be found partially in the actual changes in both the urban and suburban environments in America. The decline in the urban crime rate, the increase of mass transit in many cities, the renovations of downtown areas, the revival of older city neighborhoods, and the return of many baby-boomers and Generation Xers to city dwellings have changed the actual face of many of our large cities. Meanwhile, the suburbs have begun to look more urban, with more business offices, shopping centers, high-tech manufacturing complexes, and other "industrial campuses" locating in suburban settings, along with more ethnic diversity in the suburban population. In short, the suburb as the white middle-class haven from the evils of the city is no longer operative. The suburbs look less like Paradise; the cities look less like Hell.

However, rather than considering the actual changes in the city-suburb dichotomy, it is more germane to our study to look at the ways in which the urban environment, signified primarily by New York City, has been presented in recent years in the television medium. Television has been reshaping the urban myth before our very eyeballs. The new vision portrays city life as fun. In 1993, when David Letterman moved *Late Night with David Letterman* to a refurbished CBS studio in the Ed Sullivan Theater on Fifty-third and Broadway, he made that upper Times Square neighborhood into his playground for grown-ups. The local storekeepers—especially Rupert Jee, the genial proprietor of the Hello Deli, and Sirajul Islam and Mujibur Rahman, who run the souvenir shop on Broadway—became Dave's playmates. They used the city streets for bowling lanes and race tracks; Dave employed the corner telephone booths for adolescent practical jokes. Even the more risqué elements of the neighborhood, such as the Topless Show Palace across the street from the theater, became toys for Letterman and his viewers. By his constant interaction with city residents and tourists and by engaging in playful conversation with waiters, taxi drivers, police officers, and firefighters, Letterman contributed significantly to the new image of the Times Square area as a safe and friendly playground.

In other genres of television programming, the image of the city has blended an aura of importance with a chance to engage in good, clean fun. In 1995 NBC's *Today* moved its studios back to the street-level location it had enjoyed in its early days when Dave Garroway hosted the program and the chimpanzee J. Fred Muggs entertained passersby from his perch in the display-window. *Today's* daily presentation of happy people in Rockefeller Center waving and offering greetings to the viewers across the nation certainly sends a message. The same message was soon given by the FOX network when they relocated their news studios to the street level on the corner of Sixth Avenue and Forth-eighth Street and by ABC with the transfer of their *Good Morning America* studios to a Times Square location. Morning talk show hosts such as Regis Philbin and Rosie O'Donnell regularly offered their enthusiastic accounts of the joys of living in the city. In 1997 MTV moved its main studio to Times Square and regularly takes its young viewers out into the streets.

Meanwhile, above the fun and games on the street, the excitement of world events is captured by the network news moguls. NBC Nightly News begins its standard nightly telecast with an awe-inspiring view of the G. E. Building in Rockefeller Center as NBC's "World Headquarters" and closes each evening's news with a live shot of Tom Brokaw's image on the megascreen in Times Square, making the obvious point that these two spots in midtown Manhattan are the center of the universe. *Dateline NBC* also begins with a flashy view of the New York City skyline.

And through all of this, for more than twenty-five years, *Saturday Night Live* has begun every show with its signature announcement, "Live . . . from New York. . . . It's Saturday Night!" An entire television generation has grown up being told that the best place to spend a Saturday night is New York City. Along with these daily, nightly, and weekly messages, television provides the nation with the sight of celebratory New Yorkers and tourists at the Macy's Thanksgiving Day Parade and New Year's Eve in Times Square, major athletic championship matches at Madison Square Garden and Yankee Stadium, and legendary performances Live from Lincoln Center. Television's message is consistent: the city is fun.

The credibility of this televised presentation of urban life is enhanced by the urban situation comedies' frequent interactions with "the real world," a device not often employed in the previous eras of urban comedy. *Seinfeld's* television universe included George Steinbrenner, J. Peterman, Keith Hernandez, and a "Soup Nazi" character based closely on an actual soup-restauranteur in Manhattan. The person on whom the character of Kramer is based now gives "Kramer Reality Tours" of sites in New York City that have been featured in *Seinfeld* episodes. Several news anchors and political figures have appeared on *Murphy Brown*, whose feud with Vice President Dan Quayle in the 1992 elections mixed various levels of reality and performance. As befits a show set in a newsroom, the final episode of *Murphy Brown* presented its usual pattern of topical references, in this case, the Microsoft lawsuit; the movie blockbuster, *Titanic*; and, of course, Monica Lewinsky. Ellen DeGeneres timed the "coming out" of her sitcom character with her announcement of her own homosexuality and, during the show's last season, featured occasional appearances by her then real-life partner, Anne Heche. The overall impression was that the televised portrayal of urban fun did not differ much from the real lives of these urban celebrities.

In a similar mix of fact and fiction, these comedies employed a pattern of self-referential devices. They frequently cast television icons as guest characters. Carol Burnett and Carroll O'Connor appeared as the parents of Jamie Buchman in several episodes of *Mad About You*, and Sid Caesar and Mel Brooks played the role of other relatives of Paul Buchman. Tom Selleck, the star of the 1980s hit show *Magnum, P. I.*, appeared for several episodes as Monica's love interest on *Friends*, and, in another episode of the show, George Clooney and Noah Wylie, the sexy young doctors on *ER*, played sexy young doctors dating Rachel and Monica. Marion Ross of *Happy Days* fame appeared as Drew Carey's mother, while Tammy Faye Baker Messner played the mother of the makeup-laden character Mimi on the same show. And while not a familiar face, the veteran television producer Garry Marshall's recurring role as the television station boss on *Murphy Brown* followed the same pattern of interweaving comic fiction with references to the history of television comedy.

This comic vision of urban life as fun coexisted with prime-time drama's alternative view of the city as harsh and dangerous. Ever since 1952 when *Dragnet*'s Sergeant Joe Friday's acknowledged his Los Angeles crime beat with the cryptic expression, "This is the city," police, law, and medical dramas have exploited the possibilities for disaster that large cities offer. The 1990s did not veer from that formula, as the officers of *N.Y.P.D. Blue* and *Homicide: Life on the Street*, the doctors and nurses of *ER* and *Chicago Hope*, and the police and lawyers of *Law and Order* and *The Practice* wended their ways through the mean streets of major American cities, in some cases filming the shows in the actual urban locations. It is a nice coincidence that the same Union Square subway station is shown, to differing effects, in the opening montages of both *N.Y.P.D. Blue* and *Mad About You*.

A more problematic difference between the urban situation comedies and the melodramas was the racial composition of the casts. Many of the main characters of the nighttime dramas were African American or Latino, portrayed by respected actors such as S. Epatha Merkerson, Benjamin Bratt, André Braugher, James McDaniel, Hector Elizondo, and Jimmy Smits, along with the frequent appearance of ethnic minorities as criminals, drug dealers and users, or victims of urban violence or accidents. However, very few minority characters appeared on a regular basis in the situation comedies. The workplace ensembles of *Spin City, News Radio,* and *Veronica's Closet,* for example, included one African American each. But that pretty much completes the list of minority characters in these comedies. Of the hundreds of characters that wandered in and out of the world of *Seinfeld,* only a small percentage were Latino or African American, with the unfortunate exception of the controversial Puerto Rican Day episode near the end of the show's run. A look at the cast lists of the other urban situation comedies would almost make one think that only white people live in our major cities. Or the more disturbing message might be that only white people have a chance for any happiness in the city. Tom Carson, television critic for *The Village Voice,* may have been right when he called the world of *Seinfeld* and *Mad About You* "vanillaland."[12]

Alongside this fascination with city matters, television comedy of the 1990s did not completely desert the suburbs or small towns of America. Suburban families could still be found on the small screen; they just looked a lot different. Even the closest imitator of the traditional suburban-comedy pattern, *Home Improvement,* modified the genre by showing what the husband-father actually did at work, and, because his job was in a television studio, providing comic commentary on the television medium itself, most notably with the use of out-takes from the episode shown during the program's closing credits. It also featured a wife and mother who worked outside the home. Most of the other shows not only varied from the formula; they ridiculed it. The Bundy family of *Married . . . with Children* was a far cry from Ozzie and Harriet. The parents living across the street from Ray Barone's family on *Everybody Loves Raymond* were as quirky and annoying as the parents of the Buchmans, Jerry Seinfeld, and George Costanza in the urban comedies.

Small-town life came off even worse than the suburbs in 1990s situation comedy. Instead of the charm and nostalgia of Andy Griffith's Mayberry, the settings for *Roseanne* and *Grace under Fire* were oppressive, boring, no-opportunity worlds of strip malls and chain restaurants, best negotiated by cynical and even desperate humor.

The harshest criticism of suburbia and small towns, however, could be found in the most innovative comedy of 1990s television, the animated series. The teenage phenomenon *Beavis and Butthead* and its spin-off, *Daria,* succeeded in capturing the banality of the suburban mall-culture perfectly. The Texas suburban situation of *King of the Hill* was equally stifling. Matt Groening deliberately placed *The Simpsons* in a town named after the hometown of *Father Knows Best*, Springfield, and proceeded to ridicule it. The Colorado mountain town setting of *South Park* was drawn as cartoonishly as possible, a flattened, unidimensional world of violence and profanity that begins to resemble an animated horror film. The transgressive humor of these cartoon shows has clearly fascinated the younger segment of television viewers, articulating perhaps their own dissatisfaction with the American Eden of suburban and small-town life.

The change of locale for television situation comedies in the 1990s spawned many other changes in the comic characterizations and other codes of television entertainment. These developments mirrored changes in the real world and, perhaps, shaped some of those changes as well. First, these urban comedies offered the city, not the suburban world, as the locus for comic adventure for single adults and young married couples. Did this imply that the political and corporate power brokers were once again managing a population shift of "the white middling classes" back into the cities they had been encouraged to leave forty years ago? Was the televised "urban revival" somehow related to the Disneyfication of Times Square?

Second, the flexibility of the sitcom family structures and relationships acknowledged and encouraged diversity and tolerance in contrast to a monolithic nuclear family ideal, especially when the portrayal of the family ideal is unrealistic. Some of the cast members of those classic 1950s family comedies have gone on record to question the effect their oversimplified and narrow portrayals had on the viewers who, after watching these shows, found their real family life so inferior and disappointing.[13] Did the more flexible and imperfect family arrangements of the 1990s comedies serve at least to avoid such false and hurtful idealizations?

Third, the urban sitcoms of the 1990s showed that even the domestic comedies no longer needed to rely on zany housewives or mischievous children to create comic confusion. The adults of *Seinfeld* and the other shows were quite capable of getting into trouble on their own. The urban culture was confusing and risky even for intelligent, relatively mature men and women. Was this another acknowledgement of the indeterminacy that underlies postmodern art, science, literature, and philosophy? Is the postmodern city, with its regulation of traffic, space, rental prices, criminal activity, and so on, simply the best example of rational planning imploding on itself?

Fourth, on these shows, the comic conflicts did not need to be resolved with parental wisdom, spousal forgiveness, or any other mechanism. Comic situations were allowed to remain frustrating or confused in accordance with the general indeterminacy and unpredictability of modern life, a realization that some of the standard questions of the human condition are irresolvable. Modern urban life has exacerbated the conflicts between human freedom and social interdependence, personal values and societal demands, instinct and discipline, the very tensions that have generated comic plots throughout history.

Finally, the 1990s television comic heroes were not required to be admirable (nor, for that matter, were the heroes of the dramatic shows). Viewers got accustomed to the concept that someone like Frasier Crane or Murphy Brown, with considerable professional credentials and salaries to match, had personal problems and major inadequacies. Might this be part of the reason why the American public in the 1990s was capable of disapproving of President Clinton's personal behavior while simultaneously granting him a large vote of confidence for his job performance?

Or is Steven D. Stark correct in saying that *Seinfeld* merely "reflected a new adolescent sensibility sweeping America in the 1990s"?[14] In his analysis of the show he found Jerry's gang of male friends displaying a fourteen-year-old sensibility, allowing one girl to hang out in their clubhouse, failing to find and keep regular jobs, competing with one another sexually, and regularly engaging in anti-authoritarian mischief. Stark compares them to other cultural bad boys like Huck Finn and Holden Caulfield. He contrasts the "eccentric individualism" and "flight from adulthood" of *Seinfeld* with "the gentle ring of mainstream truth" shown in the contemporary suburban sitcom *Home Improvement*. Stark concludes that *Home Improvement* was "a better reflection of who we are, despite major social changes over decades. . . . Viewers still feel more comfortable with the Cleavers and the Bradys than they do with the *Seinfeld* alternative."[15]

But, it must be asked, did television viewers of the 1990s look to television comedy for comfort or for gentle truth? I think not. The content of 1990s urban comedy was about alternatives. It was not a rush toward a monolithic, mainstream ideal but a tumbling convergence of various channels of information and values. The style of these comedies was consistent with the wave of "urban" fashion in 1990s clothing, popular music, stand-up comedy, and film. The 1990s urban attitude thrived on diversity, wrapped its statements in irony, mixed self-aggrandizement with self-camouflage, and grooved to a funky rhythm of street sounds and movement. The fifteen-second scenes on *Seinfeld* and the non sequiturs of Phoebe on *Friends* all pulsed with the same urban beat.

I suggest that the 1990s wave of television comedy resembled in many ways the characters' situation in Shakespeare's last comedy, *The Tempest*. The play is set on an island not unlike Himmelstein's "middle-landscape," where Prospero the magician has managed to shape the primitive landscape and tame the native inhabitants to create an artificial utopia. But the island's suburban peace is disturbed by the arrival of shipwrecked sophisticates from the cities of Milan and Naples, who, in their arguments with one another and their plots against Prospero, are just as immature and self-absorbed as any of the twentieth-century urbanites on *Seinfeld, Frasier,* or *Spin City.* However, as all their plots come to their comic conclusion and they meet Prospero's daughter, Miranda, she is amazed at the sight of them. Perhaps the television viewers of the 1990s felt the same fascination as they gazed on the comic inhabitants of television city and found themselves exclaiming with Miranda:

> O wonder!
> How many goodly creatures are there here!
> How beauteous mankind is! O brave new world
> That has such people in't!
> (*Tmp.* V.i.183–186)

·12·

BACK TO THE DRAWING BOARD

The year is 1954, and in the television town of Springfield, Mr. Jim Anderson, a reputable agent for the General Insurance Company, enters his comfortable suburban home, greets his pleasant and sensible wife, Margaret, changes from his business suit to more casual attire, and spends the evening calmly dealing with their three growing children on the popular domestic comedy, *Father Knows Best*, as indeed he did, week after week for nine years in prime time and for five more years, in re-runs, during the daytime.

Click the time-travel remote four decades to 1994, and once again in a television town called Springfield, Homer Simpson checks out of his job as safety inspector at the town nuclear power plant, jumps in his car, throws a radioactive ingot out of the car window, and speeds homeward, almost running over his skateboarding son, Bart, in the family driveway, finally colliding with his frazzled wife and hyperactive children on the family couch to watch television. It is already the fifth season of *The Simpsons*, an animated comedy that has become a ratings and merchandising phenomenon. Somewhere, somehow, in those forty years the television family went crazy.

The revised picture of the American family found on television's animated comedies by the 1990s came about not only because of the talents of the new breed of animators but also, of course, because of the changes in viewers' interests. Viewers had come to expect, even in the familiar format of television situation comedy, some presentation of alternative viewpoints and more or less direct challenges to the prevailing values and social norms. John Fiske has proposed that even the most traditional television texts must now speak both to the mainstream and to the subculture:

> Television's increasingly sophisticated viewers are demanding access to television's mode of presentation. Their pleasure in television is not explained by the

ease with which [viewers] can accommodate themselves to its ideologically produced meanings and subject positions. A better explanation of the pleasure of
television lies in understanding it as a text of contestation which contains forces
of closure and of openness and which allows viewers to make meanings that are
subculturally pertinent to them, but which are made in resistance to the forces of
closure in the text, just as their subcultural identity is maintained in resistance to
the ideological forces of homogenization.[1]

It may seem excessive to portray any program appealing to millions of viewers a week as an articulation of the subculture, but, utilizing Fiske's model, one
can argue that some of the most popular comedies of the 1990s drew such
large numbers of viewers precisely because they presented a "text of contestation" that pitted an emerging viewpoint, even a subculture, against the "forces
of closure" in the text that maintained the prevailing ideology.

A case in point is the phenomenal success of the 1990s' most popular comedy, *Seinfeld*, which premiered in 1990 and ended in prime-time run in 1998. A
brief examination reveals how the show managed to reformulate the position
of young adults in the prevailing culture of urban postmodern America. In its
four main characters, *Seinfeld* dared to mirror television's own golden demographic, the 18- to 49-year-old consumers of America as, among other things,
self-centered, cynical, jaded, and opportunistic. These new quirky antiheroes
replaced the comic young adults of television in the 1970s and 1980s: the well-
meaning but flawed strugglers of *The Mary Tyler Moore Show*; the goofy singles
of *Taxi*, *Three's Company*, or *Laverne and Shirley*; and the not-so-young any-
more assortment of the lovable and the desperate on *Cheers*.

Seinfeld, employing a rapid, hostile wit and complex comic plotting, explored the options available to four contemporary young adults whose neuroses had marginalized them from a world to which, by most external standards,
they seemed entitled to belong. Jerry Seinfeld was professionally and financially successful and reasonably attractive. Elaine Benes was sensuously beautiful, sexually adventurous, and articulate and cultured, with sufficiently mar-
ketable skills to land several consecutive jobs in the publishing field. George
Costanza had come from an outwardly respectable family and had acquired a
solid college education. Cosmo Kramer was somehow financially secure, dangerously well-read, and capable of securing employment when necessary.
Rumbling underneath this layer of social stability, however, were seismic
forces of emotional disorder: Jerry was finicky and phobic; Elaine was manic;
George was paranoid and hostile; and Kramer was borderline insane.

In the show's final episode in May 1998, decent society pronounced its
judgment on them by sentencing all four to prison for violating codes of civil-
ity embodied in the Good Samaritan law of the city of Boston when they chose

to ridicule rather than help someone in need. The forces of closure in the comic text were clearly articulated. Boston, "the city on the hill" of Puritan America, had once again expelled the sinful from its community of saints. As the final scenes illustrate, however, the dissenters were unconverted. These postmodern Thoreaus continued to march to a different drummer, unapologetically maintaining their pattern of self-interested, hostile bantering and mutual criticism even in the jail cell they were sentenced to share.

Were these four misfits articulating certain tensions of the largely young, well-educated, upper-middle-class viewers who watched their show so devotedly for eight seasons? Did they reveal a hostile, frightened underside of the upwardly mobile lifestyle of young professionals in the 1990s? Was a certain resistance to the prevailing moral consensus the dirty little secret of the yuppie subculture? Fiske's study of "television pleasure" suggests such a possibility:

> For those whose accommodation to the system is less complete, an essential component of pleasure must be an evasion, or at least a negotiation, of dominant ideological practice, the ability to shake oneself free from its constraints. This then opens up spaces for subcultures or groups to find their own pleasures in relationship to the ideology they are evading. Pleasure, in this subcultural role, helps to preserve and legitimate the heterogeneity of society and is thus properly seen as oppositional to the homogenizing force of ideology and can be summed up as the pleasure/power to be different. Television, like the society it serves, contains both tendencies in active contradiction.[2]

A few months before *Seinfeld* made its début, on December 17, 1989, the fledgling FOX network dared to introduce a comedy with even more rapid and complex plots, less admirable characters, and quicker wit, and in the process managed to reinvent one of the most popular television genres, the domestic situation comedy. *The Simpsons* proceeded to become the first successful animated comedy in prime-time television since *The Flintstones* in the 1960s. Its portrayal of the typical middle-class family in the archetypal town of Springfield stood the genre on its head with Homer Simpson, the lazy, overweight, slow-witted father; his well-meaning but often hapless wife, Marge; and, most of all, their underachieving-and-proud-of-it wisecracking fourth grade son, Bart. With these characters and Bart's younger sisters, Lisa and Maggie, at the center, the show's creator, Matt Groening, filled the screen with a large cast of bizarre Springfield residents: the extended Simpson family, the faculty and staff of Bart's school, Homer's boss and coworkers at Springfield's nuclear power plant, next-door neighbors, city officials, merchants, local television personalities, and the strangely frequent celebrity visitors to the town. The technique of animation enabled the scriptwriters to include as many characters as they wanted and to switch scenes as often as possible. This increased the opportunity for much more physical comedy, rapid dialogue, and plot twists than live-action comedy could ever manage. And it also offered a new view of family life.

This animated picture of dysfunctional family life soon found imitators on both cable and broadcast networks. Four of the attempts became solid hits. A brief synopsis of the basic premise and direction of each of these shows exhibits the same subversive portrait of family life found on *The Simpsons*. More detailed examination of the animation technique in these shows demonstrates how the animated format in all of them furthered the subversive discourse.

In 1993 MTV offered viewers the adventures of two teenage slackers named Beavis and Butthead who spent most of their time watching music videos, abusing each other verbally and physically, and engaging in crude and sometimes dangerous practical jokes. Their parents were nowhere to be found. The show developed a considerable cult following among male adolescents, and in 1997 MTV aired a spin-off, *Daria*, an animated comedy aimed at a female audience. The main character, who had been a classmate of Beavis and Butthead in elementary school, went on to high school, a teen environment that the brainy, sardonic Daria could only loathe. Her parents were both successful professionals who had bequeathed their intelligence to their daughter but could not offer her any attention or quality time. Caught between the emotional sterility of her parents and the brainless frenzy of her peers, Daria had to fend for herself as a brainy nerd doomed to outsider status both at home and away.

The popularity of these cable-network efforts (along with the phenomenal success of *The Simpsons*) emboldened producers to experiment further with animated comedy appealing to the wider audience of a broadcast network, FOX. Two of these experiments succeeded. In 1996 Mike Judge, creator of *Beavis and Butthead*, used his Texas roots as the locale for his new animated comedy *King of the Hill*, featuring the family of Hank Hill residing in suburban Arlen, Texas. Conservative, lower-middle-class Hank sold propane gas and spent a lot of time drinking beer and hanging out with his neighborhood buddies. His wife, Peggy, housewife and substitute teacher, had a mind of her own, influenced by the trickle-down feminism that had made its way even into the Texas suburbs. Hank's chubby son, Bobby, was a disappointment to his father, and their live-in niece, Luanne, was too wild and frisky by Peggy's standards. This was followed in 1999 by a similar comedy on FOX, *Family Guy*, which in many ways encapsulated all the popular features of the previous animated domestic comedies but added a new level of absurdist humor. The father, Peter Griffin, was, like Homer Simpson, overweight, lazy, and irresponsible. Like Beavis and Butthead, his favorite pastime was watching television and avoiding work. His wife, Lois, like Marge Simpson and Peggy Hill, was the long-suffering wife and mother of a chaotic household, only more persistently cheerful. Their older son, Chris, was as overweight as Bobby Hill and as much of an underachiever as Bart Simpson. Their teenage daughter, Meg, was as unpopular and nerdy as Daria Morgendorffer and (sometimes) Lisa Simpson, and their one-year-old baby, Stewie, was precociously destructive enough to rival Beavis and Butthead. The elements of the absurd included the talking family dog, who spent much of the day reading the paper and offering the most sensible advice on the show, and the audible interior monologue of baby Stewie, spoken with an inexplicable British accent and expressing his paranoid hatred of his mother, who he was convinced was out to destroy him. The show outdid even *The Simpsons* in its constant references to popular culture and current events.

Meanwhile, back in cable television land, in 1997 Comedy Central had introduced a daringly transgressive comedy called *South Park*, created by two brash young newcomers, Trey Parker and Matt Stone, which followed the adventures of four foulmouthed third graders in a Colorado mountain town who constantly heaped abuse on one another; uttered racist, homophobic, and other politically insensitive epithets; and obsessed about flatulence, excretion, and other bodily functions. Their parents occasionally appeared and, when they did, were generally presented as ignorant, repressed, frantic, and otherwise unworthy of any child's respect. One of the character's mothers was regularly referred to by the other boys as a "crack whore."

The desperate copycat activity of television networks is well known, and, given the success of *The Simpsons*, it is surprising that there were not dozens of such animated prime-time families throughout the decade. Dysfunction was already in fashion for many domestic comedies. While the hip but heartwarming portrayal of family tensions and togetherness on *The Cosby Show* (1984–1992) and *Family Ties* (1982–1989) certainly appealed to the largest percentage of television viewers (*The Cosby Show* was #1 in the ratings for five years in a row, with *Family Ties* not far behind), more offbeat domestic comedies such as *Mama's Family* (1983–1990), *Roseanne* (1988–1997), and *Married . . . with Children* (1987–1997) met with considerable success, thriving on the humor of insult, anger, irresponsibility, and outrageous behavior. Steven D. Stark, in his chapter entitled "How *Roseanne* Made Trash TV Respectable," gives a good description of the typical humor::

> There was something refreshing about a loud, studiously sloppy comedy whose lead was a woman 50 pounds overweight . . . and the characters perambulated in their underwear—insulting each other and belching. . . . Where *Roseanne* really stood alone in sitcom history . . . was in her willingness to dump

on her children. . . . *Roseanne* raised verbal child-bashing to an art form. . . . "They've left for school. Quick—change the locks!" was the cry on another episode; while on yet another, she jokingly offers to trade one of her offspring for a dishwasher.[3]

Dysfunctional families like Roseanne's and the Bundys were beginning to appear often enough on television by the 1990s. It took animation, however, to present them as truly grotesque.

Even the most conventional animation techniques tend toward the grotesque. The cartoon esthetic thrives on distortion, exaggeration, vivid presentations of emotional excess, and even violence that form the language of comedy. Live performance on television or film can only approximate the comic excesses of animation. Certain television and film comedians have been gifted with an elasticity of facial expression that borders on the cartoonish; the facial distortions accomplished by comedians such as Imogene Coca, Jonathan Winters, Lucille Ball, Harpo Marx, Gilda Radner, John Belushi, or Jim Carrey usually required no clown makeup or mask. In recent years several live-action comedies have attempted to re-create cartoon grotesquerie in characters such as Glenn Close's Cruella DeVille in the live-action version of *101 Dalmations*, Dustin Hoffman's gangster Big Boy in *Dick Tracy*, Jack Nicholson's Joker in *Batman*, and the transformation of Anjelica Huston and Raul Julia into Morticia and Gomez Addams in *The Addams Family*. Yet these mighty efforts all prove how much is required for live-action filmmaking to achieve what is done so easily by a few strokes of Charles Addams's pen.

Emotional reaction in animated comedy readily approaches the grotesque. The distorted facial features of most characters lay the groundwork, but the ability to have eyes bug out in terror, faces redden and swell in anger, bodies shrink in fear, or tongues hang out with desire for food, drink, or sexual pleasure are all standard animation techniques. Violence and destruction are the daily fare in the universe of Bugs Bunny, Tom and Jerry, and the Roadrunner, who regularly encounter and survive explosions, long-distance falls, crashes, and the weight of heavy objects landing on or rolling over them. Much of the physical trickery accomplished by animation—the speeding up and slowing down of motion, appearance and disappearance of objects—can be accomplished by stop-action photography or the adjustment of camera speed, and indeed was successfully done by George Melies and Thomas Edison even in the early days of motion picture production. Yet animation is given far more liberty by the viewer to portray rapid and violent activity or overwrought emotional reactions that might be frightening or distasteful if presented in live-action film. On *The Simpsons*, for example, Homer's guzzling of beer and gorging on food, the accidents that occur at home or in the schoolyard, the larger disasters of death and destruction of property, even Homer and Marge's efforts at lovemaking, to name just a few, would tend to offend viewers if presented in graphic realism. But by their very exaggeration in animation they become ludicrous and beyond offense.

Such grotesquerie, while more acceptable in animated form, still has the capacity to provide a powerful alternative to commonly accepted viewpoints. In modern criticism the notion of the grotesque in literature and the performing arts has been given new importance by Mikhail Bakhtin's development of the concept of the carnivalesque, which he explored in the work of François Rabelais. "Carnival" is a general term for the sort of wild, sometimes orgiastic, and even lawbreaking activity that is currently most easily observed on Bourbon Street at the Mardi Gras festivities in New Orleans or the carnival celebrations in Rio de Janiero. The observance of Carnival, as a pre-Lenten revelry with roots in the Dionysian festivities of the Greeks and the Saturnalia of the Romans, according to Bakhtin:

> represented an alternative cosmovision characterized by the ludic undermining of all norms. The carnivalesque principle abolishes hierarchies, levels social classes, and creates another life free from conventional rules and restrictions. In carnival, all that is marginalized and excluded—the mad, the scandalous, the aleator—takes over the center in a liberating explosion of otherness. The principle of material body—hunger, thirst, defecation, copulation—becomes a positively corrosive force, and festive laughter enjoys a symbolic victory over death, over all that is held sacred, over all that oppresses and restricts.[4]

Early in his essay "Film, Literature, and the Carnivalesque," Robert Stam claims that contemporary mass media offer only "the simulacra of carnival-style festivity."[5] Nevertheless, he procceeds to apply elements of Bakhtinian carnival to the works of the European filmmakers Luis Bunuel, Federico Fellini, and Jean-Luc Godard, as well as the films of Monty Python, Mel Brooks, the Marx Brothers, and many others, explaining that "in some cases, the carnivalesque tradition is deployed in a purely ludic or even a commercialized manner, while elsewhere it becomes aggressive and positively subversive."[6] In general, Stam finds a certain ambivalence in the political effectiveness of carnival, wondering whether such transgressive behavior genuinely undermines or only reinforces the hegemonic structures. At one point he comments on Umberto Eco's view that such carnival activity is "an authorized transgression deeply dependent on a law that it only apparently violates."[7] In other words, the carnival festivities are usually understood as only a temporary cessation of the status-quo, and once the holiday respite has run its course, the populace returns to ordinary life, with its recognition of the legitimate authorities and structures of civilized life. Stam's response to Eco captures the same ambivalence as Fiske's "text of contestation":

> While it is true that official power has at times used carnival to channel energies that might otherwise have funneled popular revolt, it has just as often been the case that carnival itself has been the object of official repression. . . . Carnival . . . is the oppositional culture of the oppressed, a countermodel of cultural production and desire . . . a symbolic, anticipatory overthrow of oppressive social structures. . . . All carnivals must be seen as complex crisscrosssings of ideological manipulation and utopian desire.[8]

Stam suggests that the carnival may indeed have a more lasting effect, as the oppressed see in their renegade revelry a "ludic undermining" of the established order and begin to imagine and plan for alternative social orders. Hence the carnivalesque can be considerably subversive, especially if the countermodel it proposes looks like a lot of fun. The attitudes and behaviors exhibited in the new animated comedies are perhaps best understood as television's version of the carnivalesque: a countermodel that is fun. *The Simpsons* and other successful animated domestic comedies have been able to explore darker, subversive aspects of family life thanks mainly to the possibilities of the cartoon esthetic. But, like carnival, they offer their critique in a familiar and culturally acceptable environment: the traditional sitcom format. It is precisely this mixture of shock and reassurance that distinguishes the new animated television comedy.

Animated comedies have brought the oppositional esthetic of the carnival to the medium of television. Much as the carnivalesque represents the interface of the prevailing culture and various voices of opposition, so the esthetic of the new animated comedies provides opportunities within the code of domestic comedy for a countermodel of the American family ideal. Although the animation technique of *The Simpsons* is far more complex and detailed than that of the other four animated comedies under consideration, its underlying ideology shares the same subversive vision that the other, more primitive cartoons express.

In her thoroughgoing study of animation aesthetics, Maureen Furniss maintains that a choice of animation technique reflects an ideological viewpoint. She describes all motion picture production as falling within a spectrum ranging from pure mimesis—the attempt to reproduce natural reality in photographic detail—to abstraction—an interest in pure form that suggests rather than replicates nature. At the mimesis pole of the spectrum, Furniss places documentary film, using as her prime example Andy Warhol's film *Sleep*, a real-time observation of a person sleeping. Other documentaries and realistic narrative films would fit more or less closely at this end of the spectrum. At the other pole, that of abstraction, Furniss places a work such as Norman McClaren's cartoon *Hen Hop*, "which contains line drawings of hens whose bodies constantly metamorphose and break into parts" in a very stylized presentation.[9] While all attempts at animated art would naturally land closer to this pole in Furniss's spectrum, as she further examines animated film production, she soon contrasts the approaches of commercial and independent cartoon production, showing how technique can represent ideological viewpoints. In contrast to commercial animation, or what she has entitled "traditional/industrial/hegemonic forms," Furniss describes independent animation, or, in her terminology, "experimental/ independent/subversive forms." She characterizes independent animation in terms of several factors: its use of techniques other than traditional ones; tendency to alter media; abstract style; nonlinear narrative; reflection of alternative lifestyles; challenge to dominant beliefs, and its tendency to be made by artists from marginalized social groups and to reflect their concerns.[10]

The success of the new animated domestic comedies replicates the pattern described by Fiske of appealing to both mainstream and marginalized viewers. Their traditional framework presumes familiarity with the television format of the comic nuclear family from *Father Knows Best* to *Home Improvement*, which, with all its variations and even eccentricities, continues to function as a viable social unit in the real world and in television comedy. Yet the cartoon's more subversive coding proposes that all such attempts at viability must now include the recognition of the grotesque in contemporary family life. The new television animators use the techniques of independent animation described by Furniss to create another "text of contestation" over a core issue of the American ideology, the valorization of the family.

With the *The Simpsons* as primary text (even in the face of its commercial success and pop culture status), a case can be made for the function of the new animated domestic comedies as experimental/independent/subversive forms. The specific features categorized by Furnisss are apparent in the new animated comedies.

The Use of Techniques Other Than Traditional Ones, Tending to the Abstract and Nonlinear

While *The Simpsons* in its present state has become a major industry, in terms of both production and merchandizing, and while its animation is far more complex and detailed than the other four animated comedies under consideration, Groening's art is still rooted in a nontraditional style. The characters on the show still resemble the minimalist/grotesque figures (without the long rabbit ears) that populate Groening's comic strip *Life in Hell*, still in syndication in the alternative press. Perhaps the omnipresence of the Simpson characters in the media has led the public to overlook the fundamental surrealism of Marge Simpson's beehive of blue hair; the absurdity of the perpetual sucking sound of the infant Maggie Simpson; the cartoon-within-the-cartoon personae of Krusty the Clown, Sideshow Bob, and Itchy and Scratchy; the constant smoking of Marge's older sisters, the Bouvier twins; and so on. Even when celebrity guests such as Sting, John Glenn, Steven Spielberg, Darryl Strawberry, The Who, and others have appeared in certain episodes, as their actual voices were used, their images were made to conform to the general physiognomy of all *The Simpsons*'s characters: the bug eyes, the overbite, the prominent foreheads, etc. There is no attempt to aim for the naturalistic look that Disney animators sought, with the help of live human models, for Snow White, Cinderella, or Aladdin, or the animated animals in *Bambi*, *Lady and the Tramp*, and *101 Dalmations*.

Some of the animation delves even further into the abstract with the simple line drawing of the facial features of Beavis and Butthead and *South Park*'s use of paper cutout figures as their main characters. The character of Jesus Christ in *South Park* looks like a child's drawing, and some of the minor characters become almost inhuman, with blank-featured heads that resemble eggs. Daria's facial features undergo little change as she stares straight ahead through her horn-rimmed glasses that turn her face into an inscrutable mask. All of the cartoons other than *The Simpsons* tend to display a minimum of movement and of visual setting.

Of the comedies under consideration, *Beavis and Butthead* comes closest to the nonlinearity of absurdist narrative. *Beavis and Butthead* exist in a virtual Beckettian vacuum, with no familial framework, limited range of locale, and usually no sense of time of day or year. The two slackers spend most of their time on the couch watching television with no indication given of what has transpired beforehand or what awaits them. The plot of each episode often consists of repetitions of the same gag or physical schtick. *Family Guy* approaches the absurd with its talking dog and the comments of the family's resentful infant with a unexplainably British accent constantly plotting damage on his parents. *The Simpsons* has, over the years, developed a history of the family and the town as plotlines have relied on antecedent events from previous episodes. Fans of the series know that Sideshow Bob has attempted to kill Bart, Barney the town drunk has stopped drinking, and Apu, the manager of the Quickie-Mart, has married and fathered octuplets. Homer's youth and high school years have been recounted. Yet no one has grown older (particularly odd in the family sitcom genre); everyone continues in the same occupation; and practically no one (other than the Simpsons's next-door neighbor Maude Flanders) has died. The larger narrative engine is stalled.

The Tendency to Alter Media

A subtle change in the experience of the medium of television results from the self-reflexivity of the new animated comedies. Again *Beavis and Butthead* offer the clearest examples, as the inarticulate teenagers devote hours to watching, and often reviling, the music videos on MTV, the very channel that airs the program. Clips from the music videos are interspersed into the cartoon text. *King of the Hill* engages in regular references to media celebrities, current developments in pop culture, and especially the conventions of advertising texts, as, for instance, Hank and his drinking buddies imagine themselves starring in the sexy beer ads. In its broadcast of the 2001 Super Bowl, the FOX network inserted brief clips of Hank Hill and other characters from the show (which FOX also airs) to comment on the game. The intertextuality of sports news coverage, entertainment, and advertising further reshapes the viewer's understanding of the medium. The foundation of *The Simpsons* is its connection with and commentary on previous television comedy. The opening sequence of everyone's trip home honors Fred's commute to open every episode of *The Flintstones; Father Knows Best* lives on in the name of the town. The family gathers each week in front of the television set, and Homer and the children spend a great deal of their time watching the tube. Every episode is surfeited with allusions not only to familiar television texts but also to films, theater, popular music, literary classics, politics, and history. *Family Guy* raises the level of pop-cultural allusions with even more frequent references to films and other television shows, often completely unrelated to the narrative context. *The Simpsons* and *Family Guy* have turned the television medium into a repository of cultural trivia and popular folklore. In the process they encourage an oppositional reading of much of the mediated messages.

A Reflection of Alternative Lifestyles, an Expression of Marginalized Social Groups, and a Challenge to Dominant Beliefs

To a certain extent every one of the animated family comedies gives voice to a marginalized segment of society. In some cases the main characters personify a certain subculture. Beavis and Butthead's monosyllables, grunts, and chuckles speak for those isolated, inarticulate teenagers who are not on the football team, student council, or pep squad and do not face the same social dilemmas as their high school counterparts on *Beverly Hills 90210* or *Dawson's Creek*. Daria Morgendorffer, also living on the margins of her high school community, offers wry commentary on the popularity of her cheerleader sister, awkwardness of her male peers, and other features of the high school culture.

Hank Hill and his neighbors, while they may now be living in the suburbs of a Texas metropolis, still retain many of the features of their redneck roots and an America-love-it-or-leave-it mentality of disenfranchised poor whites.

The Simpson family may represent skewed variations on the American middle class, but they are surrounded by members of minority groups or other relative outsiders. Apu, the Hindu owner of the Quickie-Mart and his wife by parental arrangement, Manjula; Julius Hebert, the African American physician who in many ways resembles Bill Cosby's Dr. Huxtable character; Smithers, the Springfield tycoon's assistant, who may or may not be gay but who is clearly in love with his boss; Ned Flanders, the Simpsons's next-door neighbor who is militantly upbeat and public about his Christianity; and, finally, the foreign-born Groundskeeper Willie all add up to a diverse population for a small town, quite the opposite of the whites-only world of the earlier television Springfield.

South Park positively revels in diversity, usually with politically incorrect glee. One of the children, Cartman, is regularly reviled because he is Jewish. Timmy, the disabled child, uses his disability to serve his own purposes. Chef, the African American cook, personifies the stereotype of the "black stud." Big Gay Al minces about scantily clad and simpering, "I feel Super. Thanks for asking!" Stan's uncle is a Vietnam-vet gun-rights advocate who spouts right-wing, racist, and homophobic epithets at every opportunity. Almost every episode revolves around a delicate issue in contemporary culture wars, expressing both sides of the arguments in as tasteless a form as possible.

Most of the comedies likewise tend to challenge authority, mainly by exposing official hypocrisy and, at least, the foibles of those in power. The teenagers Beavis and Butthead seem to have no contact with their parents, while Daria's mother and father, self-absorbed and obsessed with their professional lives, are clearly deficient in their parenting skills. Beavis and Butthead's commentary on the television they watch includes cynical comments on the prevailing culture, and their occasional excursions into the mall usually involve a deliberate defiance of rules and regulations. Daria views her teachers and school administrators with thinly disguised contempt.

The Simpsons offers a full display of inept and hypocritical wielders of power: the ruthless tycoon Mr. Burns; the corrupt Mayor Quimby and Chief of Police Wiggums; the emotionally shaky elementary school principal Seymour Skinner, who does not always play by the rule book, especially if he has a chance to wreak revenge on the rebellious Bart. Bart personifies the anti-authoritarian troublemaker, impervious to school discipline and ending up in detention on a daily basis. He never addresses his father as "Dad," but as "Homer." There is added defiance of authority in the attitude of Bart's virtuous sister Lisa. Driven by her concern for the environment, her budding feminism, and sensitivity to various other social issues, she often ends up confronting the political authorities in her town and even challenging the behavior of her father. Homer defies authority whenever it gets in the way of the life of leisure he seeks, whether it means sneaking out of work at the nuclear power plant or skipping Sunday church services. The boys of *South Park* seem perpetually destined to question the status quo, especially since their parents and school authorities are so intent on controlling their lives and because they are subject to visits from aliens or other visitors who present them with alternatives to the prevailing norms of their isolated mountain town.

Is it any surprise that, in a medium with such a subversive viewpoint, the family has been reexamined as well? Animation's facility for presenting the grotesque gives it the esthetic edge in presenting an alternative view of family life, portraying both parents and children as potentially monstrous. The comic conflicts often turn violent, as Homer grabs Bart by the throat to throttle him, or Beavis pummels Butthead, or Kenny is once again killed by a citizen of South Park. The negligent parents on *Daria*; the lazy, irresponsible, nearly infantile Homer Simpson; and teenage children close to depression or criminality on *King of the Hill, Family Guy, Daria*, and *Beavis and Butthead* contribute to a grim picture of family dynamics. At the same time, the limited physiognomic range available to the simpler forms of animation chosen by Groening, Judge, Parker, and Stone also tends to portray the characters and settings as stereotypical and dangerously close to homogeneous. All the characters on *South Park* are portrayed as squat, rounded headed, and one dimensional; all the citizens of Springfield have the same bug eyes and overbite as the Simpsons. The houses in Springfield and Arlen look alike. Thus the animation technique conveys both the bizarre and mundane possibilities of contemporary family life.

However, while these animated comedies exploit the possibilities of the cartoon esthetic to present darker portrayals of family life, they also enjoy the advantage of esthetic distance typical of all film comedy. In his study of the comic hero, Maurice Charney pinpoints the distancing effect in his analysis of the familiar picture of Harold Lloyd hanging from the minute hand of a clock high up on a building in the silent film classic *Safety Last*. Charney speaks of the comic optimism of the audience, commenting, "of course, it is only a film, it is not actually happening at this very moment, and the dangers have been safely neutralized by the medium: God's in his heaven, and the film is in the can."[11] How much more carefree must the viewers feel in response to the more obviously artificial medium of animation?

In the portrayal of family interaction the cartoon esthetic has allowed viewers to have it both ways. As the new animated domestic comedies display all sorts of domestic dysfunction, they speak to viewers who feel marginalized from the dominant culture of American family life. Meanwhile, the esthetic distance of the cartoon medium allows mainstream viewers to discount the grotesquerie if they so desire. As a consequence, the presentation of the family is ambivalent. In its animated incarnation the discourse is reassuringly comic for some viewers and boldly subversive for others.

·13·

BREAKING AND ENTERING

A survey of television comedy over the years reveals that, for the most part, it has behaved itself. Even in the early days, however, a few memorable exceptions tried to break the rules. In the 1950s, when *Father Knows Best* and *The Adventures of Ozzie and Harriet* provided the models for husbandly behavior, Jackie Gleason's portrayal of a loudmouthed braggart on *The Honeymooners* approached forbidden territory in his threats to retaliate against his wife's remarks "one of these days" by punching her and sending her "to the moon, Alice, to the moon!" Milton Berle's drag routines, Red Skelton's drunken characters, and Ernie Kovacs's effeminate Percy Dovetonsils were similar mild violations of the social taboos of Middle America, while keeping well within the traditions of slapstick and vaudeville comedy. Such outlandish comedy, however, was apparently too risky for the networks. *The Ernie Kovacs Show* survived only a few months on nationwide television in 1952–1953. *The Honeymooners* lasted only one full season (1955–1956) in its situation-comedy format. Gerard Jones claims that its portrayal of a working-class couple barely making ends meet and constantly on the verge of argument "played on deep anxieties" and were a "harsh reminder of a conflict being ardently denied by popular culture."[1]

Fifteen years later Norman Lear's creations dared to speak the unspeakable, provoking frequent complaints from defenders of good taste. In Lear's breakout success *All in the Family*, Archie Bunker's bigotry, his daughter Gloria's feminism, and his son-in-law Mike's liberal atheism all served to shock sensibilities across the ideological spectrum of the 1970s.[2] Lear continued this pattern with the treatment of abortion on *Maude;* homosexuality on *Mary Hartman, Mary Hartman;* and the anger of African Americans verging on reverse racism on *Sanford and Son* and *The Jeffersons*. In more recent years two of the most popular situation comedies of the 1990s, *Roseanne* and *Married . . .*

with Children, have thrived on offensive attitudes, outrageous behavior, taboo topics, and the language of insult.

Almost all of these instances of groundbreaking comedy appeared on major networks during prime time. Most of them were cast in the conventional context of family situation comedies. They were all subject to the pressure of network Standards and Practices policies, threats of viewer boycotts, sensibilities of their sponsors, and the usual consensus in favor of "least offensive programming" to appeal to the huge viewership served by the three major networks.[3] However, a new wave of experimentation has emerged with the advent of cable television. Less burdened with FCC regulations, less dependent on sponsor support, and freer of the need to achieve blockbuster ratings, cable television has enjoyed the opportunity to appeal to a narrower demographic. In some cases this has resulted in some bold new comedy that dares to offend, a transgressive comedy that revels in shock and tastelessness. One of the most successful of these new "shock" comedies has been Comedy Central's biggest hit, *South Park*. The animated cartoon made its début on the cable network during the summer of 1997. Despite its TV-MA rating (unsuitable for children under 17) and its later time slot of 10:00 p.m., it became instantly popular, achieving a record-high rating for a cable series of 6.9 by February 1998. Its popularity has continued.

South Park, with its presentation of "alien abductions, anal probes, flaming farts, and poo," has been described as "gleefully offensive and profoundly silly, juxtaposing cute and crude, jaded and juvenile,"[4] With the use of childlike cut-out figures, the show follows the adventures of four nine-year-old boys in a small mountain town (named after an actual area in Colorado notorious for alien sightings), which the show's creators, Trey Parker and Matt Stone, portray as a "poisoned place in the heart, a taste-free zone where kids say the darndest, most fucked-up things."[5] The foulmouthed boys, Stan, Kyle, Cartman, and Kenny, constantly heap abuse on one another; utter racist and other politically insensitive epithets ("Stan's dog's a homo"); question all authority; and obsess about flatulence, excrement, and other bodily functions. Stan, the leader of the group, vomits every time he encounters his semi-girlfriend, Wendy. Kenny, who is criticized by the others because he is poor, is horribly killed in every episode only to reappear the following week. Other prominent characters include Stan's Uncle Jim, a gun-rights fanatic, and his Vietnam-vet buddy who speaks through a voice box; the school cook, Chef, the only African American in the town, who shares his fantasies and advice about sexual matters with the awestruck boys; and Cartman's Mom, described by the other boys as a "crack whore." The other adults—teachers, parents, and town officials—are generally portrayed as repressed, frantic, or otherwise unworthy of any child's respect. The one exception may be Jesus Christ, who, dressed in his familiar white robe and sandals, serves as the nice-guy host of a local cable-access show. It all adds up to a ribald, irreverent comedy with a "joyous lack of self-restraint . . . stridently, relentlessly, gloriously, and hilarious outrageous."[6]

Like the alien visitors who menace their town, these four nasty little boys have invaded the world of American pop culture and taken it by storm. The inevitable feature film, *South Park, the Movie: Bigger, Longer, and Uncut*, was released, to high critical praise and ticket sales, in the summer of 1999. Meanwhile, its phenomenal success emboldened both cable and broadcast networks to attempt their own treatments of taboo subjects with varying degrees of success. In September 1999, for example, the FOX network introduced with heavy marketing fanfare its new comedy *Action*, replete with four-letter words (bleeped but easy to lip-read), outrageous sexual misbehavior, and viciously self-absorbed characters. The network executives were counting on what they saw as "the rapid disappearance of most taste and language restrictions in mass media," with *South Park* as the prime example.[7]

Not everyone shared the general enthusiasm for *South Park*. Peggy Charren, founder of Action for Children's Television, suspected that despite the TV-MA rating, many children watch the program. She was particularly concerned about the characters' use of racial slurs, indicting such language that, in their encouragement of bigotry and discriminatory attitudes, she considered "dangerous to the democracy."[8] Dale Kunkel, professor of communications at the University of California, Santa Barbara, questioned the motives of the producers and the network. He noted that "the humor and the whole orientation of the show is adolescent-oriented humor, rejecting authority, flouting convention. . . . They say they don't want the teen audience, yet the nature of the content is significantly targeted to appeal to that audience."[9] Two elementary schools in New Jersey went so far as to send letters home to parents urging parents to stop their children from watching the show.[10]

Concern about the influence of mass communications on the general citizenry has followed every advance in mass circulation, from the penny presses and lurid dime novels of the nineteenth century to the nickelodeons at the turn of the twentieth century to the hysteria-inducing *War of the Worlds* radio broadcast and on into the present. But the debate increased in volume when television invaded the living rooms of the nation, often serving as the new babysitter. What Marshall McLuhan envisioned as the new family hearth has become unusually powerful not only in shaping but also reinforcing mainstream values. It has become the culture's primary storyteller and definer of cultural patterns through information and entertainment for an enormous and heterogeneous mass public.

The success of *South Park* and similar television comedy represents the mainstreaming of a new comic attitude, previously displayed only in more marginal settings. This attitude is new enough to television to shock the audience, yet it is creative enough to fascinate viewers. Transgressive comedy, climbing through the window of television, has broken into the American home.

This type of comedy is best identified in terms of its purpose. In his study of "the purpose of jokes," Freud first considers "innocent jokes" such as puns and other plays on words that are enjoyed for their cleverness and playfulness with no further purpose and usually evoke a chuckle of moderate amusement. He then deals with "tendentious jokes," which seem to provoke much more laughter and therefore are probably serving some deeper psychological purpose. Freud sees only two such types of purposive humor: "it is either a *hostile* joke (serving the purpose of aggressiveness, satire, or defense) or an *obscene* joke (serving the purpose of exposure)."[11] His explanation of the higher amount of pleasure derived from these two types of humor, especially the obscene, derives directly from his view of "civilization and its discontents":

> It is our belief that civilization and higher education have a large influence in the development of repression, and we suppose that, under such conditions, the psychical organization undergoes an alteration (that can also emerge as an inherited disposition) as a result of which what was formerly felt as agreeable now seems unacceptable and is rejected with all possible psychical force. The repressive activity of civilization brings it about that primary possibilities of enjoyment, which have now, however, been repudiated by the censorship in us, are lost to us. But to the human psyche all renunciation is exceedingly difficult, and so we find that tendentious jokes provide a means of undoing the renunciation and retrieving what was lost.[12]

Since civilization and education remove "the primary possibilities of enjoyment" found in uninhibited aggressive and sexual activity, in Freud's view, certain types of humor allow us to retrieve "what was lost," to regress to the more primal state of childhood with its accompanying lack of inhibitions. It is particularly pertinent to this study that, as Freud proceeds to analyze the operation of the smutty joke, he observes that its sexual material can include anything that is "common to both sexes and to which the feeling of shame extends, what is excremental in the most comprehensive sense."[13] He specifically refers to "the sense covered by sexuality in childhood, an age at which there is, as it were, a cloaca within which what is sexual and what is excremental are barely or not at all distinguished."[14] The farting, vomiting, and verbal spewing of the South Park boys vividly display such an interconnection.

It is important for the purposes of this discussion to emphasize the distinction Freud makes between the purpose of the smutty or "exposure" jokes

(jokes about farting, vomiting, sexual activity) from the hostile humor which serves an aggressive or defensive purpose. Satirical comedy is one form of such aggression, attacking its target from a sense of outrage and with the hope of some reform. Juvenal catalogued the moral corruption of Rome; Molière ridiculed the religious hypocrites, lying doctors, and miserly parental tyrants of Louis XIV's Paris; Pope and Dryden derided the vanity and foppery of London society; Heller, Vonnegut, Kubrick, and other twentieth-century artists have employed absurdist techniques to oppose the stupidities of modern warfare and military culture. Such is the grand aggressive tradition of satire: human reason's warfare on human folly.

Transgressive humor has no such moralistic purpose. Instead of trying to change or eliminate human foolishness, certain comic writers and performers deliberately revel in the lower forms of social behavior. Unlike the intellectual wit and verbal sophistication of the satirical tradition, transgressive humor regresses to the infantile. Rather than portraying the objects of its humor in hopes that witty ridicule and public shame might provoke change, transgressive humor does not expect or even desire a change, for then the fun would end.

Transgressive humor does share one element with satire. Both comic methods depend on a basic consensus of standards and boundaries; otherwise the joke would not be pleasurable. The societal taboos must remain, especially in transgressive humor, so that one can experience the delight of the entry into forbidden realms, a childish joy in simply breaking all the adult taboos and a pleasure indulged in for the sake of exposure of the impulses we have all been forced to repress.

In another overlap with satire, sometimes transgressive humor, purposely or not, can serve general satirical purposes by its faux–innocent or playful criticism of ignorance, prejudice, or stereotypes. For example, in a transgressive context the articulation of an offensive word or the performance of an offensive action operates to transform stigmatization into empowerment. The appropriation of the insult by the intended target disempowers the insult. The use of the word "nigger" by black comedians and rappers and in urban street talk in general and the use of the epithet "queer" in gay discourse from academia to performance art serve precisely this purpose while adding an element of threat to those who would attempt to use these words against them. Gay comedy reverts to "camp," and black comedy employs "homey" style for much the same purposes.[15] Appropriation of the insulting attack disempowers the attacker.

Transgressive humor sometimes adds a subtle twist to this formula of insult appropriation. While the comic speaker may not be a member of the target group, the speaker's humor attempts to signify his or her solidarity with the group by joining in their appropriation of the hostile or outrageous language or actions. Such seems to have been the intent of a case of some famous transgressive humor that resulted in considerable confusion and offense, a blackface act performed by the television star Ted Danson at a Friars Club roast of the African American comedian Whoopi Goldberg in 1993. The routine had been written primarily by Goldberg, who was in a relationship with Danson at the time. In the long tradition of the Friars Club roasts, Danson's routine was sexually explicit, with many references to black sexual stereotypes, outrageous sexual positions, and Goldberg's anatomy. Danson also joked about racist social stereotypes, reporting that, when he took Whoopi to meet his family, they asked her to do the laundry and wash the dishes and offered to drive her to the nearest bus stop when she had finished. Many prominent African Americans in the audience were deeply offended, including former Mayor David Dinkins and television talk-show host Montel Williams, who cancelled his membership in the Friars.[16]

In the ensuing controversy Goldberg defended the routine as their response to the volume of hate mail and openly racist threats she and Danson had received. "We thought it would be a good idea if we sort of dispelled that word."[17] The comedy writer Bruce Vilanch, who may have contributed material to the sketch, added: "Ted's plan was to defuse the whole (racial) thing with jokes up front."[18] The actor Burt Reynolds offered two arguments in favor of the humor: the traditionally raucous context of Friars roasts that combine tastelessness with affection, and Goldberg's sensitivity to racial offensiveness, saying "She's tuned in to what would be degrading to blacks. Times have changed, and we've gone past that."[19] In an interview on the Black Entertainment Television network, Danson added another argument in defense of the sketch, saying, "We are a racist nation. It's time maybe we started talking."[20] In other words, such humor brings unpleasant realities into public consciousness and, perhaps, provokes some corrective discourse. Even academic experts offered some defense of Danson's comedy. Elise A. Williams, associate professor of English at the University of the District of Columbia and an expert on African American humor, commented that even though jokes based on racial stereotypes are particularly troublesome in a mixed-race setting, "I would rather have a comedian push the truth as far as he or she possibly can . . . tease, or move the stereotype to a kind of caricature as a way of *deflating* it."[21]

Another oblique technique is to place the transgressive remarks or actions in the mouth or body of a character for ironic effect. For instance, in *All in the Family* when Archie Bunker refers to "jungle bunnies," "chinks," or "fags," his obvious ignorance was intended by Lear to serve as a satire of racism. However, audience surveys at the time of the show's initial run indicated that many viewers identified with Archie's bigotry and failed to see the irony that Lear intended, seeing the show not as satire but as outrageous expression of many viewers' socially forbidden racial resentments.[22] Similarly, the South Park children's emotional and mental immaturity and undeveloped impulse control allow them to speak the unspeakable and act out the forbidden behavior. The adults to whom the program is ostensibly targeted are presumed to understand and enjoy the irony and satire, but such a viewer reaction cannot be guaranteed. One viewer's satire may be another viewer's secret truths.

In fact, if the humor is truly outrageous it is not properly considered satire, but it is merely a case of truly bad taste. Freedom to engage in such transgressive humor has even found a legal basis, most famously in the case of Larry Flynt, who was sued by Jerry Falwell for intention to inflict emotional distress when, in 1983, Flynt's *Hustler* magazine ran a parody Campari liquer advertisement depicting the famous televangelist as intoxicated and confessing that his first sexual experience had been with his mother in an outhouse. This crude joke qualifies as transgressive rather than satirical. It was not intended as a criticism of any specific behavior of the Reverend Falwell; there was no evidence or public awareness in 1983 of any alcoholic or sexual misbehavior by Mr. Falwell. Since the advertisement was not based on fact, it had no satirical intent to change such behavior. If indeed there is any misbehavior it is more accurately understood as mischief on the part of the magazine, a besmirching of a respected moral authority, like the eternal practice of students lampooning their teachers or administrators by portraying them engaging in outrageous behavior. In the same spirit, Flynt could just as easily have decided to target Mother Teresa or the Dalai Lama. Such was the understanding behind the decision in the first court's decision on the case before it finally made its way to the Supreme Court as a First Amendment case. It was precisely the general understanding that the portrayal of Falwell was not intended to be taken as truth that robbed the joke of any satirical or libelous power and made the prosecution change its case to one of "emotional distress." The unanimous Supreme Court decision reaffirmed the protection of parody as included in "the recognition of the free flow of ideas." Chief Justice Rehnquist's opinion stated that "freedom to speak one's mind is not only an aspect of individual liberty, but essential to the quest for truth and the vitality of society as a whole.[23] It is worth noting in this context that the Supreme Court decision came at a time when many of the Reverend Falwell's televangelist colleagues were being exposed for financial fraud and sexual misconduct, and such a portrayal of Falwell could have been interpreted as an accusation of guilt by association, yet the Supreme Court ignored such an interpretation.

While precedents for the outrageous comedy of *South Park* and other shows are readily found in the practices of various folk cultures, the more mainstream influence can be traced to the long tradition in European societies of organized periods of anarchy and the formation of official societies that regularly violated, and often criticized, the standards and practices of their culture.

In Enid Welsford's classic study of the social and literary history of the fool in Western culture, she describes the phenomenon of "misrule" that appeared in European culture from Roman days until the Renaissance. She refers us to Lucan's *Saturnalia* and its description of the "Liberties of December" at the time of the winter solstice, when "for a short while masters and slaves changed places, laws lost their force, and a mock-king ruled over a topsy-turvy world."[24]

Welsford even recounts examples of the Roman Catholic clergy engaging in public folly, in which "mighty persons were humbled, sacred things profaned, laws relaxed and ethical ideals reversed, under the leadership of a Patriarch, Pope, or Bishop of Fools."[25] In the cathedral towns of twelfth-century France, the Feast of Fools was an annual occurrence, during which even the Mass was burlesqued. Instead of waving censers of incense, the clergy would swing chains of sausages. Instead of sprinkling the congregation with holy water, some of the sacred ministers would be doused with buckets of water. Sometimes an ass was brought into the church, and "on these occasions solemn Mass was punctuated with brays and howls."[26] The mock-priest would conclude the liturgy by braying three times and the people would respond in similar fashion. According to Welsford such sacrilegious frivolity was often accompanied by satirical verse, topical plays, and burlesque sermons as expressions of the lower clergy's criticism of the church for whom they were the official exponents.

The official church, of course, persistently condemned such behavior, so that eventually secular associations took up the role of seasonal fools. Groups such as the *Societes Joyeuses* flourished from the end of the fifteenth century to the middle of the seventeenth century. Welsford describes them as

> associations of young men who adapted the traditional fool's dress of motley, eared hoods, bells and baubles and organized themselves into kingdoms under the rule of an annually elected monarch known as *Prince des Sots, Mere-Folle*, etc. . . . which enabled them to keep up a running commentary on the affairs of their neighbours and to indulge a taste for satire and social criticism.[27]

Welsford offers considerable documentation of the continuation of such frivolity especially among the more educated classes and members of the royal households. This pattern of annual interruptions of the ordinary routine, with temporary suspension of law and order, remained popular in England, with the traditional feast of the "boy-bishop" among the choirboys of the English cathedrals and in the Christmas Revels of the Lord of Misrule among university students, at the Inns of Court, and in the English and Scottish royal courts of the fifteenth and sixteenth centuries. In France the holiday tradition became a permanent feature among the upper classes. What had been seen as a social safety valve, an "annual interruption of the ordinary routine, marked by a temporary suspension of law and order" developed into a "permanent and legal recognized institution, whose members . . . were pledged to more or less continuous representation of the whole of society as a 'great stage of fools'" and the social satire that had been "the occasional by-product of the Feast of Fools became the whole business of the *Societes Joyeuses*.'"[28] Welsford describes the development as a change in the understanding of the purpose of a fool: "The *Enfants-sans-souci* emphasized the idea of folly as a mask for the wise and armour of the critic. Their 'Misrule' was no temporary relaxation of law and order, but a more subtle and permanent reversal of ordinary judgments. It was the wisdom of *Mere-Folle* to display the folly of the wise."[29]

One is left with the question of whether the transgressive humor of *South Park* and similar television shows is meant to be a mere relaxation of all prevailing norms, like the early Saturnalia and Feasts of Fools, or as a constant satirical commentary on the powerful and famous. Should the foulmouthed children of *South Park* be considered our boy-bishops (fools for a day) or our *Enfants-sans-souci* (year-round fools)? Since such comedies appear on a weekly basis throughout the year, should they be understood as a break in the week's routine or the regular weekly meetings of the global-village idiots? Can the viewing of such programming offer an opportunity for a "more subtle and permanent reversal of ordinary judgments"? Can such programming be truly oppositional and not just a holiday from the prevailing hegemony?

John Fiske's approach to the pleasure and play of television viewing opts for the oppositional interpretation, describing some readings of the television texts as expressions of resistance to the prevailing norms. Fiske comments:

> This sort of pleasure lies in the refusal of the social control inscribed in the "bounds." While there is clearly a pleasure in exerting social power, the popular pleasures of the subordinate are necessarily found in resisting, evading, or offending this power. Popular pleasures are those that empower the subordinate, and they thus offer political resistance, even if only momentarily and even if only in a limited terrain.[30]

The crude language and offensive actions of the characters on *South Park* develop what Fiske goes on to describe as "an alternative semiotic strategy of resistance or evasion." As a model of such cultural resistance, Fiske applies the term "resistance" to the typical behavior of carnival:

> [N]ot in its more overtly political or even revolutionary [sense] of attempting to overthrow the social system. Rather it refers to the refusal to accept the social identity proposed by the dominant ideology and the social control that goes with it. The refusal of ideology, of its meanings and control, may not of itself

challenge the dominant social system but it does resist incorporation and it does maintain and strengthen a sense of social difference that is a prerequisite to any more direct social challenge.[31]

As Fiske describes it, the carnival humor of *South Park* and other transgressive comedies, acted out on the small screens in the very living rooms of the American home, offer a particularly empowering pleasure for the viewers. Television comedy allows them, if only for half an hour at a time, the opportunity to imagine and enjoy alternatives to the prevailing ideology. When the televised revels are ended, the viewers will not simply return to their previous behavior and attitudes. They have enjoyed what they saw and experienced, and the pleasure of the program's challenge to the social system—of family life, gender relations, racial and class identities—is likely to lead to further exploration and further resistance to the status quo. Many a revolution has started with less.

One final observation of Fiske's is particularly relevant to the comedy of *South Park* and other animated comedies of recent years. The self-referential nature of much of the humor creates what Fiske has called an "empowering inversion of viewer relations."[32] Beavis and Butthead spend considerable time watching and commenting on the music videos typical of MTV, the very channel that carries the show. *The Simpsons*, *Family Guy*, and *King of the Hill* provide frequent visual jokes about the art of animation and the existence of their characters as products of animators and not actual persons. One of the most sophisticated examples was *The Simpsons* episode that took the viewers behind the show, as MTV does with *Behind the Music*, and interviewed each of the main characters as if they were actual actors looking for other work. This conspiracy between the creators and viewers to acknowledge the artifice of television primes the viewer to question the legitimacy of any televised versions of "reality." This could prove truly subversive.

If the comedy of *South Park* can be understood as genuinely oppositional, how long can it continue? Will its ability to shock and offend be somehow disempowered and "domesticated," as Todd Gitlin maintains happened to the Norman Lear comedies of the 1970s?[33] Will it spawn enough successful imitators, as television mega-hits tend to do, that eventually the irreverence, irony, and shock will become the familiar comic landscape of television? Since Gitlin ascribes the softening of *All in the Family*'s edges to commercial decisions, perhaps the greatest hope for transgressive comedy lies in the viewer-driven nature of cable television as opposed to the broadcast networks' subservience to their advertisers. Alan Ball, the Academy Award–winning writer of *American Beauty*, has remarked that he chose to write his dark comedy *Six Feet Under* for HBO because "network TV works as a vehicle for marketing. . . . They want as large an audience as possible . . . primed by the fantasy in the shows for the fantasy of the products."[34] Ball and others believe that commercial-free cable television offers an alternative situation, connecting more esoteric programming with a more select but highly appreciative target audience. This is borne out by the popularity of several taboo-breaking cable programs such as *Oz*, *Sex and the City*, *The Osbournes*, *The Sopranos*, *Queer as Folk*, and *Queer Eye for the Straight Guy*, as well as the less sophisticated revelry of *WWF Smackdown* and *The Man Show*. If this is the case, cable television offers viewers who delight in the violation of cultural taboos their best hope of indulging their antisocial appetites. Every week they can join the foolish company of Stan, Kenny, Cartman, and Kyle and enjoy the carnival while it lasts.

Or it might be instructive to return to the imagery of Nathaniel Hawthorne's tale of the culture wars of early New England in his short story, "The Maypole of Merry Mount," which was discussed in Chapter 1. Many viewers—as good, responsible citizens—may prefer that the comedy that comes into their homes on the television screen offer familiar and reassuring images of the ideological consensus even in its exhibition of human folly and playfulness. The broadcast networks are happy to provide such material. Others—dissatisfied with or even resentful of the demands of polite society—are more eager to explore the frontiers of human experience, even in such playful modes as television comedy offers. Nowadays they can find plenty of such opportunities on the cable channels.

The broadcast networks, with their concern for standards and practices and the upbringing of children, are the modern equivalent of the attempts at a well-ordered community of saints in the Massachusetts Bay Colony and other Puritan settlements. The cable stations, meanwhile, are operating out in the forests on the electronic fringe, inviting viewers to dance around the maypole on Merry Mount Channel. This time around, one can hope, the concerns of the upright citizens and the laughter of the frivolous revelers might manage to coexist, even in the same living room.

NOTES

Chapter 1

1. Darrel Y. Hamamoto. *Nervous Laughter: Television Situation Comedy and Liberal Democratic Ideology*. New York; Westport, CT; London: Praeger Publishers, 1989, p. 15.
2. Lynn Spigel. *Make Room for TV: Television and the Family Ideal in Postwar America*, Chicago: University of Chicago Press, 1992, p. 32.
3. Ibid., p. 33.
4. J. Ronald Oakley. *God's Country: America in the Fifties*, New York: Dembner, 1986, pp. 319–320.
5. Ibid., p. 320.
6. Ralph Barton Perry. *Puritanism and Democracy*, New York: Harper and Row, 1944, p. 66.
7. Ibid., p. 78.
8. Ibid., p. 81.
9. See, for instance, John Demos. *A Little Commonwealth: Family Life in the Plymouth Colony*, New York: Oxford University Press, 1970; Perry Miller. *Errand into the Wilderness*, Cambridge, MA: Harvard University Press, 1956; and Edmund S. Morgan. *The Puritan Family*, New York: Harper and Row, 1944.
10. Francis J. Bremer. *The Puritan Experiment*, New York: St. Martin's, 1976, p. 23.
11. Ibid., p. 23.
12. Ibid., pp. 24–25.
13. Perry, *Puritanism and Democracy*, p. 627, 628.
14. Ibid., p. 678.
15. Nathaniel Hawthorne. "The Maypole of Merry Mount," in *Hawthorne's Short Stories*, ed. and intro. Newton Arvin, New York: Alfred A. Knopf, 1969, pp. 23–33.
16. One document recounting the Puritan reaction to Morton's misbehavior can be found in Alden T. Vaughan. *The Puritan Tradition in America*, Columbia: University of South Carolina Press, 1972, pp. 205–87.
17. Perry, *Puritanism and Democracy*, pp. 327, 328, 330.
18. Ibid., p. 329.

19. Kenneth T. Jackson. *Crabgrass Frontier: The Suburbanization of the United States*, New York: Oxford University Press, 1985, pp. 199–203, 178, 208–9.
20. Spigel, *Make Room for TV*, p. 39.
21. Cecelia Tichi. *The Electronic Hearth*, New York: Oxford University Press, 1991, pp. 47- 56.
22. Morgan, *The Puritan Family*, p. 133.
23. Ibid. p. 146.
24. Ibid.
25. Spigel, *Make Room for TV*, pp. 38,39.
26. Ibid., p. 40.
27. Hugh F. Rankin. *The Theater in Colonial America*, Chapel Hill: University of North Carolina Press, 1965, pp. 2–3; and S. E. Wilmer. *Theatre, Society and the Nation: Staging American Identities*, Cambridge: Cambridge University Press, 2002, p. 16.
28. Tichi, *The Electronic Hearth*, p. 50.
29. Ibid., p. 90.
30. Ibid., p. 94.
31. Ibid., p. 103.
32. Ibid., p. 103.
33. Max Weber. *The Protestant Ethic and the Spirit of Capitalism*, intro. and trans. Stephen Kalberg, Chicago and London: Fitzroy Dearborn, 2001.
34. Gerald Mast. *Comedy and the Movies*, 2nd ed., Chicago: University of Chicago Press, 1979, p. 21.

Chapter 2

1. Tim Brooks and Earle Marsh. *The Complete Directory to Prime Time Network and Cable TV Shows 1946–Present*, 7th ed., New York: Ballantine, 1999, p. 665.
2. *Newsweek*, 16 May 1949, p. 6.
3. Steven D. Stark. *Glued to the Set*, New York: Free Press, 1997, p. 10.
4. Philip Hamburger, *The New Yorker*, 29 October, 1949, p. 91.
5. Arthur Frank Wertheim. "The Rise and Fall of Milton Berle," in *American History/American Television*, ed. John E. O'Connor, New York: Frederick Unger, 1983, p. 59.
6. Ibid., p. 70.
7. Gerard Jones. *Honey, I'm Home! Sitcoms: Selling the American Dream*, New York: St. Martin's, 1992, pp. 32, 33.
8. Wertheim, "The Rise and Fall of Milton Berle," p. 63.
9. Ibid., p. 62.
10. Stark, *Glued to the Set*, p. 8.
11. David Marc. *Comic Visions: Television Comedy and American Culture*, 2nd ed., Malden, MA: Blackwell, 1997, pp. 32, 36.
12. Lawrence Van Gelder. "Milton Berle, TV's First Star as 'Uncle Miltie,' Dies at 93," *The New York Times*, 28 March 2002, p. A29.
13. Wertheim, "The Rise and Fall of Milton Berle," pp. 67,68.
14. Ibid., p. 71.

15. Ibid., p. 76.
16. Marc, *Comic Visions*, p. 58.
17. See Stark, *Glued to the Set*, p. 13, for a listing of various reasons for the decline of the variety show, especially Berle's.
18. Ted Sennett. *Your Show of Shows*, New York: Macmillan, 1977, p. 12.
19. Ibid., p. 12.
20. Ibid., p. 21.
21. Mark Williams. "Caesar, Sid," in *Encyclopedia of Television*, ed. Horace Newcomb, Cary O'Dell, and Noelle Watson, Chicago: Fitzroy Dearborn, 1997, p. 273.
22. Sennett, *Your Show of Shows*, p. 37.
23. *TV Guide*, April 1950, quoted in Sennett, *Your Show of Shows*, p. 38.
24. Sennett, *Your Show of Shows*, p. 41.
25. Quoted in Sennett, *Your Show of Shows*, pp. 171–72.
26. Max Wilk. *The Golden Age of Television*, New York: Delacorte, 1976, p. 173.
27. Quoted in Sennett, *Your Show of Shows*, p. 172.
28. Wilk, *The Golden Age of Television*, p. 174.
29. Virginia Wright Wexman. "Returning from the Moon: Jackie Gleason, the Carnivalesque, and Television Comedy," *Journal of Film and Video* 42 (Winter 1990): p. 20.
30. Wexman, "Returning from the Moon," p. 23.
31. Brooks and Marsh, *The Complete Directory*, pp. 503–4.
32. See Wexman, "Returning from the Moon," pp. 20–32, for her observations about the Rabelasian comedy and the comedy of the grotesque in Gleason's performances.

Chapter 3

1. Maurice Zolotow. *No People Like Show People*, New York: Random House, 1951, p. 180.
2. Ibid., p. 186.
3. Ibid., pp. 186, 187.
4. Ibid., p. 186.
5. Ibid., p. 155.
6. Tinky Weisblat. "Benny, Jack," in *Encyclopedia of Television*, ed. Horace Newcomb, Cary O'Dell, and Noelle Watson, Chicago: Fitzroy Dearborn, 1997, p. 158.
7. Tim Brooks and Earle Marsh. *The Complete Directory to Prime Time Network and Cable TV Shows 1946–Present*, 7th ed., New York: Ballantine, 1999, p. 502.
8. Ibid., p. 501.
9. Weisblat, "Benny, Jack," p. 157.
10. Zolotow, *No People Like Show People*, pp. 160, 171.
11. David Smith. "Jack Benny Checklist," unpublished manuscript, The New York Public Library for the Performing Arts, pp. 11–17.
12. Robert Lemieux. "Skelton, Red," in *Encyclopedia of Television*, ed. Horace Newcomb, Cary O'Dell, and Noelle Watson, Chicago: Fitzroy Dearborn, 1997, p. 1506.
13. Brooks and Marsh, *The Complete Directory*, p. 847,

14. Arthur Marx. *Red Skelton*, New York: E. P. Dutton, 1979, pp. 169–70.
15. Ibid., p. 170.
16. Ibid., p. 211.
17. Ibid., p. 308.
18. Ibid., p. 305
19. Arthur J. Singer. *Arthur Godfrey: The Adventures of an American Broadcaster*, Jefferson, NC, and London: McFarland, 2000, p. 1.
20. Douglas Gomery. "Arthur Godfrey Shows," in *Encyclopedia of Television*, ed. Horace Newcomb, Cary O'Dell, and Noelle Watson, Chicago: Fitzroy Dearborn, 1997, p. 92.
21. Steve Allen. *The Funny Men*, New York: Simon and Schuster, 1956, pp. 188–89.
22. Douglas Gomery. "Godfrey, Arthur," in *Encyclopedia of Television*, ed. Horace Newcomb, Cary O'Dell, and Noelle Watson, Chicago: Fitzroy Dearborn, 1997, p. 697.
23. Singer, *Arthur Godfrey*, pp. 116–17.
24. Ibid., p. 77.
25. Ibid., p. 117.
26. Ibid., p. 89.
27. Allen, *The Funny Men*, pp. 192–94.
28. David Marc. *Demographic Vistas: Television in American Culture*, rev. ed., Philadelphia: University of Pennsylvania Press, 1996, pp. 99–100.
29. Ibid., p. 102.
30. Singer, *Arthur Godfrey*, pp. 138–39.
31. Ibid., p. 157.
32. Ibid., p. 156.
33. Donald Bogle. *Primetime Blues*, New York: Farrar, Straus and Giroux, 2001, p. 178.
34. Kathryn D. D'Allesandro. "The Carol Burnett Show," in *Encyclopedia of Television*, ed. Horace Newcomb, Cary O'Dell, and Noelle Watson, Chicago: Fitzroy Dearborn, 1997, p. 315.

Chapter 4

1. David Grote. *The End of Comedy: The Sit-Com and the Comedic Tradition*, Hamden, CT: Archon, 1983, p. 158.
2. Ibid., p. 158.
3. Gerard Jones. *Honey I'm Home! Sitcoms: Selling the American Dream*, New York: St. Martin's, 1992, p. 84.
4. David Marc. *Comic Visions: Television Comedy and American Culture*, 2nd ed., Malden, MA: Blackwell, 1997, p. 18.
5. Jones, *Honey I'm Home! Sitcoms*, p. 69.
6. Ibid., p. 69.
7. Ibid., p. 70.
8. Ibid., p. 68.
9. Ibid., p. 71.
10. Ibid., p. 68.

11. Betty Friedan, *The Feminine Mystique* (Twentieth Anniversary Edition). New York and London: W. W. Norton and Company, 1982. p. 15.
12. Ibid., p. 378.
13. Northrop Frye. *The Anatomy of Criticism*, New York: Atheneum, 1966, p. 163.
14. Grote, *The End of Comedy*, pp. 66, 67.
15. Ibid., p. 68.
16. Steven D. Stark. *Glued to the Set*, New York: Free Press, 1997, p. 28.
17. Grote, *The End of Comedy*, pp. 68–69.
18. Jones, *Honey I'm Home! Sitcoms*, pp. 67–68.
19. Ibid., p. 71.
20. Ibid., p. 108.
21. Ibid., pp. 108, 109.
22. Virginia Wright Wexman. "Returning from the Moon: Jackie Gleason, the Carnivalesque, and Television Comedy," *Journal of Film and Video* 42 (Winter 1990): p. 26.
23. Ibid., p. 25.
24. Jones, *Honey I'm Home! Sitcoms*, p. 110.
25. Tim Brooks and Earle Marsh. *The Complete Directory to Prime Time Network and Cable TV Shows 1946–Present*, 7th ed., New York: Ballantine, 1999, p. 504.
26. Grote, *The End of Comedy*, pp. 92, 93.
27. Ibid., pp. 93–94.
28. Jones, *Honey I'm Home! Sitcoms*, p. 113.
29. Ibid., p. 73.
30. Wexman, "Returning from the Moon," p. 22.
31. Jones, *Honey I'm Home! Sitcoms*, p. 113.
32. Stark, *Glued to the Set*, p. 29.
33. Ibid., p. 29.
34. Alan Wolfe, quoted in Elizabeth Bumiller. "Why America Has Gay Marriage Jitters," *The New York Times*, 10 August 2003, Section 4, p. 1.

Chapter 5

1. Lynn Spigel. *Make Room for TV: Television and the Family Ideal in Postwar America*, Chicago: University of Chicago Press, 1992, p. 2.
2. David Halberstam. *The Fifties*, New York: Villard, 1993, p. 58.
3. Mary Beth Haralovich. "Sitcoms and Suburbs: Positioning the 1950s Homemaker," *Quarterly Review of Film and Video* 11 (Spring 1989), p. 61.
4. Nina C. Leibman. *Living Room Lectures: The Fifties Family in Film and Television*, Austin: University of Texas Press, 1995.
5. Spigel, *Make Room for TV*, p. 179.
6. Halberstam, *The Fifties*, p. 509.
7. Ibid., p. 516.
8. Ibid., p. 515.
9. Gerard Jones. *Honey, I'm Home! Sitcoms: Selling the American Dream*, New York: St. Martin's, 1992, pp. 88, 89.
10. Ibid., p. 90.

11. Ibid., p. 90.
12. Ibid., p. 94.
13. Diana Meehan. *Ladies of the Evening: Women Characters in Prime Time*, Metuchen, NJ: Scarecrow Press, 1983, pp. 34–39, 153–54.
14. Halberstam, *The Fifties*, p. 510.
15. Rick Mitz. *The Great TV Sitcom Book*, New York: Perigee, 1988, p. 95.
16. Dave Marsh. *Elvis*, New York: Thunder's Mouth, 1992, p. 186.
17. Joel Selvin. *Ricky Nelson: Idol for a Generation*, Chicago: Contemporary, 1990, p. 67.
18. Hal Himmelstein. *Television Myths and the American Mind*, 2nd ed. Westport, CT: Praeger, 1994, p. 125.
19. See *Consumer Reports 23* (July 1958): pp. 384–86, for a listing of some of the features of adolescents as a distinct consumer group. See also Reuell Denny's report on 1950s teenagers in "American Youth Today: A Bigger Cast, A Wider Screen," in *Youth: Change and Challenge*, ed. Erick Erikson, New York: Basic, 1963, pp. 131–51, and J. S. Coleman. *The Adolescent Society*, New York: Free Press, 1961.
20. *TV Guide*, 29 July 1995, p. 11, reported that television viewers between the ages of twelve and seventeen reported the lowest number of viewing hours per week (22.7) in contrast with their mothers, who averaged 29.9 hours a week, and the top group, women over fifty-five, who averaged twice as much viewing, 45.2 hours a week. A study of a "typical teenager" in suburban Chicago in the early 1980s reported that the young man, Rob Miranda, spent 8 percent of his time watching television, less than two hours a day, compared to the 35 percent of his time he spent socializing. See Mihaly Csikszentmilhalyi and Reed Larson. *Being Adolescent*, New York: Basic, 1984, p. 38.
21. Halberstam, *The Fifties*, pp. 515–16.

Chapter 6

1. Steven D. Stark. *Glued to the Set*, New York: Free Press, 1997. p. 115.
2. Ibid., p. 108.
3. Tim Brooks and Earle Marsh. *The Complete Directory to Prime Time Network and Cable TV Shows 1946–Present*, 7th ed., New York: Ballantine, 1999, p. 477.
4. Gerard Jones. *Honey I'm Home! Sitcoms: Selling the American Dream*, New York: St. Martin's Press, 1992, p. 179.
5. Stark, *Glued to the Set*, p. 115.
6. Ibid., p. 118.
7. Brooks and Marsh, *The Complete Directory*, p. 1015.
8. Marc, *Comic Visions*, p. 122.
9. Hal Himmelstein. *Television Myth and the American Mind*, 2nd ed., Westport, CT: Praeger Publishers, 1994.
10. "Smothers Out: A Wise Decision," editorial, *TV Guide*. 19 April, 1969, p. A1.
11. Ibid., p. 191.

Chapter 7

1. Richard P. Adler, ed. *All in the Family: A Critical Appraisal*. New York: Praeger Publishers, 1979, p. xxi; Gerard Jones. *Honey, I'mHome*. New York: St. Martin's Press, 1992, p. 205; Steven D. Stark. *Glued to the Set*. New York: The Free Press, 1997, p. 164, p. 164.
2. Jones, *Ibid.*
3. Adler, *op. cit*, pp. xv–xvi.
4. Jack Gould. "Can Bigotry Be Laughed Away? It's Worth a Try," *The New York Times*, 21. January 1971, reprinted in *All in the Family: A Critical Appraisal*, ed. Adler, p. 73.
5. Ibid., p. 74.
6. Stephanie Harrington. "The Message Sounds Like 'Hate Thy Neighbor,'" *The New York Times*, 24 January 1971, reprinted in *All in the Family: A Critical Appraisal*, ed. Adler, p. 76, 77.
7. *Variety*, 13 January 1971, reprinted in *All in the Family: A Critical Appraisal*, ed. Adler, pp. 69.
8. Alan Bunce. "'All in the Family': TV Social Departure," *Christian Science Monitor*, 18 January 1971, reprinted in *All in the Family: A Critical Appraisal*, ed. Adler, pp. 82.
9. Whitney M. Young, Jr. "Irresponsible Television Production Aids Racism," *Los Angeles Sentinel*, 4 February 1971, reprinted in *All in the Family: A Critical Appraisal*, ed. Adler, pp. 85–87.
10. Pamela Haynes. "New TV Comedy Takes Hard, Realistic Poke at Bigotry," *Los Angeles Sentinel*, 28 January 1971, reprinted in *All in the Family: A Critical Appraisal*, ed. Adler, pp. 84–85.
11. Janet Staiger. *Blockbuster TV: Must-See Sitcoms in the Network Era*, New York and London: New York University Press, 2000, p. 93.
12. See Adler, *op. cit*, p. xxvi for a more detailed report on the ratings.
13. Adler, ed., *All in the Family*, p. xxvi.
14. Gould, "Can Bigotry Be Laughed Away?," p. 15.
15. Ibid.
16. Laura Z. Hobson. "As I Listened to Archie Say 'Hebe'. . . ," *The New York Times*, 12 September 1971, reprinted in *All in the Family: A Critical Appraisal*, ed. Adler, pp. 97–106.
17. Adler, ed., *Ibid.*, p. xxviii.
18. Marc, *Comic Visions*, p. 148.
19. Ibid., p. 149.
20. Adler, ed., *All in the Family*, pp. xxxiv, xxxv.
21. Marc, *Comic Visions*, p. 151.
22. Ibid., p. 150.
23. Adler, ed., *All in the Family*, pp. xxxiv–xxxv.
24. Tim Brooks and Earle Marsh. *The Complete Directory of Prime Time Network and Cable TV Shows 1946–Present*, 7th ed., New York: Ballantine, 1999, p. 30.
25. Quoted in Adler, ed., *All in the Family*, pp. xix–xx.
26. Ibid., p. xxxiv.
27. Ibid., p. xxxix.

28. Timothy P. Meyer. "The Impact of 'All in the Family' on Children," *Journal of Broadcasting* 20 (Winter 1976), reprinted in *All in the Family: A Critical Appraisal,* ed. Adler, pp. 159–69.

29. Hobson, "As I Listened to Archie Say 'Hebe,'" p. 27.

30. Adler, ed. *All in the Family,* p. xxxiv.

Chapter 8

1. David Marc. *Comic Visions: Television Comedy and American Culture,* 2nd ed., Malden, MA: Blackwell, 1997, pp. 71–73; and Gerard Jones. *Honey I'm Home! Sitcoms: Selling the American Dream,* New York: St. Martin's, 1992, pp. 142–44.

2. James Goodman. *US Magazine,* 18 September 1979, p. 58.

3. John O'Connor. "'Taxi' Rolls into Superior Sit-Com," *The New York Times,* 19 June 1979, p. C21.

4. Frank Lovece with Jules Franco. *Taxi: The Official Fan's Guide,* New York: Citadel, 1996, pp. 22–23.

5. Bob Zmuda with Matthew Scott Hansen. *Andy Kaufman Revealed,* New York: Little, Brown, 1999, pp. 99, 106.

6. See the description of the mimetic central character in Hal Himmelstein. *Television Myths and the American Mind,* 2nd ed., Westport, CT: Praeger, 1994, p. 117.

7. Robert S. Alley and Irby B. Brown. *Murphy Brown: The Anatomy of a Sitcom,* New York: Delta, 1990, p. 19.

8. Ibid., p. 20.

9. Ibid., p. 20.

10. Ibid., p. 21.

11. Tim Brooks and Earle Marsh. *The Complete Directory of Prime Time Network and Cable TV Shows 1946–Present,* 7th ed., New York: Ballantine, 1999, p. 694.

12. Alley and Brown, *Murphy Brown,* p. 179.

Chapter 9

1. *TV Guide,* 29 July 1995, p. 17

2. Robert Metz. *The Tonight Show,* New York: Playboy, 1980, pp. 74–75, 80.

3. Ibid., p. 75.

4. Tim Brooks and Earle Marsh. *The Complete Directory to Prime Time Network and Cable TV Shows 1946–Present,* 7th ed., New York: Ballantine, 1999, p. 1037.

5. Metz, *The Tonight Show,* p. 95.

6. Ibid., p. 101.

7. Ibid., p. 127.

8. Ibid., p. 161.

9. Ibid., p. 270.

10. Ibid., pp. 217, 219.

11. Jill Gerston. "Here's Everybody! After Carson, A Host of Late-Night Wannabees," *The New York Times,* 16 August 1992., Section 2, p. 1.

12. Bernard M. Timberg. *Television Talk: A History of the TV Talk Show*, Austin: University of Texas Press, 2002, p. 151.
13. Brooks and Marsh, *Complete Directory to Prime Time*, p. 562.
14. Bernard M. Timberg. "Talk Shows," in *Encyclopedia of Television*, ed. Horace Newcomb, Cary O'Dell, and Noelle Watson, Chicago: Fitzroy Dearborn, 1997, p. 1621.
15. Tom Shales and James Andrew Miller. *Live from New York: An Uncensored History of* Saturday Night Live, New York: Little, Brown, 2002, pp. 19–20.
16. Ibid., p. 9.
17. Ibid., p. 6.
18. Michael Cader. *Saturday Night Live: The First Twenty Years*, New York: Houghton Mifflin, 1994, pp. 124–27.
19. Ibid., pp. 52–69.
20. Ibid., p. 134.

Chapter 10

1. Donald Bogle. *Primetime Blues*, New York: Farrar, Straus and Giroux, 2001, p. 23.
2. Mel Watkins. *On the Real Side*, New York: Simon and Schuster, 1994, pp. 304–5.
3. Bogle, *Primetime Blues*, pp. 34–35.
4. Watkins, *On the Real Side*, pp. 305, 306.
5. Ibid., p. 277.
6. Ibid.
7. Ibid., p. 278.
8. Ibid., p. 276.
9. Ibid., p. 279.
10. Gerard Jones. *Honey I'm Home! Sitcoms: Selling the American Dream*, New York: St. Martin's Press, 1992, p. 51.
11. Bogle, *Primetime Blues*, p. 33.
12. Thomas Cripps. "*Amos 'n' Andy* and the Debate over American Racial Integration," in *American History/American Television*, ed. John E. O'Connor, New York: Frederick Unger, 1983, pp. 43, 44.
13. J. Fred MacDonald. *Blacks and White TV*, 2nd ed., Chicago: Nelson-Hall, 1992, pp. 30–34.
14. Ibid., p. 35.
15. Jones, *Honey, I'm Home! Sitcoms*, p. 54.
16. Ibid., p. 57.
17. Ibid., p. 55.
18. Watkins, *On the Real Side*, pp. 313, 314.
19. Jones, *Honey, I'm Home! Sitcoms*, p. 59.
20. Bogle, *Primetime Blues*, p. 6.
21. Ibid., p. 6.
22. Ibid., p. 5.
23. Ibid., p. 286.
24. Ibid., p. 292.
25. Jones, *Honey, I'm Home! Sitcoms*, p. 260.

26. Bogle, *Primetime Blues*, p. 301.
27. Ibid., pp. 301–2.
28. Ibid., p. 301.
29. Ibid., p. 297.
30. Jones, *Honey, I'm Home! Sitcoms*, pp. 260–61.
31. Robin R. Means Coleman. *African American Viewers and the Black Situation Comedy*, New York and London: Garland, 1998, p. 111.
32. Ibid., pp. 113–14.
33. Ibid., p. 131.
34. Ibid., p. 130.
35. Ibid., p. 125.
36. MacDonald, *Blacks and White TV*, p. 268.
37. James Sterngold. "A Racial Divide Widens on Network TV," *The New York Times*, 29. December 1998, A1.
38. "Blacks Prefer TV Fare with Black Casts, but Tastes of Blacks and Whites Are Converging, Study Says," *The New York Times* 21 April 2003, p. C12.
39. Walter Kerr. *The Silent Clowns*, New York: Knopf, 1975, p. 62.
40. Bogle, *Primetime Blues*, p. 33.
41. "Blacks Prefer TV Fare with Black Casts," p. C12.
42. Bogle, *Primetime Blues*, p. 7.

Chapter 11

1. Hal Himmelstein. *Television Myth and the American Mind*, 2nd ed., Westport, CT: Praeger, 1994, p. 123.
2. Ibid.
3. Ibid.
4. David Marc. *Comic Visions: Television Comedy and American Culture*, 2nd ed., Malden, MA: Blackwell, 1997, p. 43.
5. Gerard Jones. *Honey, I'm Home! Sitcoms: Selling the American Dream*, New York: St. Martin's, 1992, p. 42.
6. Marc, *Comic Visions*, p. 42.
7. Himmelstein, *Television Myths*, p. 125.
8. Marc, *Comic Visions*, p. 42.
9. Steven D. Stark. *Glued to the Set*, New York: Free Press, 1997, p. 171.
10. Marc, *Comic Visions*, p. 190.
11. F. Scott Fitzgerald. *The Great Gatsby*, New York: Scribner, 1925, p. 75.
12. Tom Carson. "Degrees of Separation," *The Village Voice*, 2 June 1998, p. 169.
13. Christopher Paul Denis and Michael Denis. *Favorite Families of TV*, New York: Citadel, 1992, pp. 50–52.
14. Stark, *Glued to the Set*, p. 284.
15. Ibid., pp. 286, 287.

Chapter 12

1. John Fiske. *Television Culture*, London and New York: Routlege, 1987, p. 239.
2. Ibid., p. 234.
3. Steven D. Stark. *Glued to the Set*, New York: Free Press, 1997, pp. 264, 265.
4. Robert Stam. *Subversive Pleasures: Bakhtin, Cultural Criticism, and Film*, Baltimore, MD: Johns Hopkins University Press, 1989, p. 86.
5. Ibid., p. 92.
6. Ibid., p. 111.
7. Ibid., p. 91.
8. Ibid., pp. 91, 95, 96.
9. Maureen Furniss. *Art in Motion: Animation Aesthetics*, Sydney, Australia: John Libbey, 1998, p. 6.
10. Ibid., p. 30.
11. Maurice Charney. *Comedy High and Low*, New York: Oxford University Press, 1978, pp. 145–46.

Chapter 13

1. Gerard Jones. *Honey, I'm Home! Sitcoms: Selling the American Dream*, New York: St. Martin's, 1992, p. 113.
2. Neil Vidmar and Milton Rokeach. "Archie Bunker's Bigotry: A Study in Selective Perception and Exposure," in *All in the Family: A Critical Appraisal*, ed. Richard P. Adler, New York: Praeger, 1979, pp. 123–138.
3. The development of the broadcast networks' mass audience mentality is well described in J. Fred MacDonald. *One Nation under Television: The Rise and Decline of Network TV*, Chicago: Nelson-Hall, 1994, pp. 118–24.
4. Rick Marin. "The Rude Tube," *Newsweek*, 23 March 1998, pp. 56–57.
5. David Wilde, "South Park's Evil Geniuses and the Triumph of No-Brow Culture," *Rolling Stone* 19 February 1998, p. 34.
6. Eric Mink. "'South Park' Comes Up a Hallo-winner," *New York Daily News*, 29 October 1997, p. 89.
7. Bill Cartier and Lawrie Mifflin. "Mainstream TV Bets on 'Gross-Out' Humor," *The New York Times*, 19 July 1999, p. C10.
8. Richard Huff. "'South Park' Fuels Truth-in-Labeling Debate," *New York Daily News*, 5 March 1998, p. 103.
9. Ibid., p. 103.
10. Michael Starr. "'South Park' Net Cries 'Foul,'" *The New York Post*, 20 March 1998, p. 20.
11. Sigmund Freud. *Jokes and Their Relation to the Unconscious*, New York and London: W. W. Norton, 1960, p. 97.
12. Ibid., p. 101.
13. Ibid., p. 101.
14. Ibid., pp. 97–98.
15. See Philip Core. *Camp: The Lie That Tells the Truth*, New York: Delilah, 1984, especially the foreword by George Melly for his description of "camp" as expressive

of "a significant minority whose unacceptable characteristics . . . render them vulnerable to the world's brutal laughter" (p. 9).

16. Jeanine Williams. "Whoopi's Shock Roast/Danson in Blackface Leaves Many Fuming." *USA Today*, 11 October 1993, D2.
17. Ibid., p. D2.
18. Ibid., p. D2.
19. Karen Thomas. "Friars Take the Heat for Their Tradition of Tasteless Humor," *USA Today*, 12 October 1993, D3.
20. "Danson 'Proud' of Racist Act at Roast," *The Arizona Republic*, 25 October 1993, p. B8.
21. David Mills. "What's So Funny?" *The Washington Post*, 26 October 1993, p. 5 (emphasis mine).
22. John C. Brigham and Linda W. Giesbrecht. "*All in the Family:* Racial Attitudes," in *All in the Family: A Critical Appraisal*, ed. Richard P. Adler, New York: Praeger, 1979, pp. 139–46.
23. Supreme Court of the United States, No.86–1278, *Hustler Magazine, Inc. et al. v. Jerry Falwell*, 485 U.S. 46. Argued 2 December 1987. Decided 24 February 1988.
24. Enid Welsford. *The Fool: His Social and Literary History*, Gloucester, MA: Peter Smith, 1966, p. 201.
25. Ibid., p. 201.
26. Ibid., p. 202.
27. Ibid., p. 205.
28. Ibid., p. 205.
29. Ibid., p. 218.
30. John Fiske. *Television Culture*, London and New York: Routledge, 1987, p. 230.
31. Ibid., p. 241.
32. Ibid., p. 242.
33. Todd Gitlin. "Prime-Time Ideology: The Hegemonic Process in Television Entertainment," in *Television: The Critical View*, 5th ed., ed. Horace Newcomb, New York: Oxford University Press, 1994, pp. 516–36.
34. Tad Friend. "The Next Big Bet," *The New Yorker*, 14 May 2001, p. 83.

BIBLIOGRAPHY

Books

Adler, Richard P., ed. *All in the Family: A Critical Appraisal*, New York: Praeger, 1979.

Allen, Steve. *The Funny Men*, New York: Simon and Schuster, 1956.

Alley, Robert S., and Irby B. Brown. *Murphy Brown: The Anatomy of a Sitcom*, New York: Delta, 1990.

Bogle, Donald. *Primetime Blues*, New York: Farrar, Straus and Giroux, 2001.

Bremer, Francis J. *The Puritan Experiment*, New York: St. Martin's, 1976.

Brigham, John C., and Linda W. Giesbrecht. *"All in the Family:* Racial Attitudes," in *All in the Family: A Critical Appraisal*, ed. Richard P. Adler, pp. 139–146. New York: Praeger, 1979.

Brooks, Tim, and Earle Marsh. *The Complete Directory to Prime Time Network and Cable TV Shows 1946–Present*, 7th ed., New York: Ballantine, 1999.

Cader, Michael. *Saturday Night Live: The First Twenty Years*, New York: Houghton Mifflin, 1994.

Charney, Maurice. *Comedy High and Low*, New York: Oxford University Press, 1978.

Coleman, J. S. *The Adolescent Society*, New York: Free Press, 1961.

Core, Philip. *Camp: The Lie That Tells the Truth*, New York: Delilah, 1984.

Cripps, Thomas. *"Amos 'n' Andy* and the Debate over American Racial Integration," in *American History/American Television*, ed. John E. O'Connor, pp. 35–54. New York: Frederick Unger, 1983.

Csikszentmilhalyi, Mihaly, and Reed Larson. *Being Adolescent*, New York: Basic, 1984.

D'Allesandro, Kathryn D. "The Carol Burnett Show," in *Encyclopedia of Television*, ed. Horace Newcomb,, Cary O'Dell, and Noelle Watson, pp. 314–316. Chicago: Fitzroy Dearborn, 1997.

Demos, John. *A Little Commonwealth: Family Life in the Plymouth Colony*, New York: Oxford University Press, 1970.

Denis, Christopher Paul, and Michael Denis. *Favorite Families of TV*, New York: Citadel, 1992.

Denny, Reuell. "American Youth Today: A Bigger Cast, A Wider Screen," in *Youth: Change and Challenge*, ed. Erik H. Erikson, pp. 131–51, New York: Doubleday, 1963.

Erikson, Erik H., ed. *Youth: Change and Challenge*, New York: Doubleday, 1963.

Fiske, John. *Television Culture*, London and New York: Routledge, 1987.

Fitzgerald, F. Scott. *The Great Gatsby*, New York, Scribner, 1925.

Freud, Sigmund. *Jokes and Their Relation to the Unconscious*, New York and London: W. W. Norton, 1960.

Frye, Northrop. *The Anatomy of Criticism*, New York: Atheneum: 1966.

Furniss, Maureen. *Art in Motion: Animation Aesthetics*, Sydney: John Libbey, 1998.

Gitlin, Todd. "Prime-Time Ideology: The Hegemonic Process in Television Entertainment," in *Television: The Critical View*, 5th ed., ed. Horace Newcomb, pp. 516–36, New York: Oxford University Press, 1994.

Gomery, Douglas. "Arthur Godfrey Shows," in *Encyclopedia of Television*, ed. Horace Newcomb, Cary O'Dell, and Noelle Watson, pp. 91–93. Chicago: Fitzroy Dearborn, 1997.

Gomery, Douglas. "Godfrey, Arthur," in *Encyclopedia of Television*, ed. Horace Newcomb, Cary O'Dell, and Noelle Watson, pp. 696–697. Chicago: Fitzroy Dearborn, 1997.

Grote, David. *The End of Comedy: The Sit-Com and the Comedic Tradition*, Hamden, CT: Archon, 1983.

Halberstam, David. *The Fifties*, New York: Villard, 1993.

Hamamoto, Darrell Y. *Nervous Laughter: Television Situation Comedy and Liberal Democratic Ideology*. New York; Westport, Connecticut; London: Praeger Publishers, 1989.

Hawthorne, Nathaniel. *Hawthorne's Short Stories*, ed. and intro. Newton Arvin, New York: Alfred A. Knopf, 1969.

Himmelstein, Hal. *Television Myths and the American Mind*, 2nd ed., Westport, CT: Praeger, 1994.

Jackson, Kenneth T. *Crabgrass Frontier: The Suburbanization of the United States*, New York: Oxford University Press, 1985.

Jones, Gerard. *Honey I'm Home! Sitcoms: Selling the American Dream*, New York: St. Martin's, 1992.

Kerr, Walter. *The Silent Clowns*, New York: Knopf, 1975.

Leibman, Nina C. *Living Room Lectures: The Fifties Family in Film and Television*, Austin: University of Texas Press, 1995.

Lemieux, Robert. "Skelton, Red," in *Encyclopedia of Television*, ed. Horace Newcomb, Cary O'Dell, and Noelle Watson, pp. 1505–1507. Chicago: Fitzroy Dearborn, 1997.

Lovece, Frank, with Jules Franco. *Taxi: The Official Fan's Guide*, New York: Citadel, 1996.

MacDonald, J. Fred. *One Nation under Television: The Rise and Decline of Network TV*, Chicago: Nelson-Hall, 1994.

MacDonald, J. Fred. *Blacks and White TV*, 2nd ed., Chicago: Nelson-Hall, 1992.

Marc, David. *Demographic Vistas, Television in American Culture*, rev. ed., Philadelphia: University of Pennsylvania Press, 1996.

Marc, David. *Comic Visions: Television Comedy and American Culture*, 2nd ed., Malden, MA: Blackwell, 1997.

Marsh, Dave. *Elvis*, New York: Thunder's Mouth Press, 1996.

Marx, Arthur. *Red Skelton*, New York: E. P. Dutton, 1979.

Mast, Gerald. *Comedy and the Movies*, 2nd ed., Chicago: University of Chicago Press, 1979.

Means Coleman, Robin R. *African American Viewers and the Black Situation Comedy*, New York and London: Garland, 1998.

Meehan, Diana. *Ladies of the Evening: Women Characters in Prime Time*, Metuchen, NJ: Scarecrow, 1983.

Metz, Robert. *The Tonight Show*, New York: Playboy, 1980.

Miller, Perry. *Errand into the Wilderness*, Cambridge, MA: Harvard University Press, 1956.

Mitz, Rick. *The Great TV Sitcom Book*, New York: Perigee, 1988.

Morgan, Edmund S. *The Puritan Family*, New York: Harper and Row, 1944.

Newcomb, Horace, ed. *Television: The Critical View*, 5th ed., New York: Oxford University Press, 1994.

Newcomb, Horace, Cary O'Dell, and Noelle Watson, eds. *Encyclopedia of Television*, Chicago: Fitzroy Dearborn, 1997.

Oakley, J. Ronald. *God's Country: America in the Fifties*, New York: Dembner, 1986.

O'Connor, John E., ed. *American History/American Television*. New York: Frederick Unger, 1983.

Perry, Ralph Barton. *Puritanism and Democracy*, New York: Harper and Row, 1944.

Rankin, Hugh F. *The Theater in Colonial America*, Chapel Hill: University of North Carolina Press, 1965.

Selvin, Joel. *Rick Nelson: Idol for a Generation*, Chicago: Contemporary, 1990.

Sennett, Ted. *Your Show of Shows*, New York: Macmillan, 1977.

Shales, Tom, and James Andrew Miller. *Live from New York: An Uncensored History of Saturday Night Live*, New York: Little, Brown, 2002.

Singer, Arthur J. *Arthur Godfrey: The Adventures of an American Broadcaster*, Jefferson, NC, and London: McFarland, 2000.

Spigel, Lynn. *Make Room for TV: Television and the Family Ideal in Postwar America*, Chicago: University of Chicago Press, 1992.

Staiger, Janet. *Blockbuster TV: Must-See Sitcoms in the Network Era*, New York and London: New York University Press, 2000.

Stam, Robert. *Subversive Pleasures: Bakhtin, Cultural Criticism, and Film*, Baltimore, MD: Johns Hopkins University Press, 1989.

Stark, Steven D. *Glued to the Set*, New York: Free Press, 1997.

Tichi, Cecelia. *The Electronic Hearth*, New York: Oxford University Press, 1991.

Timberg, Bernard M. *Television Talk: A History of the TV Talk Show*, Austin: University of Texas Press, 2002.

Vaughan, Alden T. *The Puritan Tradition in America*, Columbia: University of South Carolina Press, 1972.

Vidmar, Neil, and Milton Rokeach. "Archie Bunker's Bigotry: A Study in Selective Perception and Exposure," in *All in the Family: A Critical Appraisal*, ed. Richard P. Adler, pp. 13–138, New York: Praeger, 1979.

Watkins, Mel. *On the Real Side*, New York: Simon and Schuster, 1994.

Weber, Max. *The Protestant Ethic and the Spirit of Capitalism*, intro. and trans. Stephen Kalberg, Chicago and London: Fitzroy Dearborn, 2001.

Weisblat, Tinky. "Benny, Jack," in *Encyclopedia of Television*, ed. Horace Newcomb, Cary O'Dell, and Noelle Watson, pp. 157–158. Chicago: Fitzroy Dearborn, 1997.

Welsford, Enid. *The Fool: His Social and Literary History*, Gloucester, MA: Peter Smith, 1966.

Wertheim, Arthur Frank. "The Rise and Fall of Milton Berle," in *American History/ American Television*, ed. John E. O'Connor, pp. 55–78. New York: Frederick Unger, 1983.

Wilk, Max. *The Golden Age of Television*, New York: Delacorte, 1976.

Williams, Mark. "Caesar, Sid," in *Encyclopedia of Television*, ed. Horace Newcomb, Cary O'Dell, and Noelle Watson, pp. 272–274. Chicago: Fitzroy Dearborn Publishers, 1997.

Wilmer, S. E. *Theatre, Society and the Nation: Staging American Identities*, Cambridge: Cambridge University Press, 2002.

Zmuda, Bob, with Matthew Scott Hansen. *Andy Kaufman Revealed*, New York: Little, Brown, 1999.

Zolotow, Maurice. *No People Like Show People*, New York: Random House, 1951.

Periodicals

"Blacks Prefer TV Fare with Black Casts, But Tastes of Blacks and Whites Are Converging, Study Says," *The New York Times*, 21 April 2003, p. C12.

Bumiller, Elizabeth. "Why America Has Gay Marriage Jitters," *The New York Times*, 10 August 2003, Section 4, p. 1.

Carson, Tom. "Degrees of Separation," *The Village Voice*, 2 June 1998, p. 169.

Cartier, Bill, and Lawrie Mifflin. "Mainstream TV Bets on 'Gross-Out' Humor," *The New York Times*, 19 July 1999, p. C1, 10.

"Danson 'Proud' of Racist Act at Roast," *The Arizona Republic*, 25 October 1993, p. B8.

Friend, Tad. "The Next Big Bet," *The New Yorker*, 14 May 2001, p. 83.

Gerston, Jill. "Here's Everybody! After Carson, A Host of Late-Night Wannabees," *The New York Times*, 16 August 1992, Section 2, pp. 1, 21.

Goodman, James. *US* Magazine, 18 September 1979, p. 58.

Hamburger, Philip. *The New Yorker*, 29 October 1949, p. 91

Haralovich, Mary Beth. "Sitcoms and Suburbs: Positioning the 1950s Homemaker," *Quarterly Review of Film and Video* 11 (Spring 1989): pp. 61–83.

Huff, Richard. "'South Park' Fuels Truth-in-Labeling Debate," *New York Daily News,* 5 March. 1998, p. 103.

Jacobson, Mark. "Night-Shifting for the Hip Fleet," *New York Magazine,* 22 September 1975.

Marin, Rick. "The Rude Tube," *Newsweek,* 23 March 1998, pp. 55–62.

Mills, David. "What's So Funny?" *The Washington Post,* 26 October 1993, p. 5.

Mink, Eric. "'South Park' Comes Up a Hallo-winner," *New York Daily News,* 29 October 1997, p. 89.

O'Connor, John. "'Taxi' Rolls into Superior Sit-Com," *The New York Times,* 19 June 1979, p. C21.

Smith, David. "Jack Benny Checklist," unpublished manuscript, The New York Public Library for the Performing Arts.

"Smothers Out: A Wise Decision," editorial, *TV Guide,* 19 April 1969, p. A1.

Starr, Michael. "'South Park' Net Cries 'Foul,'" *The New York Post,* 20 March 1998, p. 20.

Sterngold, James. "A Racial Divide Widens on Network TV," *The New York Times,* 29 December 1998, p. A1.

Thomas, Karen. "Friars Take the Heat for Their Tradition of Tasteless Humor," *USA Today,* 12 October 1993, p. D3.

Timberg, Bernard M. "Talk Shows," in *Encyclopedia of Television,* ed. Horace Newcomb, Cary O'Dell, and Noelle Watson, pp. 1617–1623, Chicago: Fitzroy Dearborn, 1997.

Van Gelder, Lawrence. "Milton Berle, TV's First Star as 'Uncle Miltie,' Dies at 93," *The New York Times,* 28 March 2002, p. A29.

Wexman, Virginia Wright. "Returning from the Moon: Jackie Gleason, the Carnivalesque, and Television Comedy," *Journal of Film and Video* 42 (Winter 1990): pp. 20–32.

Wilde, David. "South Park's Evil Geniuses and the Triumph of No-Brow Culture," *Rolling Stone,* 19 February 1998, p. 34.

Williams, Jeanine. "Whoopi's Shock Roast/Danson in Blackface Leaves Many Fuming," *USA Today,* 11 October 1993, p. D2.

INDEX

Toby Miller
General Editor

Popular Culture and Everyday Life is the new place for critical books in cultural studies. The series stresses multiple theoretical, political, and methodological approaches to commodity culture and lived experience by borrowing from sociological, anthropological, and textual disciplines. Each volume develops a critical understanding of a key topic in the area through a combination of thorough literature review, original research, and a student-reader orientation. The series consists of three types of books: single-authored monographs, readers of existing classic essays, and new companion volumes of papers on central topics. Fields to be covered include: fashion, sport, shopping, therapy, religion, food and drink, youth, music, cultural policy, popular literature, performance, education, queer theory, race, gender, and class.

For additional information about this series or for the submission of manuscripts, please contact:

Toby Miller
Department of Cinema Studies
New York University
721 Broadway, Room 600
New York, New York 10003

To order other books in this series, please contact our Customer Service Department:

(800) 770-LANG (within the U.S.)
(212) 647-7706 (outside the U.S.)
(212) 647-7707 FAX

Or browse online by series: